CIVIL WAR

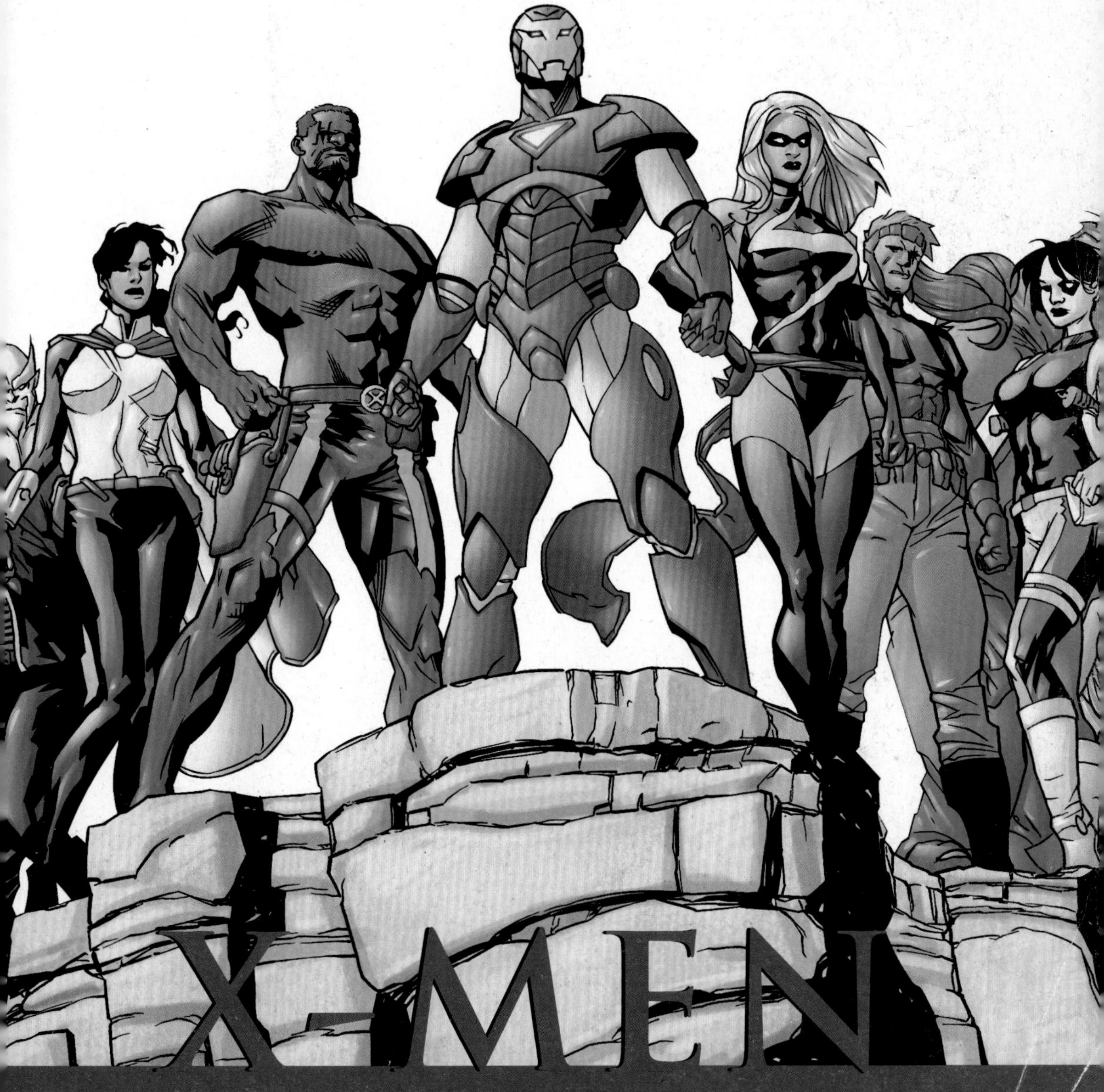

X-MEN

A

MARVEL COMICS

PRESENTATION

CIVIL

WRITER
DAVID HINE

PENCILER
YANICK PAQUETTE WITH
AARON LOPRESTI (ISSUE #3)

INKERS
SERGE LAPOINTE WITH
JAY LEISTEN (ISSUE #3)

COLORIST
STEPHANE PERU

LETTERER
VC'S RUS WOOTON

ASSISTANT EDITOR
SEAN RYAN

ASSOCIATE EDITOR
NICK LOWE

EDITOR
MIKE MARTS

COLLECTION EDITOR
JENNIFER GRÜNWALD

ASSISTANT EDITORS
MICHAEL SHORT &
CORY LEVINE

ASSOCIATE EDITOR
MARK D. BEAZLEY

SENIOR EDITOR, SPECIAL PROJECTS
JEFF YOUNGQUIST

SENIOR VICE PRESIDENT OF SALES
DAVID GABRIEL

PRODUCTION
JERRY KALINOWSKI

BOOK DESIGNER
DAYLE CHESLER

VICE PRESIDENT OF CREATIVE
TOM MARVELLI

EDITOR IN CHIEF
JOE QUESADA

PUBLISHER
DAN BUCKLEY

WAR

X-MEN

CIVIL WAR
X-MEN

PREVIOUSLY...

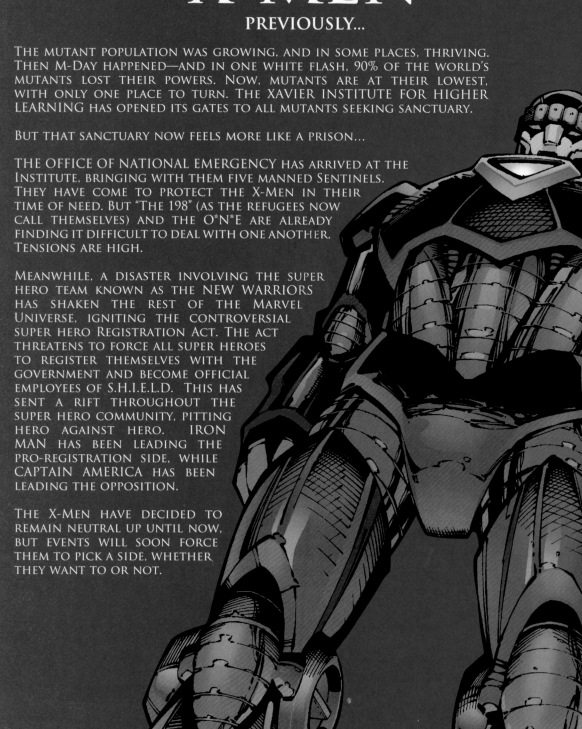

THE MUTANT POPULATION WAS GROWING, AND IN SOME PLACES, THRIVING. THEN M-DAY HAPPENED—AND IN ONE WHITE FLASH, 90% OF THE WORLD'S MUTANTS LOST THEIR POWERS. NOW, MUTANTS ARE AT THEIR LOWEST, WITH ONLY ONE PLACE TO TURN. THE XAVIER INSTITUTE FOR HIGHER LEARNING HAS OPENED ITS GATES TO ALL MUTANTS SEEKING SANCTUARY.

BUT THAT SANCTUARY NOW FEELS MORE LIKE A PRISON...

THE OFFICE OF NATIONAL EMERGENCY HAS ARRIVED AT THE INSTITUTE, BRINGING WITH THEM FIVE MANNED SENTINELS. THEY HAVE COME TO PROTECT THE X-MEN IN THEIR TIME OF NEED. BUT "THE 198" (AS THE REFUGEES NOW CALL THEMSELVES) AND THE O*N*E ARE ALREADY FINDING IT DIFFICULT TO DEAL WITH ONE ANOTHER. TENSIONS ARE HIGH.

MEANWHILE, A DISASTER INVOLVING THE SUPER HERO TEAM KNOWN AS THE NEW WARRIORS HAS SHAKEN THE REST OF THE MARVEL UNIVERSE, IGNITING THE CONTROVERSIAL SUPER HERO REGISTRATION ACT. THE ACT THREATENS TO FORCE ALL SUPER HEROES TO REGISTER THEMSELVES WITH THE GOVERNMENT AND BECOME OFFICIAL EMPLOYEES OF S.H.I.E.L.D. THIS HAS SENT A RIFT THROUGHOUT THE SUPER HERO COMMUNITY, PITTING HERO AGAINST HERO. IRON MAN HAS BEEN LEADING THE PRO-REGISTRATION SIDE, WHILE CAPTAIN AMERICA HAS BEEN LEADING THE OPPOSITION.

THE X-MEN HAVE DECIDED TO REMAIN NEUTRAL UP UNTIL NOW, BUT EVENTS WILL SOON FORCE THEM TO PICK A SIDE, WHETHER THEY WANT TO OR NOT.

X-MEN

A MARVEL COMICS EVENT

CIVIL WAR

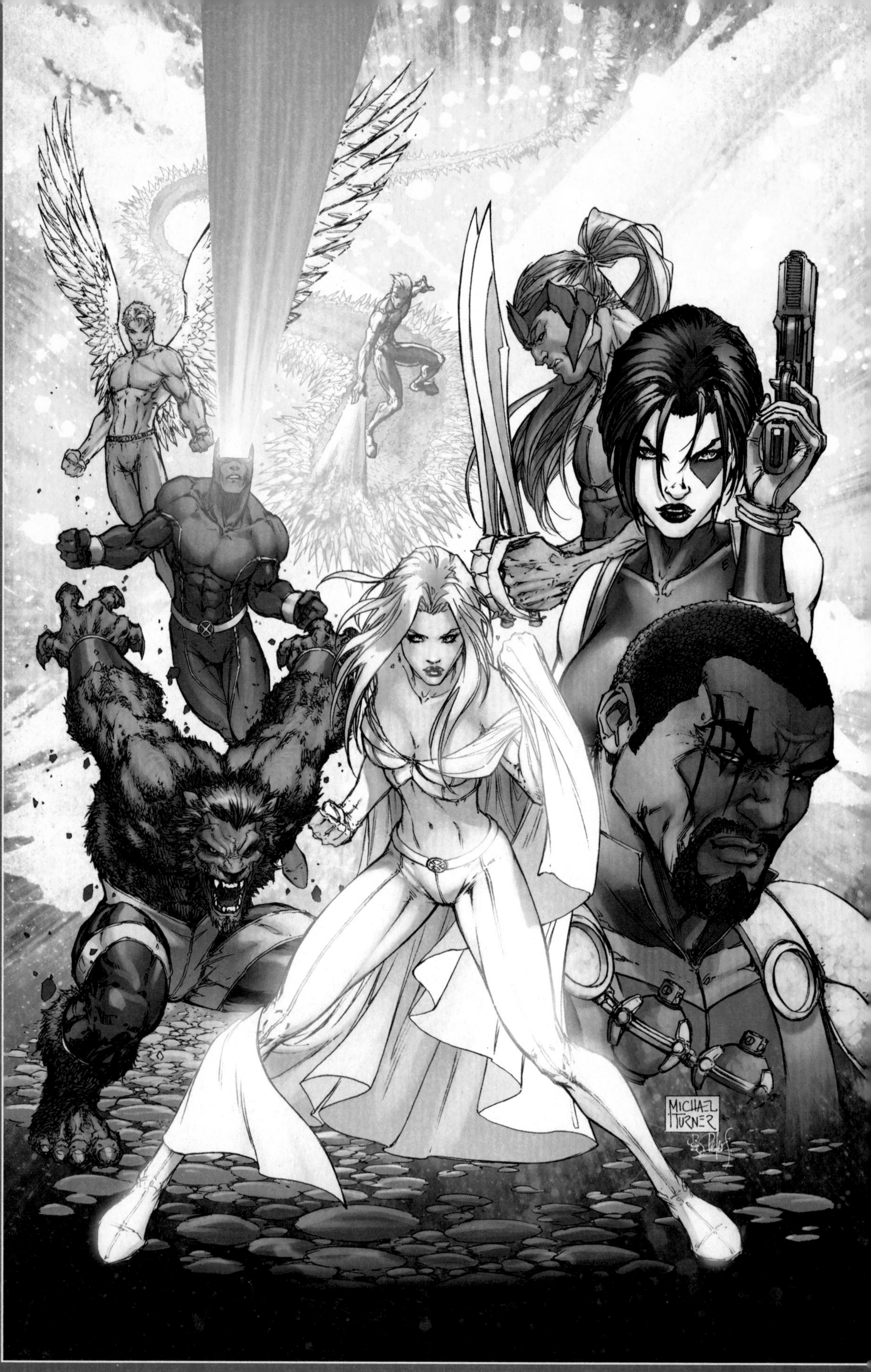
MICHAEL TURNER

CIVIL WAR: X-MEN #1 ASPEN VARIANT BY MICHAEL TURNER

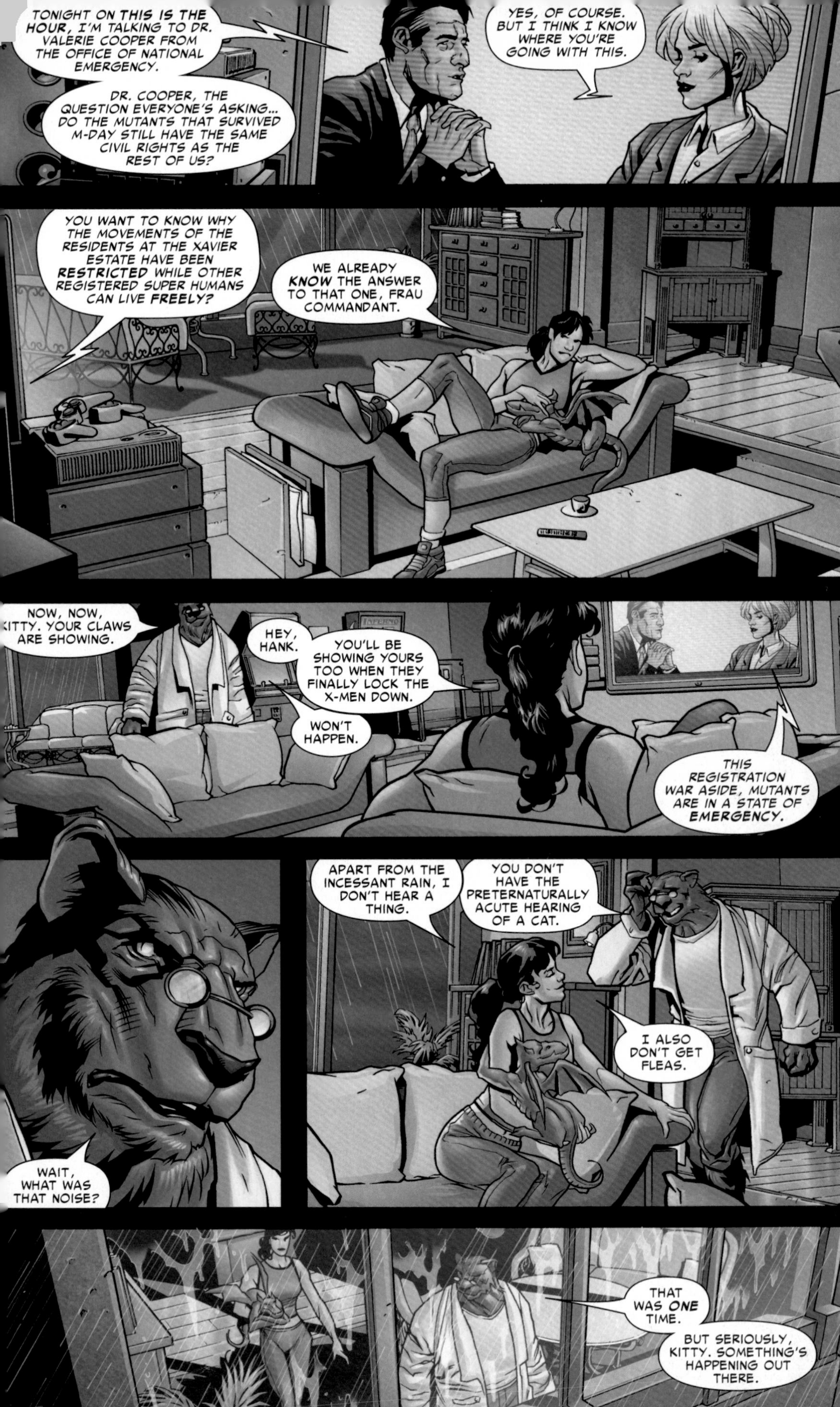
TONIGHT ON THIS IS THE HOUR, I'M TALKING TO DR. VALÉRIE COOPER FROM THE OFFICE OF NATIONAL EMERGENCY.
DR. COOPER, THE QUESTION EVERYONE'S ASKING... DO THE MUTANTS THAT SURVIVED M-DAY STILL HAVE THE SAME CIVIL RIGHTS AS THE REST OF US?
YES, OF COURSE. BUT I THINK I KNOW WHERE YOU'RE GOING WITH THIS.
YOU WANT TO KNOW WHY THE MOVEMENTS OF THE RESIDENTS AT THE XAVIER ESTATE HAVE BEEN RESTRICTED WHILE OTHER REGISTERED SUPER HUMANS CAN LIVE FREELY?
WE ALREADY KNOW THE ANSWER TO THAT ONE, FRAU COMMANDANT.
NOW, NOW, KITTY. YOUR CLAWS ARE SHOWING.
HEY, HANK.
YOU'LL BE SHOWING YOURS TOO WHEN THEY FINALLY LOCK THE X-MEN DOWN.
WON'T HAPPEN.
THIS REGISTRATION WAR ASIDE, MUTANTS ARE IN A STATE OF EMERGENCY.
WAIT, WHAT WAS THAT NOISE?
APART FROM THE INCESSANT RAIN, I DON'T HEAR A THING.
YOU DON'T HAVE THE PRETERNATURALLY ACUTE HEARING OF A CAT.
I ALSO DON'T GET FLEAS.
THAT WAS ONE TIME.
BUT SERIOUSLY, KITTY. SOMETHING'S HAPPENING OUT THERE.

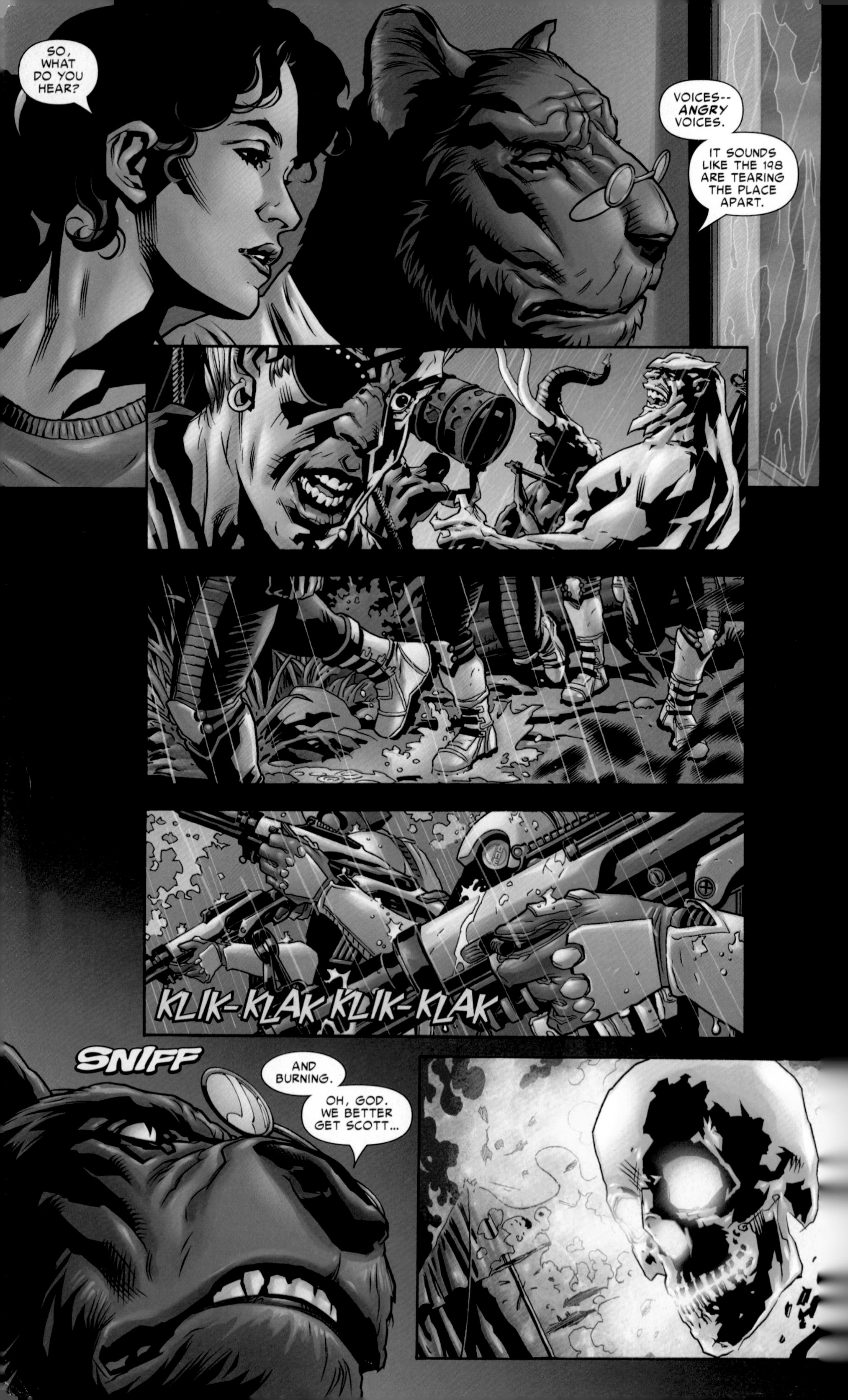
SO, WHAT DO YOU HEAR?
VOICES-- ANGRY VOICES.
IT SOUNDS LIKE THE 198 ARE TEARING THE PLACE APART.
KLIK-KLAK KLIK-KLAK
SNIFF
AND BURNING.
OH, GOD. WE BETTER GET SCOTT...

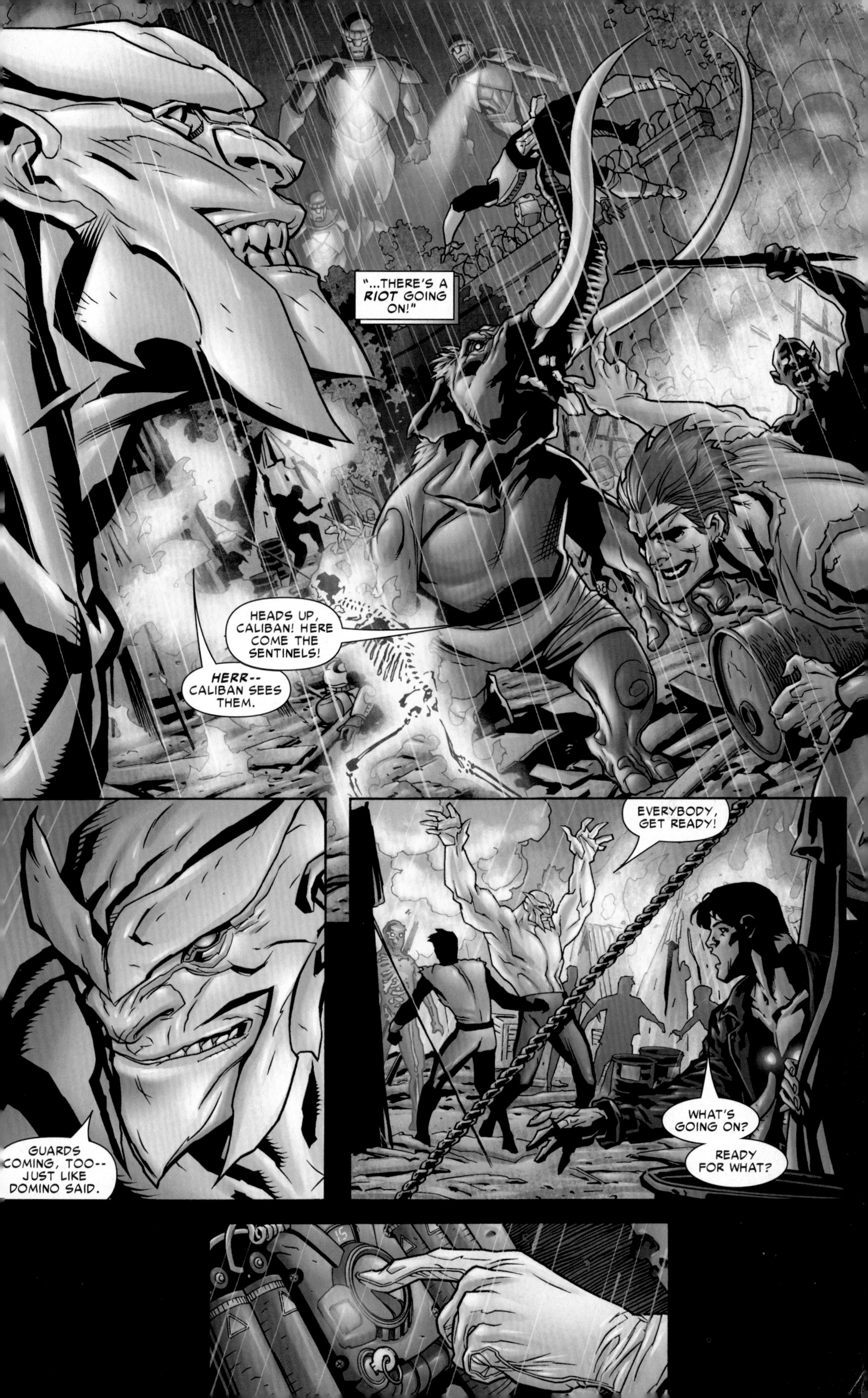
"...THERE'S A *RIOT* GOING ON!"
HEADS UP, CALIBAN! HERE COME THE SENTINELS!
HERR-- CALIBAN SEES THEM.
GUARDS COMING, TOO-- JUST LIKE DOMINO SAID.
EVERYBODY, GET READY!
WHAT'S GOING ON?
READY FOR WHAT?

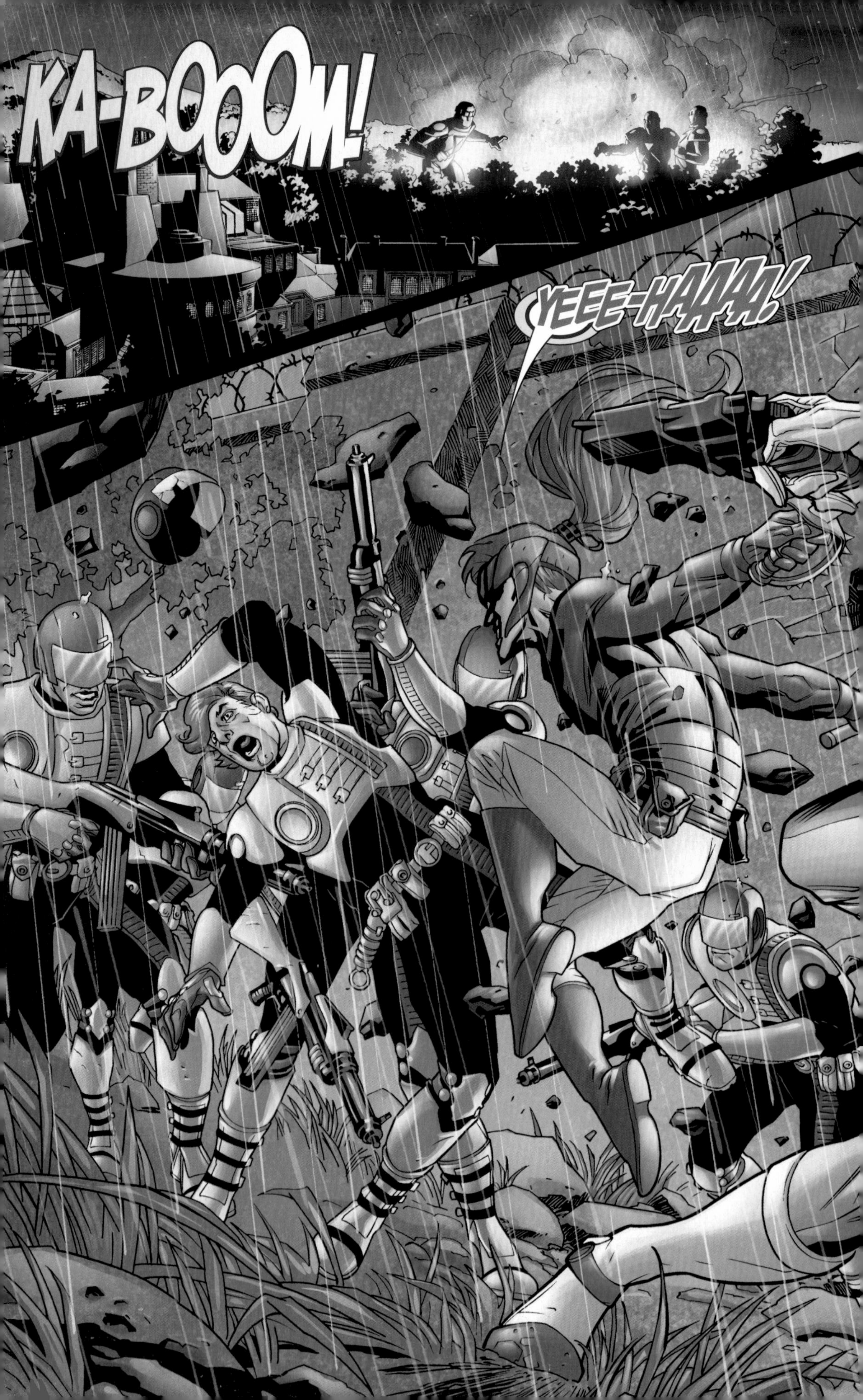
KA-BOOOM!
YEEE-HAAAA!

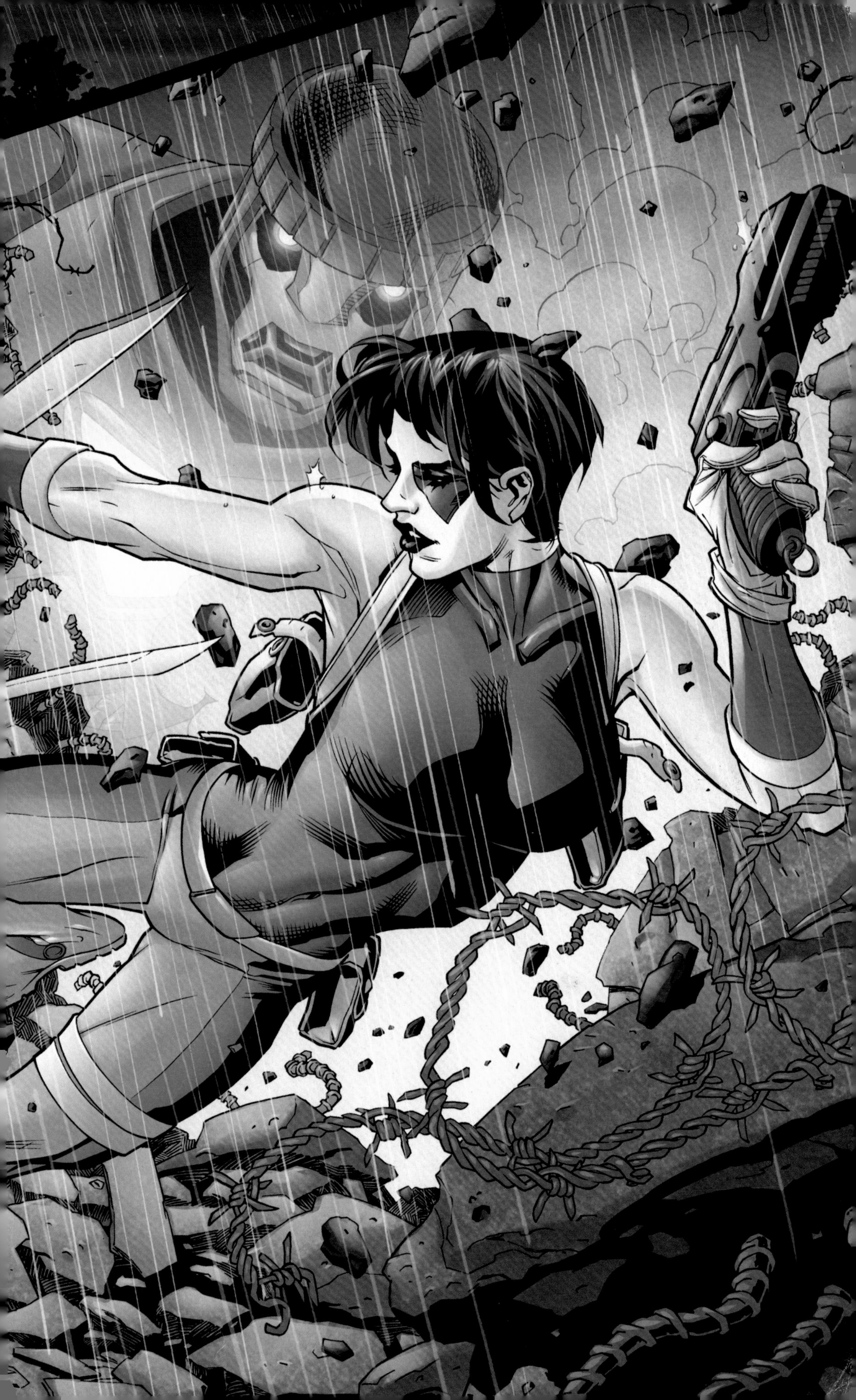

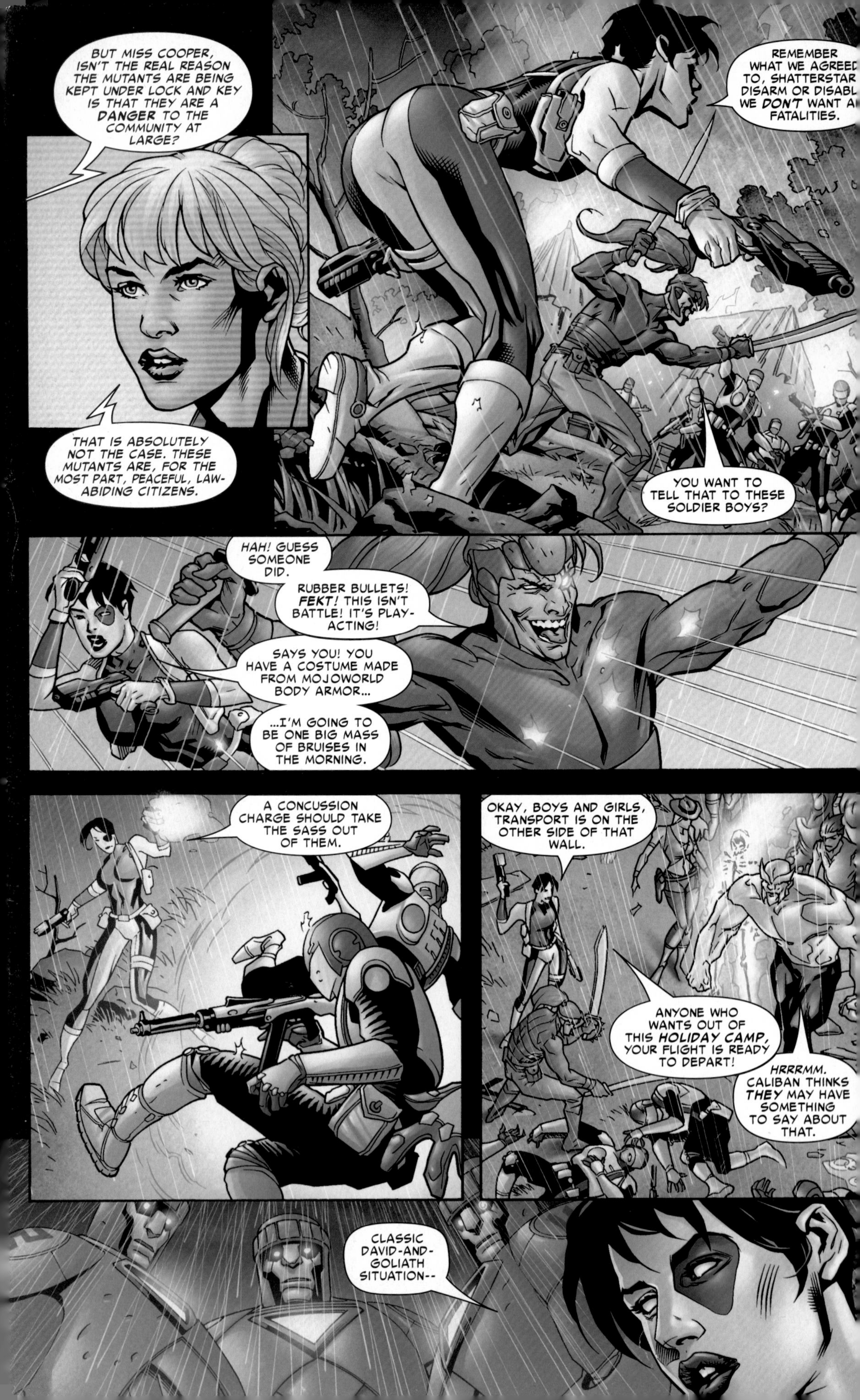
BUT MISS COOPER, ISN'T THE REAL REASON THE MUTANTS ARE BEING KEPT UNDER LOCK AND KEY IS THAT THEY ARE A DANGER TO THE COMMUNITY AT LARGE?
THAT IS ABSOLUTELY NOT THE CASE. THESE MUTANTS ARE, FOR THE MOST PART, PEACEFUL, LAW-ABIDING CITIZENS.
REMEMBER WHAT WE AGREED TO, SHATTERSTAR DISARM OR DISABL WE DON'T WANT A FATALITIES.
YOU WANT TO TELL THAT TO THESE SOLDIER BOYS?
HAH! GUESS SOMEONE DID.
RUBBER BULLETS! FEKT! THIS ISN'T BATTLE! IT'S PLAY-ACTING!
SAYS YOU! YOU HAVE A COSTUME MADE FROM MOJOWORLD BODY ARMOR...
...I'M GOING TO BE ONE BIG MASS OF BRUISES IN THE MORNING.
A CONCUSSION CHARGE SHOULD TAKE THE SASS OUT OF THEM.
OKAY, BOYS AND GIRLS, TRANSPORT IS ON THE OTHER SIDE OF THAT WALL.
ANYONE WHO WANTS OUT OF THIS HOLIDAY CAMP, YOUR FLIGHT IS READY TO DEPART!
HRRRMM. CALIBAN THINKS THEY MAY HAVE SOMETHING TO SAY ABOUT THAT.
CLASSIC DAVID-AND-GOLIATH SITUATION--

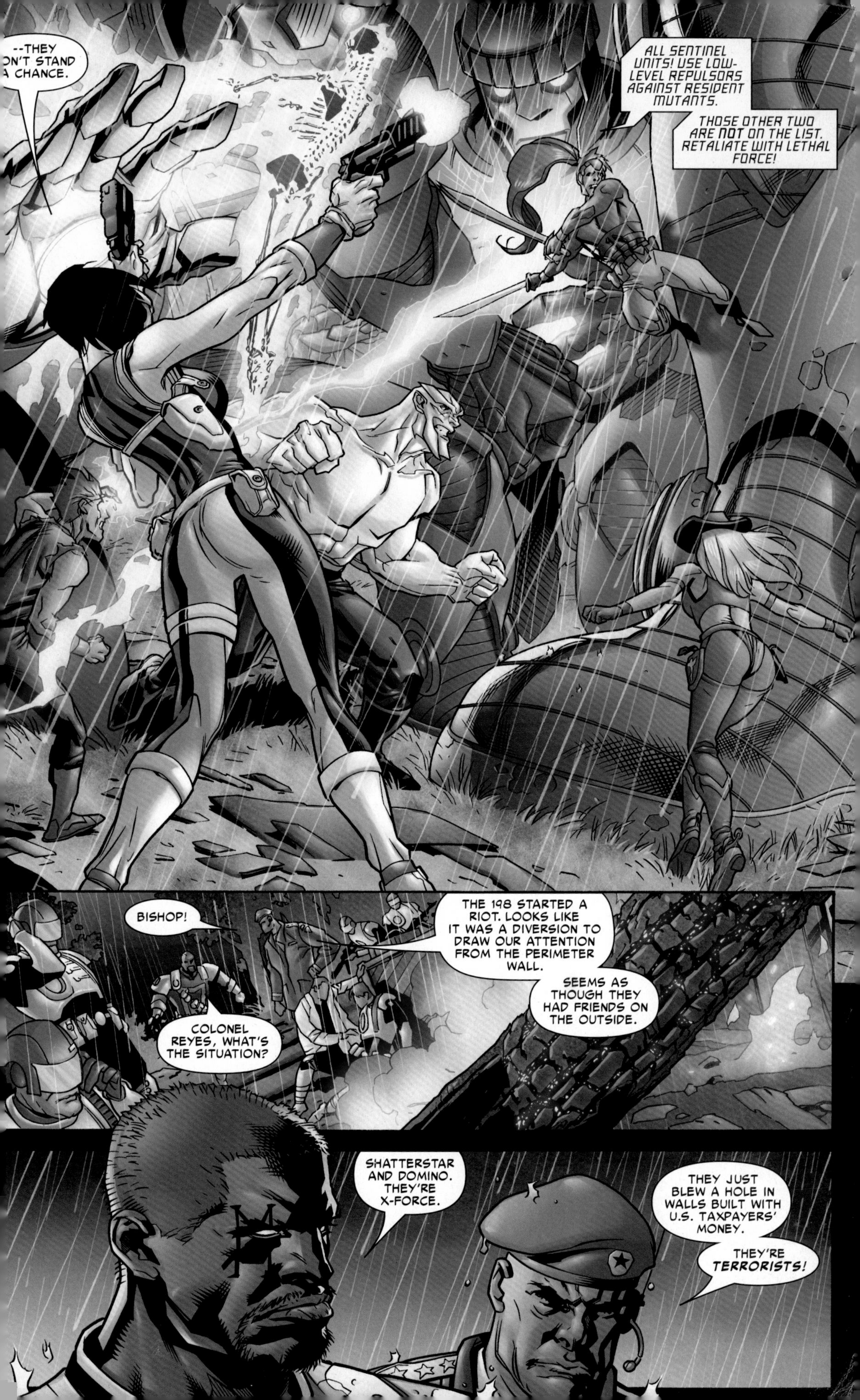
--THEY
ON'T STAND
A CHANCE.
ALL SENTINEL UNITS! USE LOW-LEVEL REPULSORS AGAINST RESIDENT MUTANTS.
THOSE OTHER TWO ARE NOT ON THE LIST. RETALIATE WITH LETHAL FORCE!
BISHOP!
COLONEL REYES, WHAT'S THE SITUATION?
THE 198 STARTED A RIOT. LOOKS LIKE IT WAS A DIVERSION TO DRAW OUR ATTENTION FROM THE PERIMETER WALL.
SEEMS AS THOUGH THEY HAD FRIENDS ON THE OUTSIDE.
SHATTERSTAR AND DOMINO. THEY'RE X-FORCE.
THEY JUST BLEW A HOLE IN WALLS BUILT WITH U.S. TAXPAYERS' MONEY.
THEY'RE TERRORISTS!

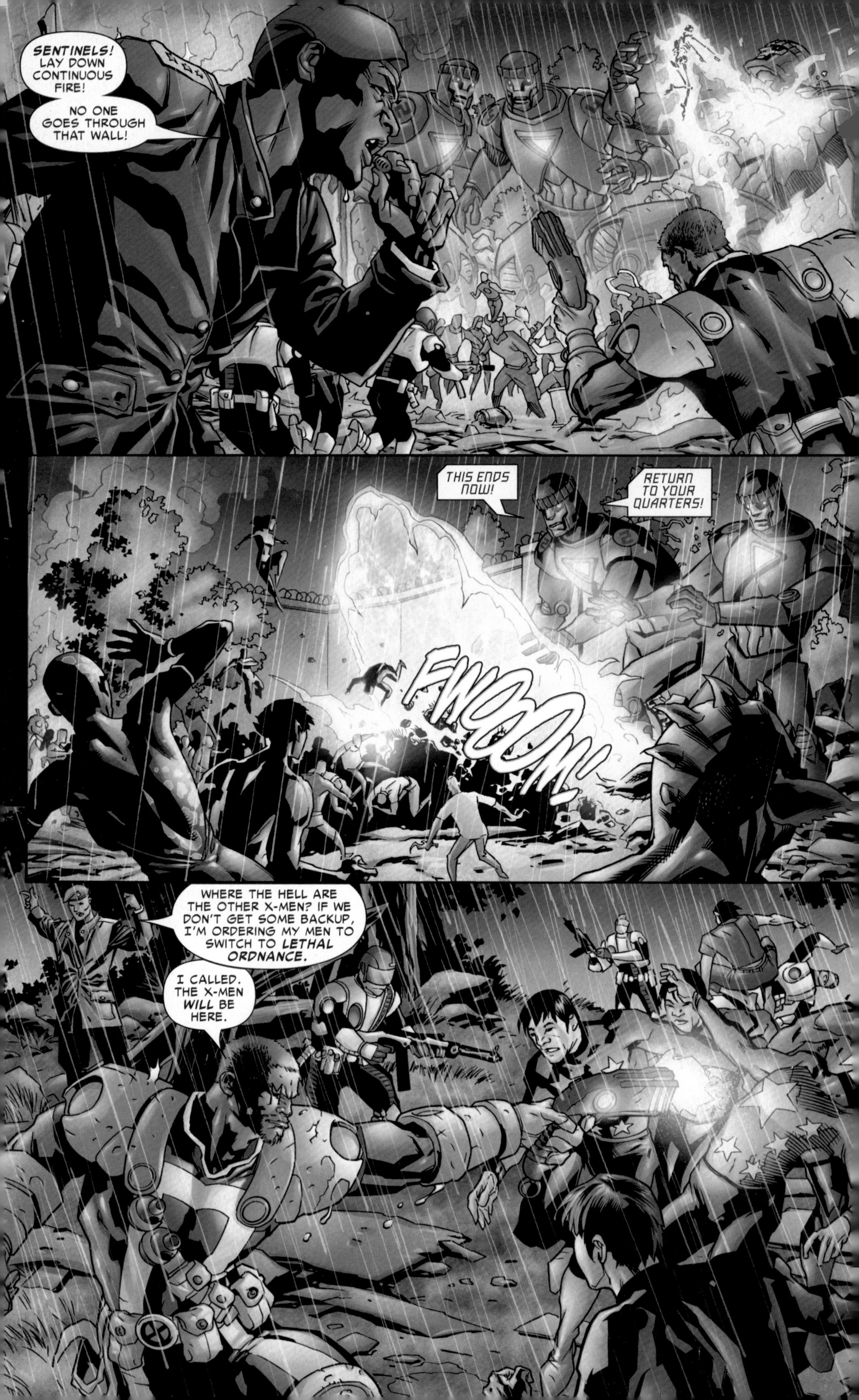
SENTINELS! LAY DOWN CONTINUOUS FIRE!
NO ONE GOES THROUGH THAT WALL!
THIS ENDS NOW!
RETURN TO YOUR QUARTERS!
FWOOOM!
WHERE THE HELL ARE THE OTHER X-MEN? IF WE DON'T GET SOME BACKUP, I'M ORDERING MY MEN TO SWITCH TO LETHAL ORDNANCE.
I CALLED. THE X-MEN WILL BE HERE.

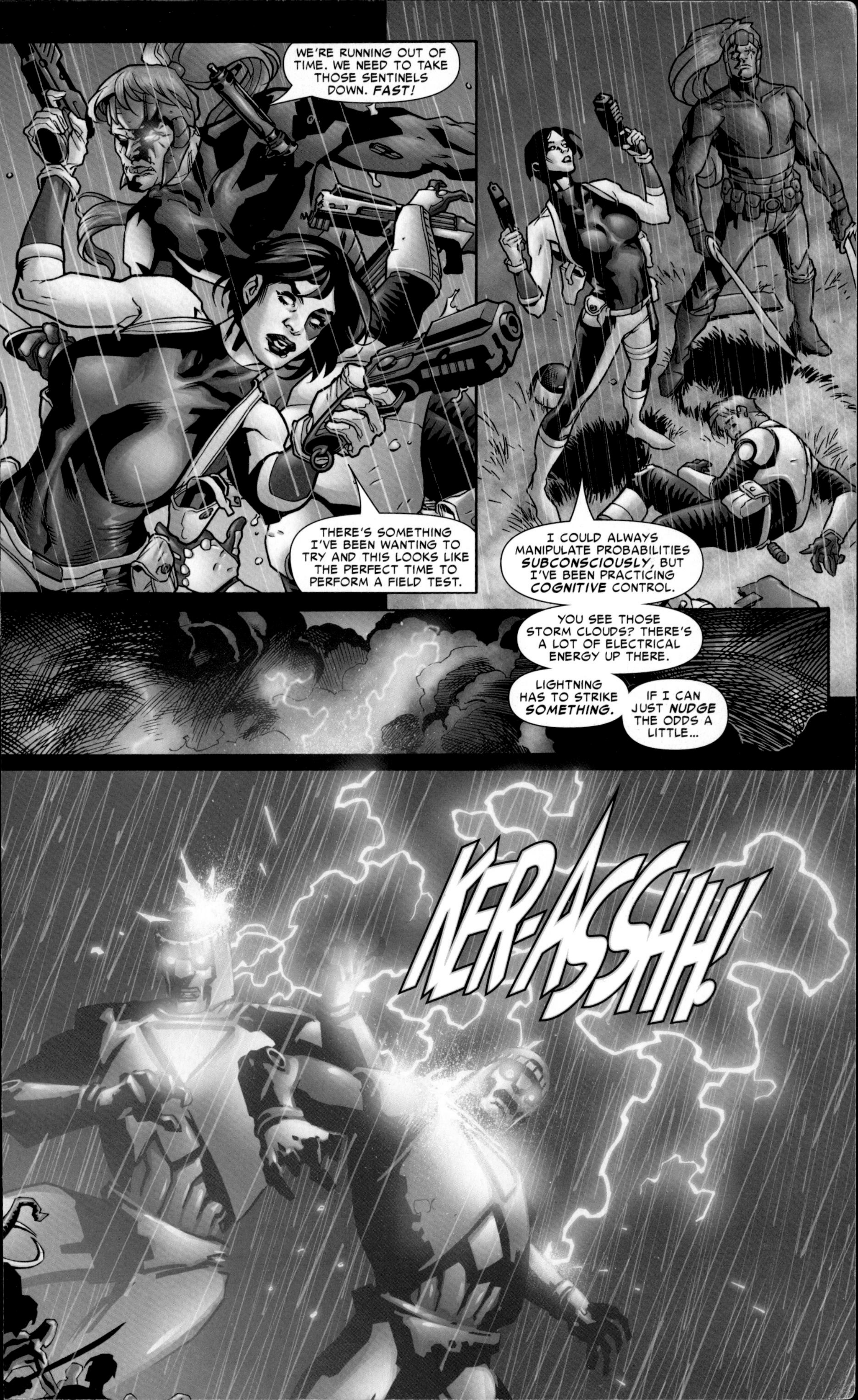
WE'RE RUNNING OUT OF TIME. WE NEED TO TAKE THOSE SENTINELS DOWN. FAST!
THERE'S SOMETHING I'VE BEEN WANTING TO TRY AND THIS LOOKS LIKE THE PERFECT TIME TO PERFORM A FIELD TEST.
I COULD ALWAYS MANIPULATE PROBABILITIES SUBCONSCIOUSLY, BUT I'VE BEEN PRACTICING COGNITIVE CONTROL.
YOU SEE THOSE STORM CLOUDS? THERE'S A LOT OF ELECTRICAL ENERGY UP THERE.
LIGHTNING HAS TO STRIKE SOMETHING.
IF I CAN JUST NUDGE THE ODDS A LITTLE...
KER-ASSHH!

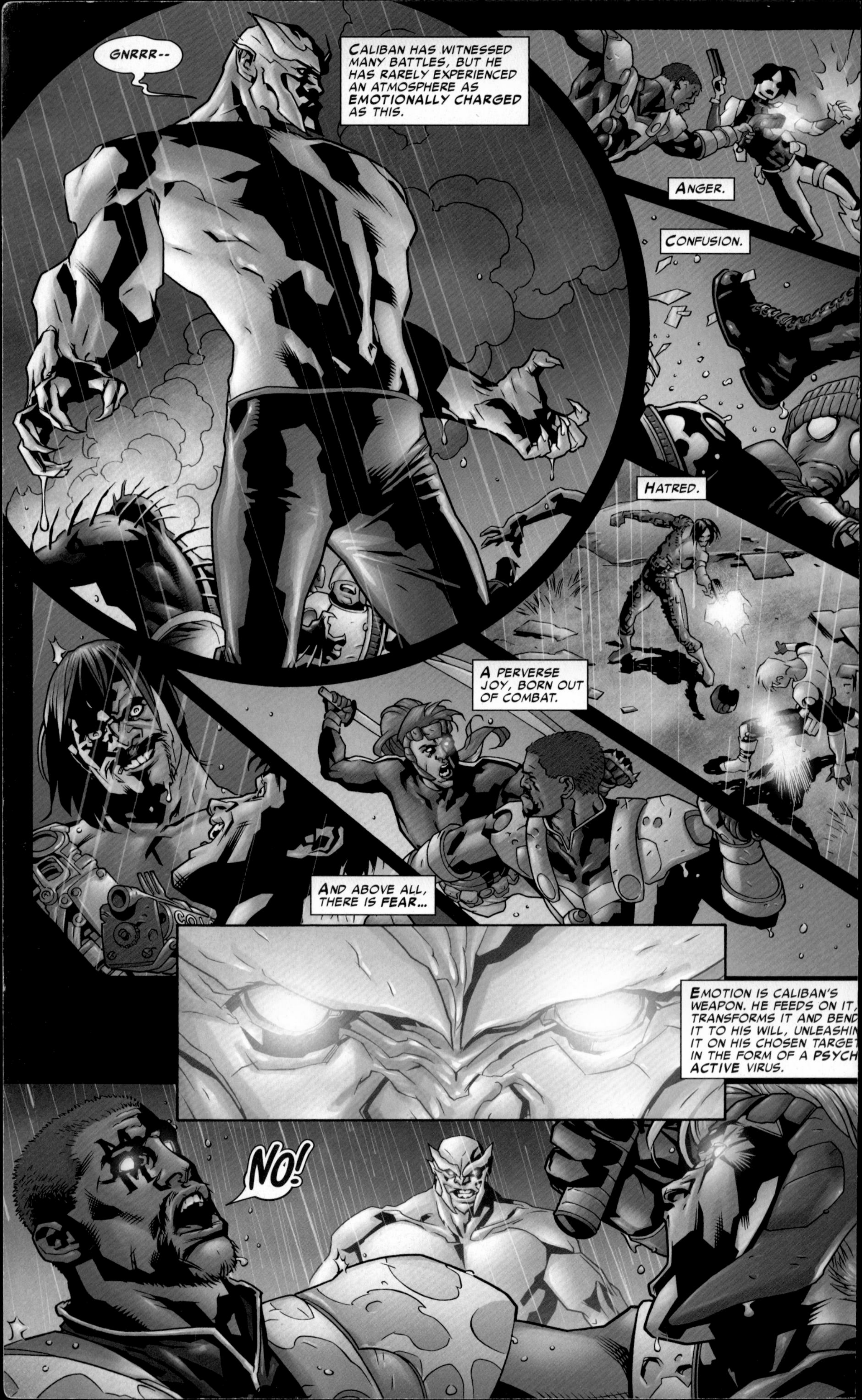
GNRRR--
CALIBAN HAS WITNESSED MANY BATTLES, BUT HE HAS RARELY EXPERIENCED AN ATMOSPHERE AS EMOTIONALLY CHARGED AS THIS.
ANGER.
CONFUSION.
HATRED.
A PERVERSE JOY, BORN OUT OF COMBAT.
AND ABOVE ALL, THERE IS FEAR...
EMOTION IS CALIBAN'S WEAPON. HE FEEDS ON IT, TRANSFORMS IT AND BEND IT TO HIS WILL, UNLEASHIN IT ON HIS CHOSEN TARGE IN THE FORM OF A PSYCH ACTIVE VIRUS.
NO!

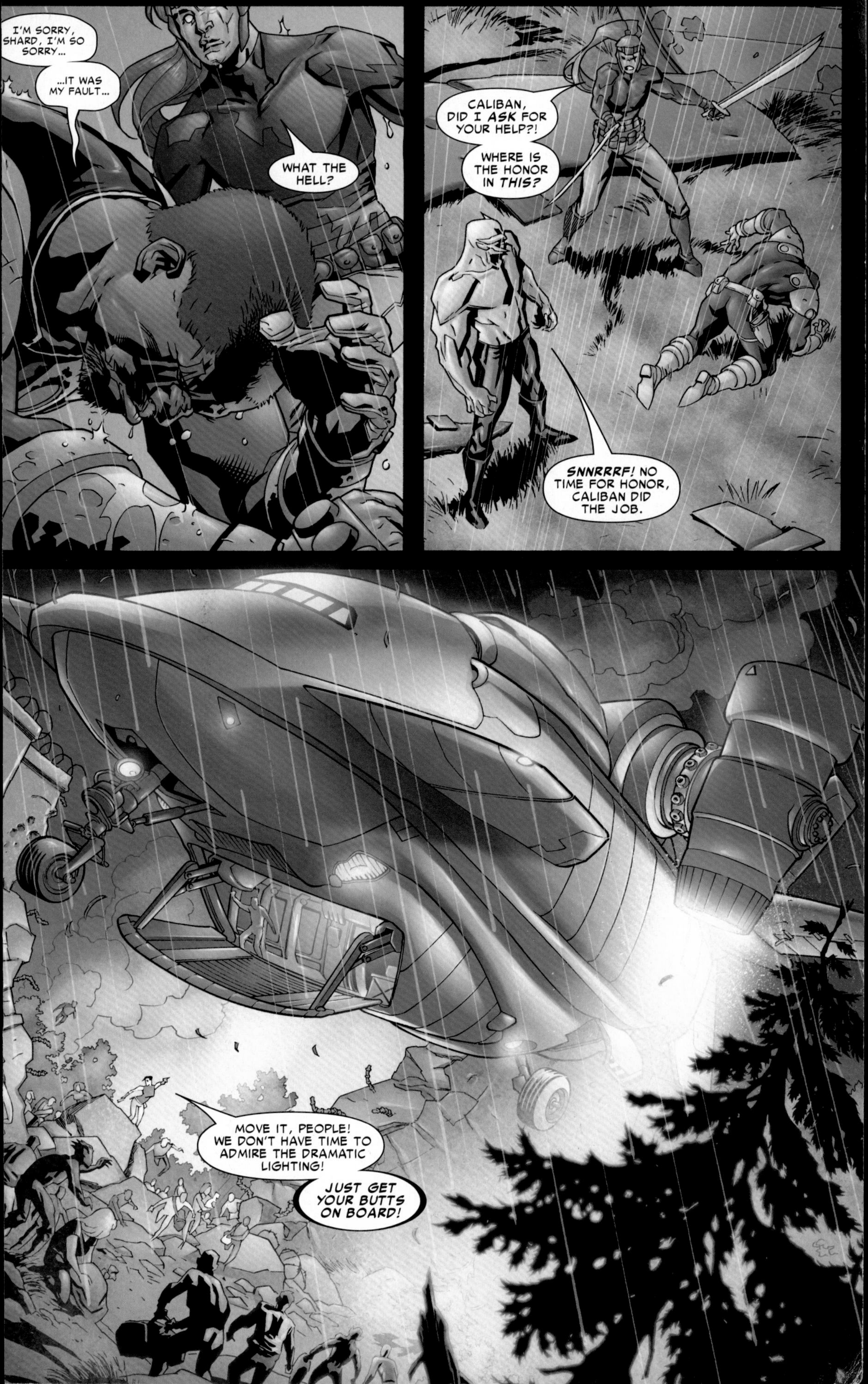

I'M SORRY, SHARD, I'M SO SORRY...
...IT WAS MY FAULT...
WHAT THE HELL?
CALIBAN, DID I ASK FOR YOUR HELP?!
WHERE IS THE HONOR IN THIS?
SNNRRRF! NO TIME FOR HONOR, CALIBAN DID THE JOB.
MOVE IT, PEOPLE! WE DON'T HAVE TIME TO ADMIRE THE DRAMATIC LIGHTING!
JUST GET YOUR BUTTS ON BOARD!

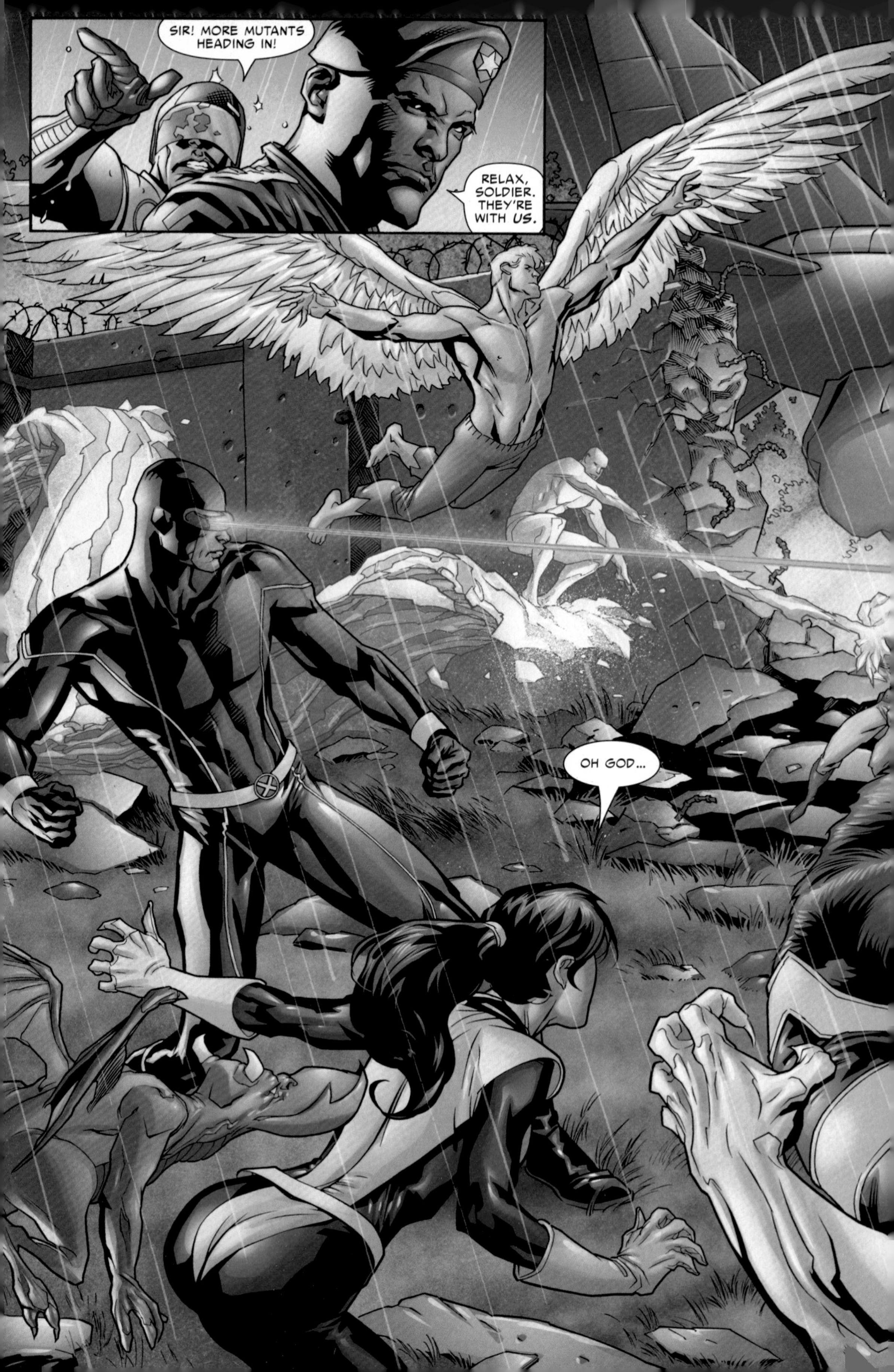
SIR! MORE MUTANTS HEADING IN!
RELAX, SOLDIER. THEY'RE WITH US.
OH GOD...

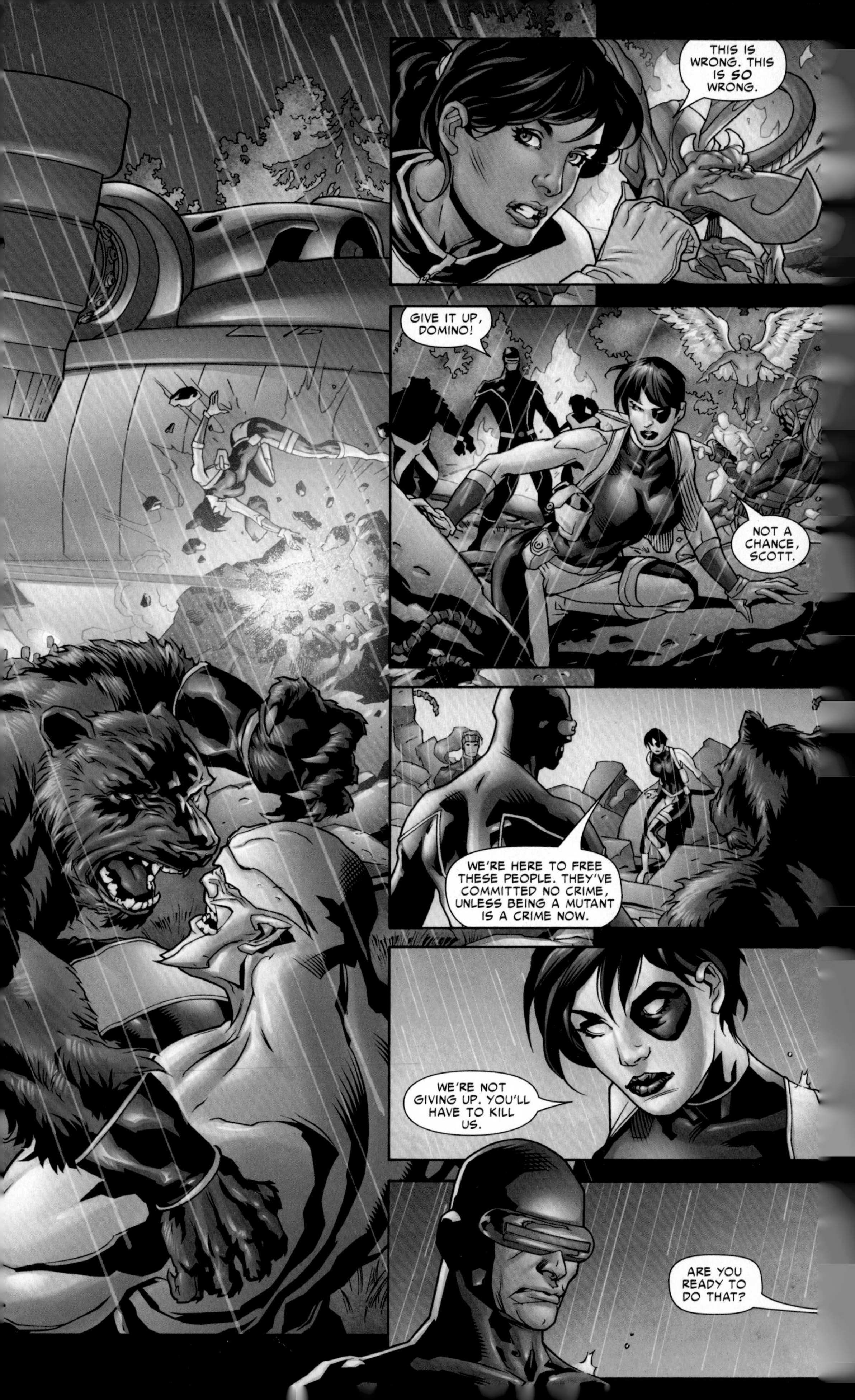
THIS IS WRONG. THIS IS SO WRONG.
GIVE IT UP, DOMINO!
NOT A CHANCE, SCOTT.
WE'RE HERE TO FREE THESE PEOPLE. THEY'VE COMMITTED NO CRIME, UNLESS BEING A MUTANT IS A CRIME NOW.
WE'RE NOT GIVING UP. YOU'LL HAVE TO KILL US.
ARE YOU READY TO DO THAT?

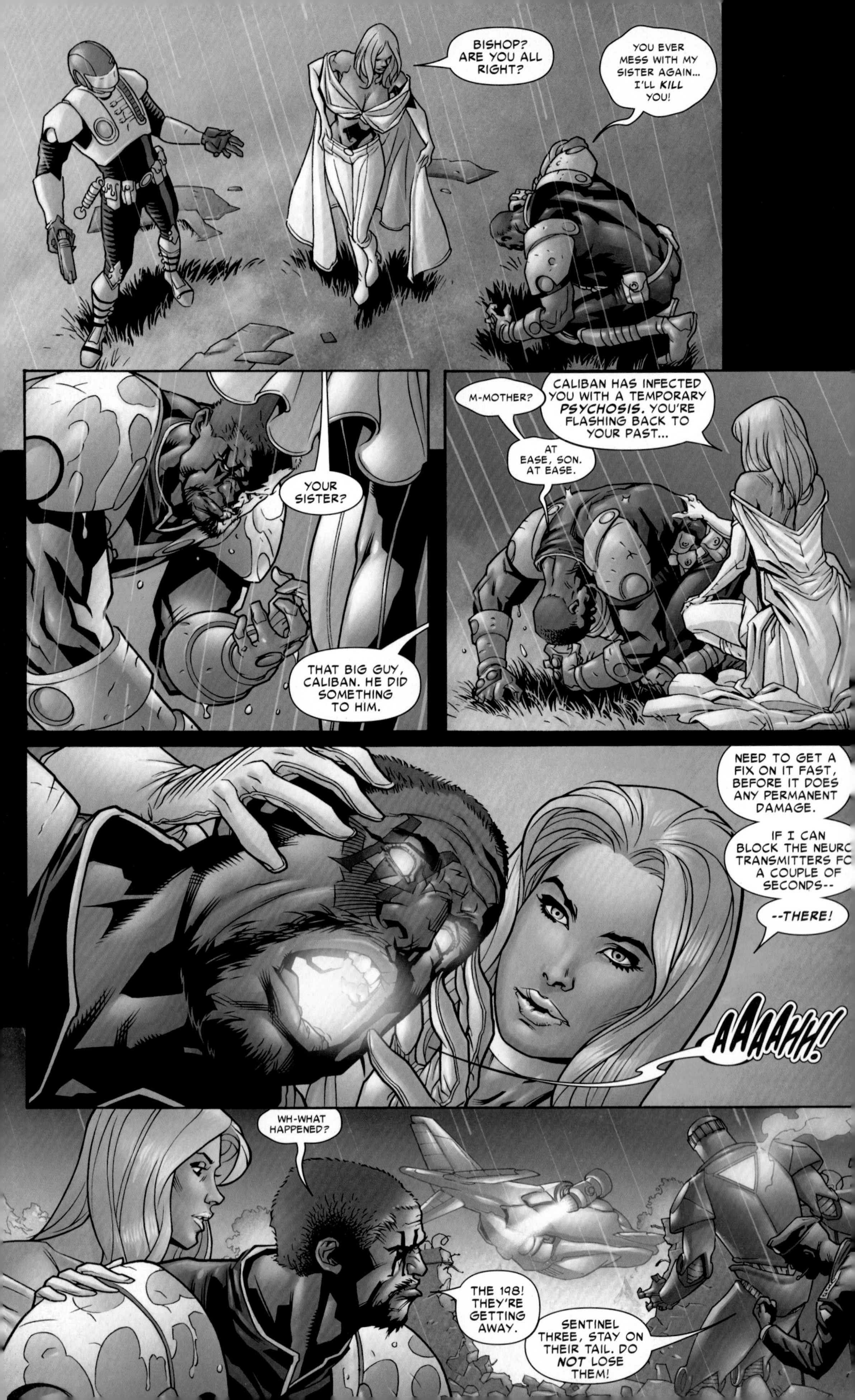
BISHOP? ARE YOU ALL RIGHT?
YOU EVER MESS WITH MY SISTER AGAIN... I'LL KILL YOU!
YOUR SISTER?
THAT BIG GUY, CALIBAN. HE DID SOMETHING TO HIM.
M-MOTHER?
CALIBAN HAS INFECTED YOU WITH A TEMPORARY PSYCHOSIS. YOU'RE FLASHING BACK TO YOUR PAST...
AT EASE, SON. AT EASE.
NEED TO GET A FIX ON IT FAST, BEFORE IT DOES ANY PERMANENT DAMAGE.
IF I CAN BLOCK THE NEURO TRANSMITTERS FO A COUPLE OF SECONDS--
--THERE!
AAAAHH!
WH-WHAT HAPPENED?
THE 198! THEY'RE GETTING AWAY.
SENTINEL THREE, STAY ON THEIR TAIL. DO NOT LOSE THEM!

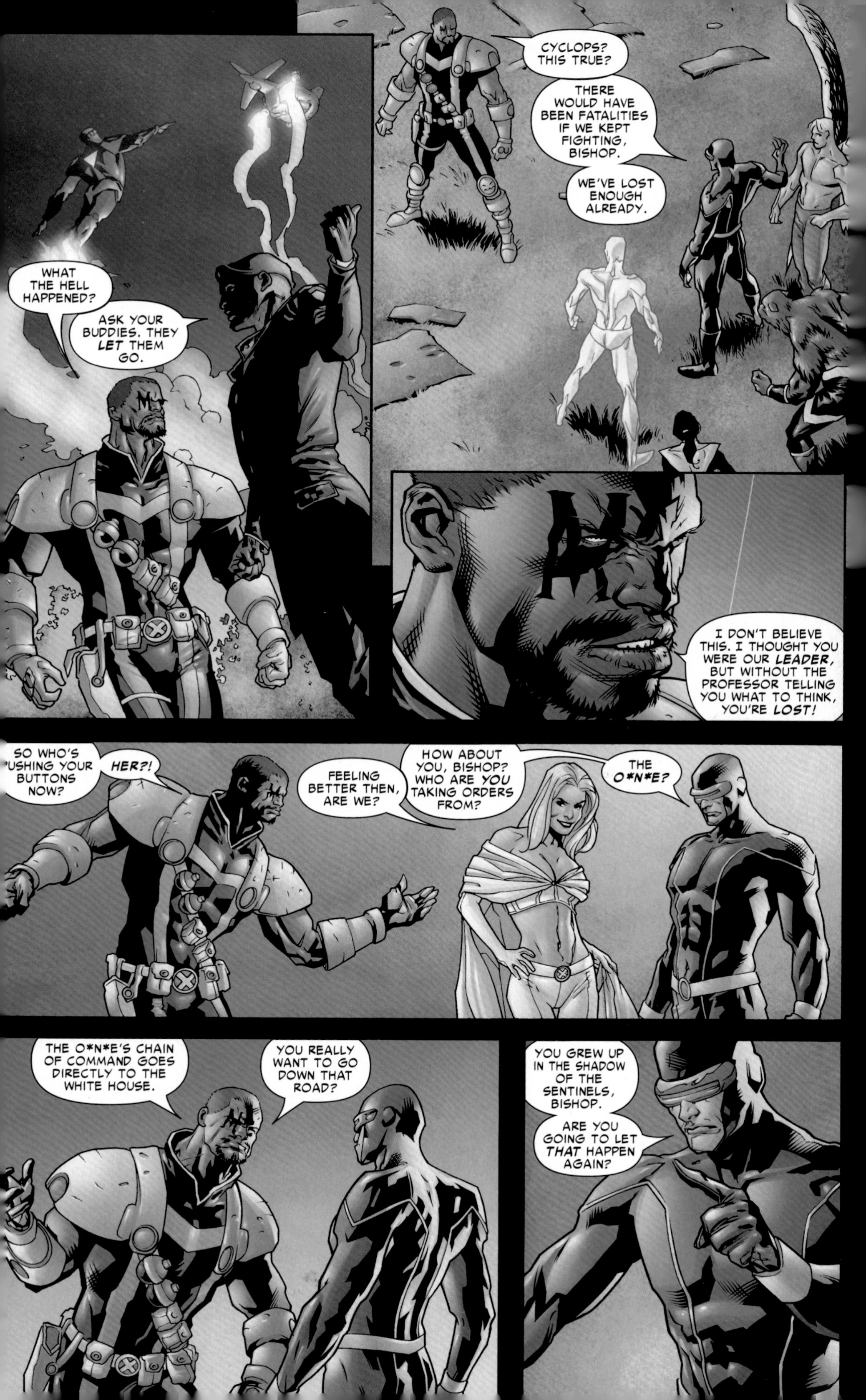
CYCLOPS? THIS TRUE?
THERE WOULD HAVE BEEN FATALITIES IF WE KEPT FIGHTING, BISHOP.
WE'VE LOST ENOUGH ALREADY.
WHAT THE HELL HAPPENED?
ASK YOUR BUDDIES. THEY LET THEM GO.
I DON'T BELIEVE THIS. I THOUGHT YOU WERE OUR LEADER, BUT WITHOUT THE PROFESSOR TELLING YOU WHAT TO THINK, YOU'RE LOST!
SO WHO'S PUSHING YOUR BUTTONS NOW?
HER?!
FEELING BETTER THEN, ARE WE?
HOW ABOUT YOU, BISHOP? WHO ARE YOU TAKING ORDERS FROM?
THE O*N*E?
THE O*N*E'S CHAIN OF COMMAND GOES DIRECTLY TO THE WHITE HOUSE.
YOU REALLY WANT TO GO DOWN THAT ROAD?
YOU GREW UP IN THE SHADOW OF THE SENTINELS, BISHOP.
ARE YOU GOING TO LET THAT HAPPEN AGAIN?

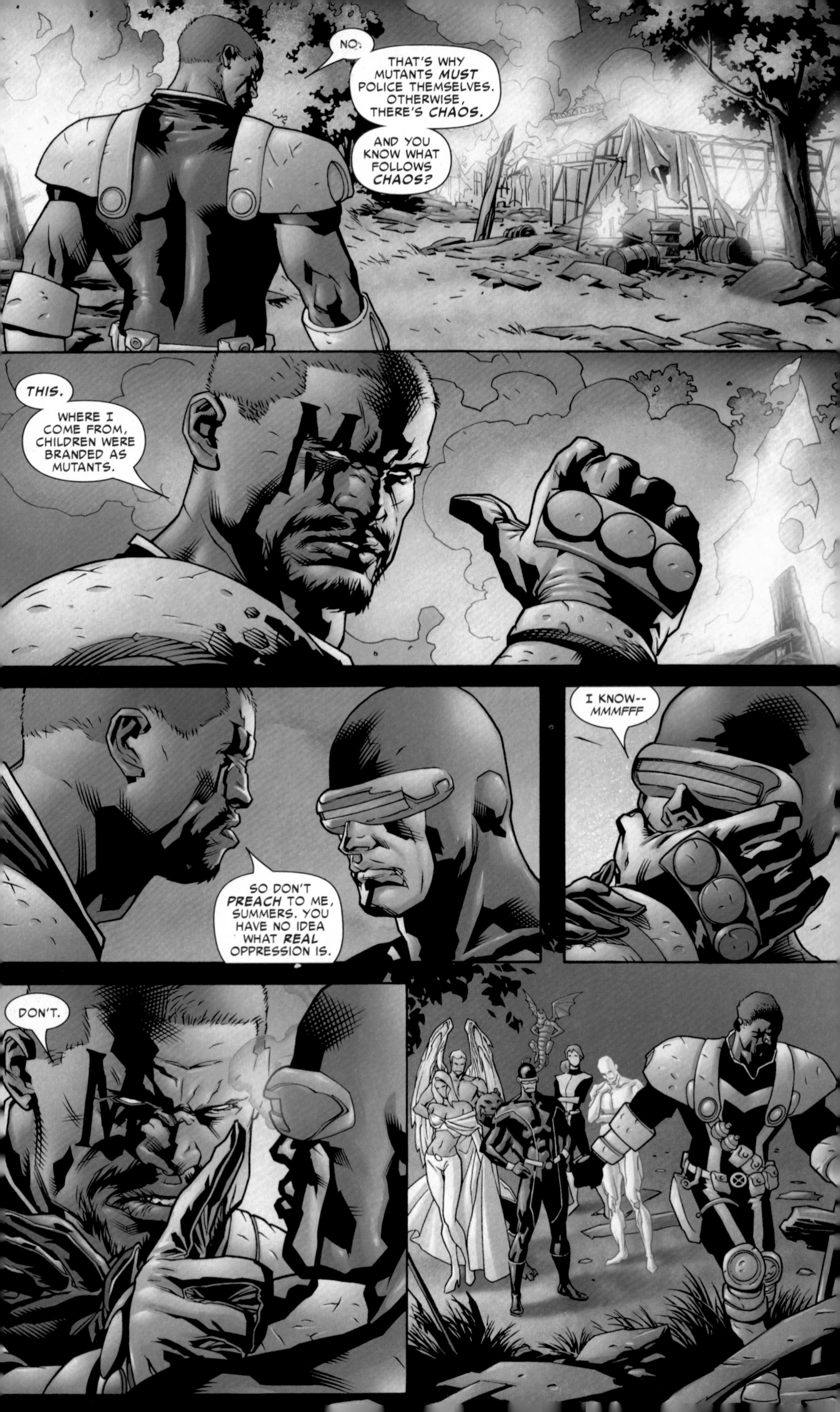
NO.
THAT'S WHY MUTANTS MUST POLICE THEMSELVES. OTHERWISE, THERE'S CHAOS.
AND YOU KNOW WHAT FOLLOWS CHAOS?
THIS.
WHERE I COME FROM, CHILDREN WERE BRANDED AS MUTANTS.
SO DON'T PREACH TO ME, SUMMERS. YOU HAVE NO IDEA WHAT REAL OPPRESSION IS.
I KNOW-- MMMFFF
DON'T.

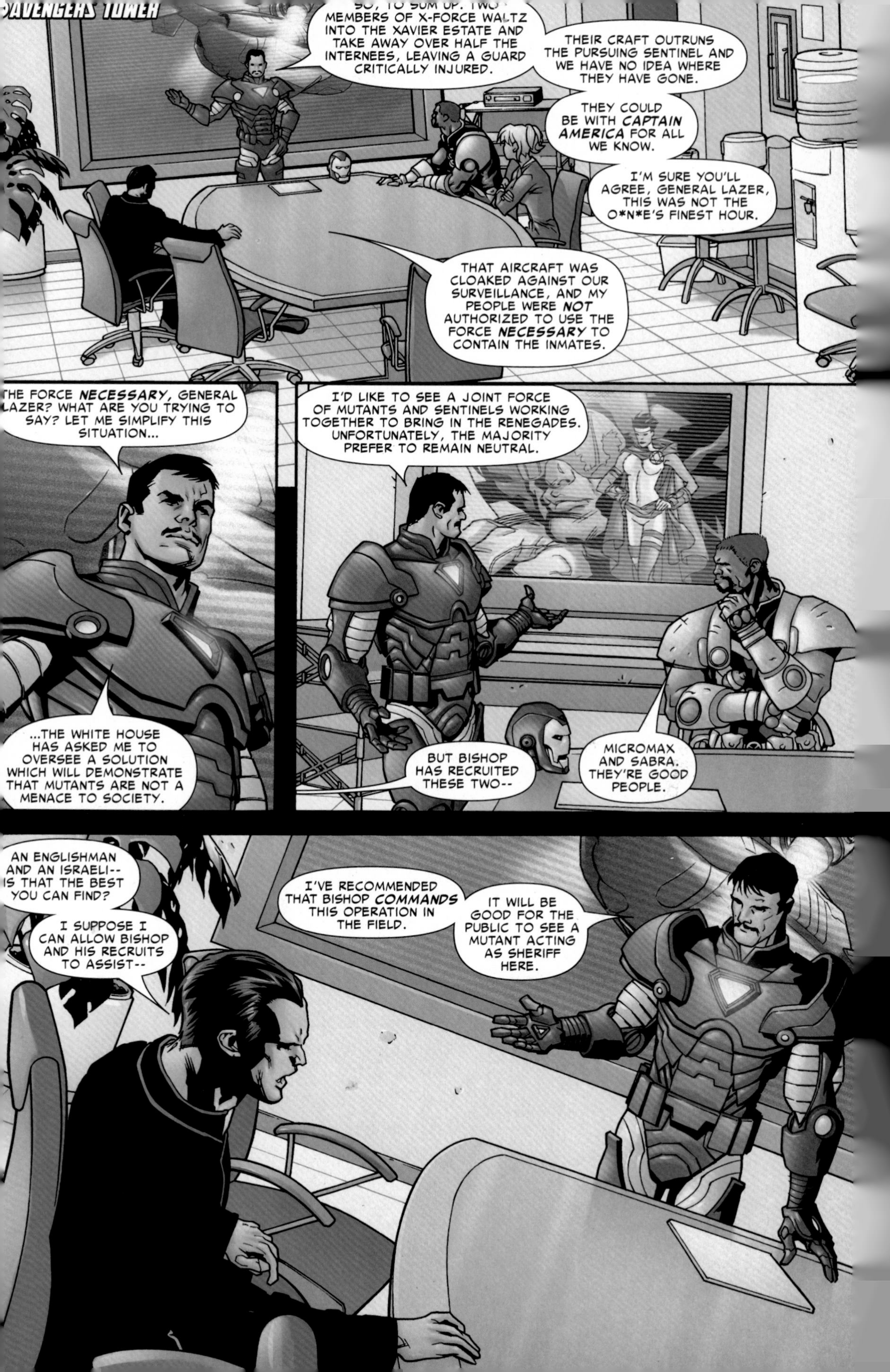
AVENGERS TOWER
SO, TO SUM UP. TWO MEMBERS OF X-FORCE WALTZ INTO THE XAVIER ESTATE AND TAKE AWAY OVER HALF THE INTERNEES, LEAVING A GUARD CRITICALLY INJURED.
THEIR CRAFT OUTRUNS THE PURSUING SENTINEL AND WE HAVE NO IDEA WHERE THEY HAVE GONE.
THEY COULD BE WITH CAPTAIN AMERICA FOR ALL WE KNOW.
I'M SURE YOU'LL AGREE, GENERAL LAZER, THIS WAS NOT THE O*N*E'S FINEST HOUR.
THAT AIRCRAFT WAS CLOAKED AGAINST OUR SURVEILLANCE, AND MY PEOPLE WERE NOT AUTHORIZED TO USE THE FORCE NECESSARY TO CONTAIN THE INMATES.
THE FORCE NECESSARY, GENERAL LAZER? WHAT ARE YOU TRYING TO SAY? LET ME SIMPLIFY THIS SITUATION...
...THE WHITE HOUSE HAS ASKED ME TO OVERSEE A SOLUTION WHICH WILL DEMONSTRATE THAT MUTANTS ARE NOT A MENACE TO SOCIETY.
I'D LIKE TO SEE A JOINT FORCE OF MUTANTS AND SENTINELS WORKING TOGETHER TO BRING IN THE RENEGADES. UNFORTUNATELY, THE MAJORITY PREFER TO REMAIN NEUTRAL.
BUT BISHOP HAS RECRUITED THESE TWO--
MICROMAX AND SABRA. THEY'RE GOOD PEOPLE.
AN ENGLISHMAN AND AN ISRAELI-- IS THAT THE BEST YOU CAN FIND?
I SUPPOSE I CAN ALLOW BISHOP AND HIS RECRUITS TO ASSIST--
I'VE RECOMMENDED THAT BISHOP COMMANDS THIS OPERATION IN THE FIELD.
IT WILL BE GOOD FOR THE PUBLIC TO SEE A MUTANT ACTING AS SHERIFF HERE.

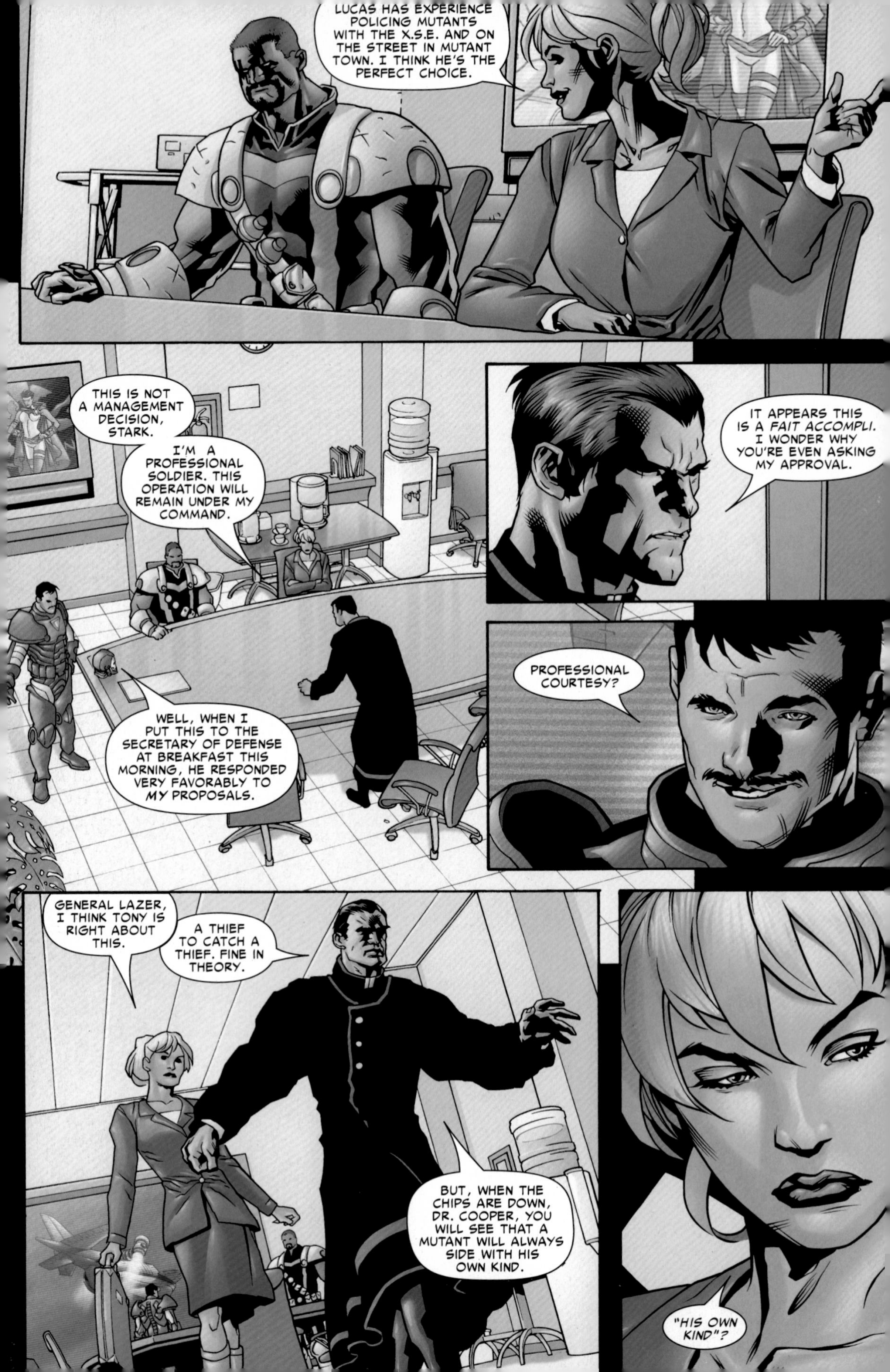
LUCAS HAS EXPERIENCE POLICING MUTANTS WITH THE X.S.E. AND ON THE STREET IN MUTANT TOWN. I THINK HE'S THE PERFECT CHOICE.
THIS IS NOT A MANAGEMENT DECISION, STARK.
I'M A PROFESSIONAL SOLDIER. THIS OPERATION WILL REMAIN UNDER MY COMMAND.
WELL, WHEN I PUT THIS TO THE SECRETARY OF DEFENSE AT BREAKFAST THIS MORNING, HE RESPONDED VERY FAVORABLY TO MY PROPOSALS.
IT APPEARS THIS IS A FAIT ACCOMPLI. I WONDER WHY YOU'RE EVEN ASKING MY APPROVAL.
PROFESSIONAL COURTESY?
GENERAL LAZER, I THINK TONY IS RIGHT ABOUT THIS.
A THIEF TO CATCH A THIEF. FINE IN THEORY.
BUT, WHEN THE CHIPS ARE DOWN, DR. COOPER, YOU WILL SEE THAT A MUTANT WILL ALWAYS SIDE WITH HIS OWN KIND.
"HIS OWN KIND"?

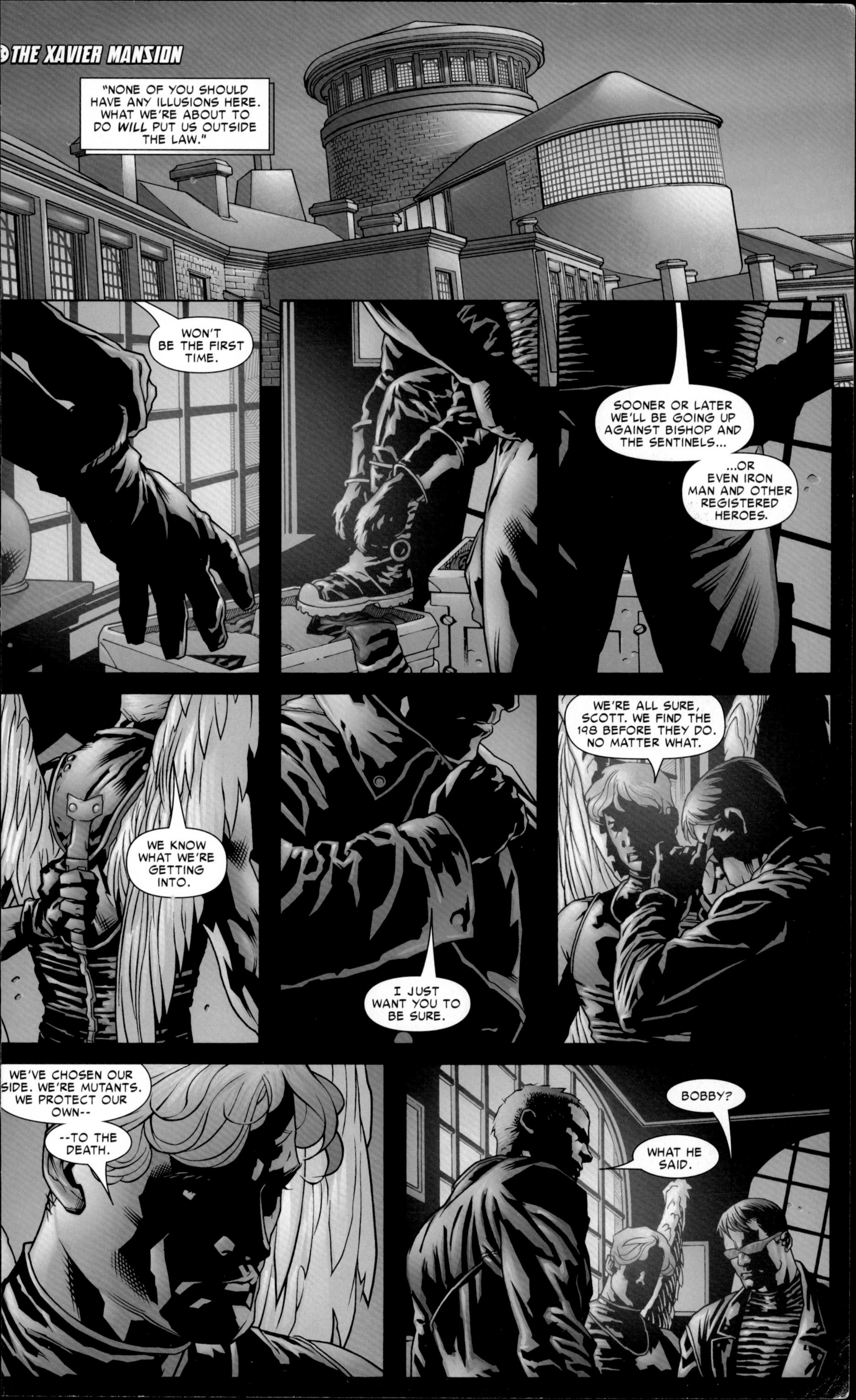
THE XAVIER MANSION
"NONE OF YOU SHOULD HAVE ANY ILLUSIONS HERE. WHAT WE'RE ABOUT TO DO *WILL* PUT US OUTSIDE THE LAW."
WON'T BE THE FIRST TIME.
SOONER OR LATER WE'LL BE GOING UP AGAINST BISHOP AND THE SENTINELS...
...OR EVEN IRON MAN AND OTHER REGISTERED HEROES.
WE KNOW WHAT WE'RE GETTING INTO.
I JUST WANT YOU TO BE SURE.
WE'RE ALL SURE, SCOTT. WE FIND THE 198 BEFORE THEY DO. NO MATTER WHAT.
WE'VE CHOSEN OUR SIDE. WE'RE MUTANTS. WE PROTECT OUR OWN--
--TO THE DEATH.
BOBBY?
WHAT HE SAID.

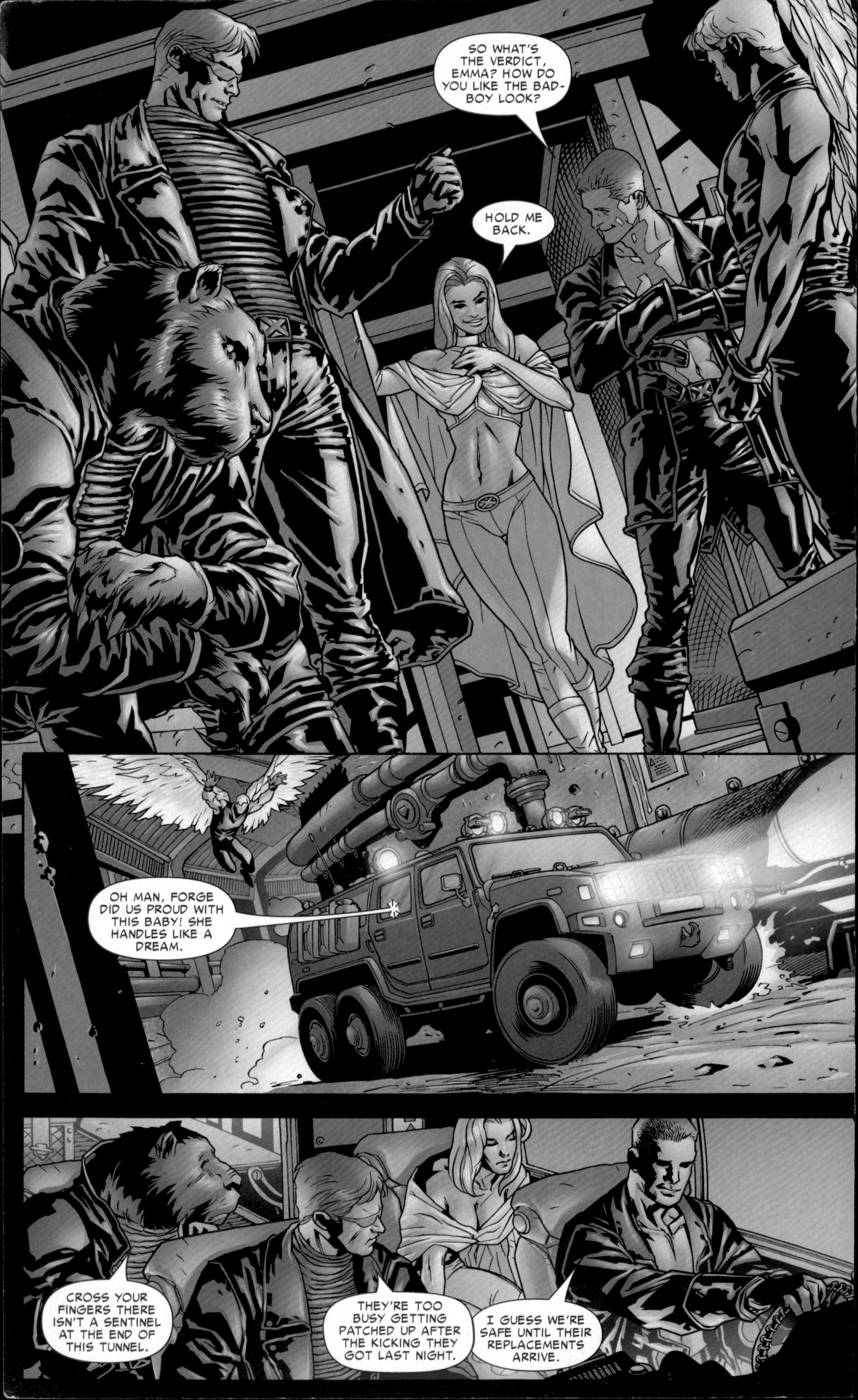
SO WHAT'S THE VERDICT, EMMA? HOW DO YOU LIKE THE BAD-BOY LOOK?
HOLD ME BACK.
OH MAN, FORGE DID US PROUD WITH THIS BABY! SHE HANDLES LIKE A DREAM.
CROSS YOUR FINGERS THERE ISN'T A SENTINEL AT THE END OF THIS TUNNEL.
THEY'RE TOO BUSY GETTING PATCHED UP AFTER THE KICKING THEY GOT LAST NIGHT.
I GUESS WE'RE SAFE UNTIL THEIR REPLACEMENTS ARRIVE.

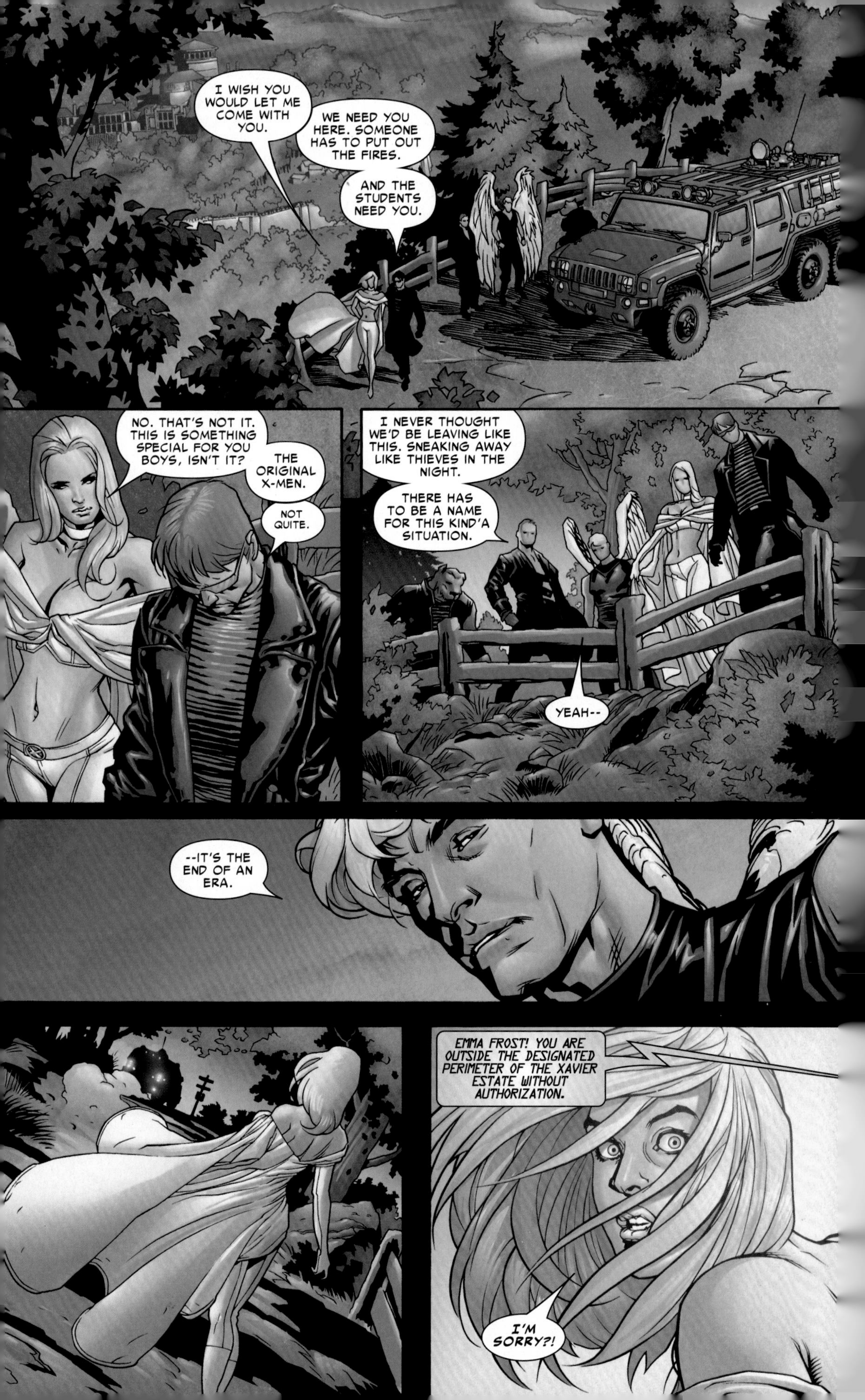
I WISH YOU WOULD LET ME COME WITH YOU.
WE NEED YOU HERE. SOMEONE HAS TO PUT OUT THE FIRES.
AND THE STUDENTS NEED YOU.
NO. THAT'S NOT IT. THIS IS SOMETHING SPECIAL FOR YOU BOYS, ISN'T IT?
THE ORIGINAL X-MEN.
NOT QUITE.
I NEVER THOUGHT WE'D BE LEAVING LIKE THIS. SNEAKING AWAY LIKE THIEVES IN THE NIGHT.
THERE HAS TO BE A NAME FOR THIS KIND'A SITUATION.
YEAH--
--IT'S THE END OF AN ERA.
EMMA FROST! YOU ARE OUTSIDE THE DESIGNATED PERIMETER OF THE XAVIER ESTATE WITHOUT AUTHORIZATION.
I'M SORRY?!

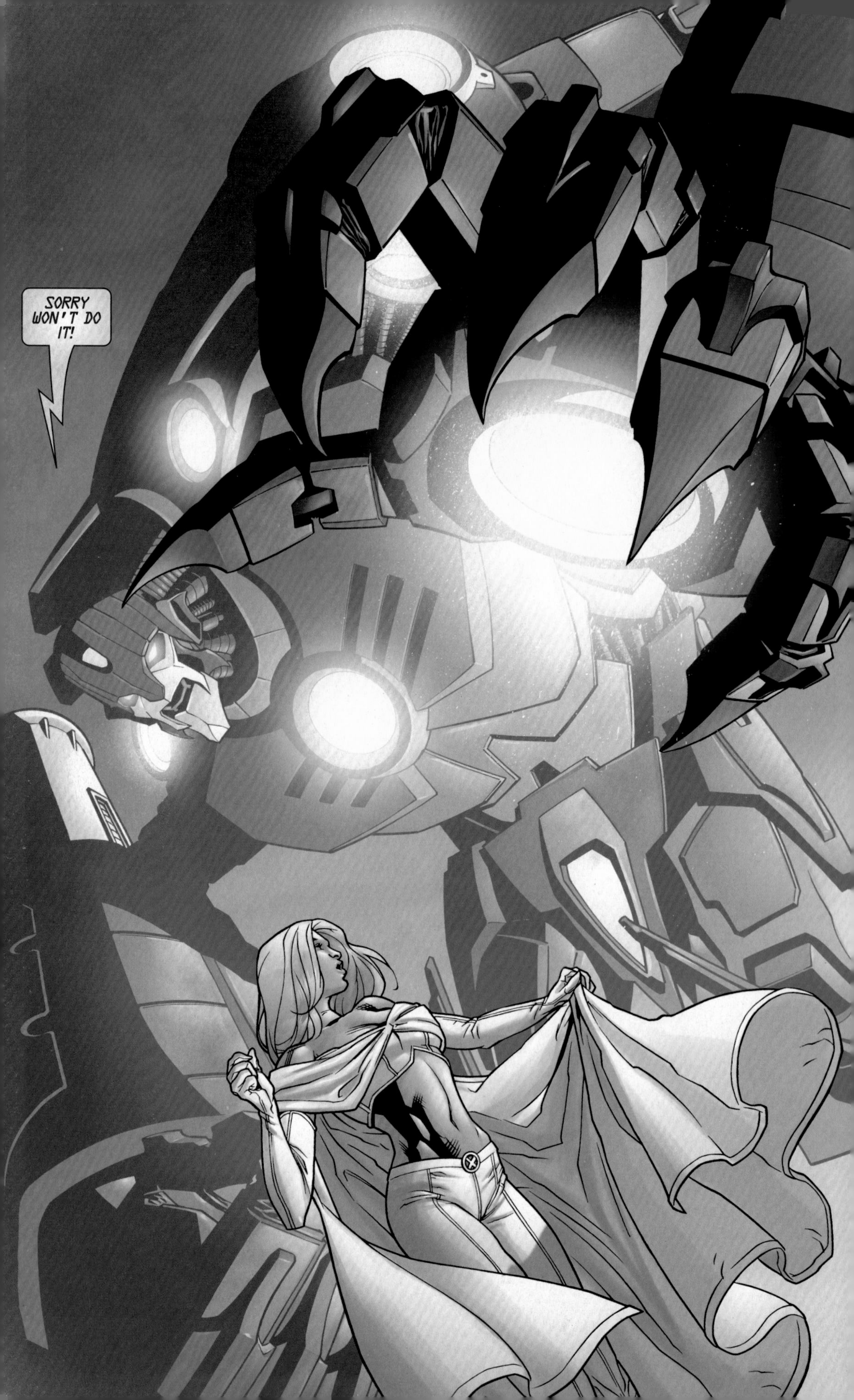
SORRY WON'T DO IT!

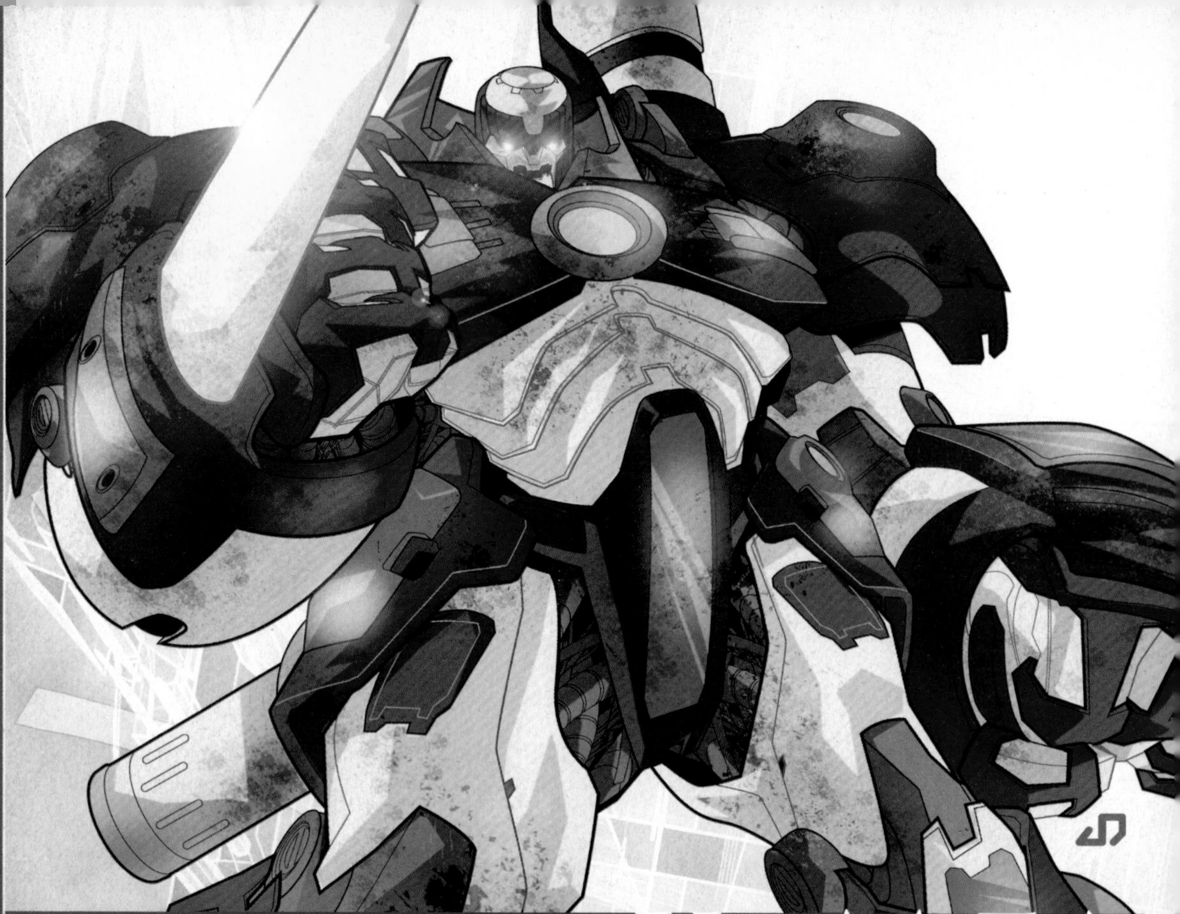

X-MEN

A MARVEL COMICS EVENT

CIVIL WAR

CIVIL WAR: X-MEN #2

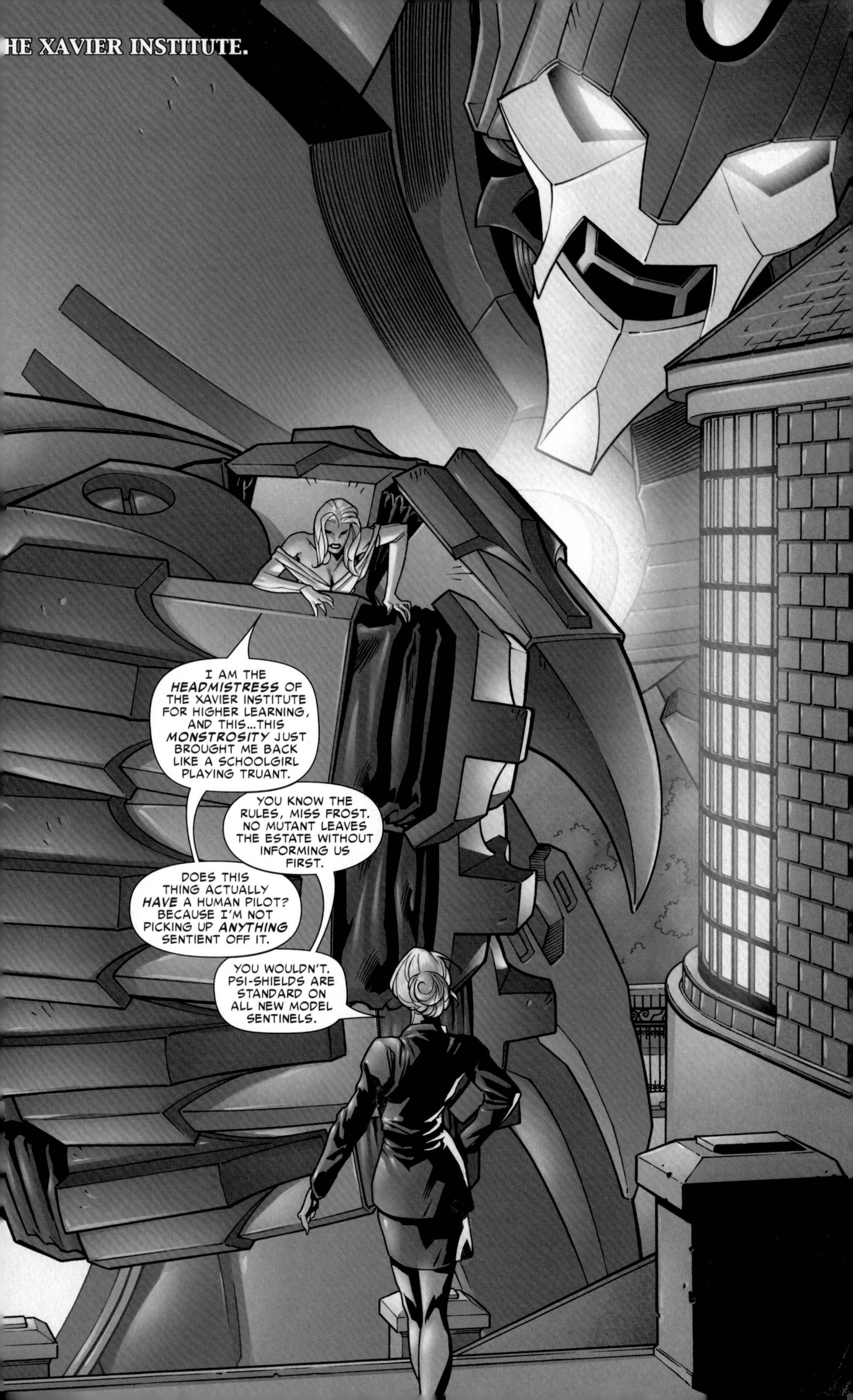
HE XAVIER INSTITUTE.
I AM THE HEADMISTRESS OF THE XAVIER INSTITUTE FOR HIGHER LEARNING, AND THIS...THIS MONSTROSITY JUST BROUGHT ME BACK LIKE A SCHOOLGIRL PLAYING TRUANT.
YOU KNOW THE RULES, MISS FROST. NO MUTANT LEAVES THE ESTATE WITHOUT INFORMING US FIRST.
DOES THIS THING ACTUALLY HAVE A HUMAN PILOT? BECAUSE I'M NOT PICKING UP ANYTHING SENTIENT OFF IT.
YOU WOULDN'T. PSI-SHIELDS ARE STANDARD ON ALL NEW MODEL SENTINELS.

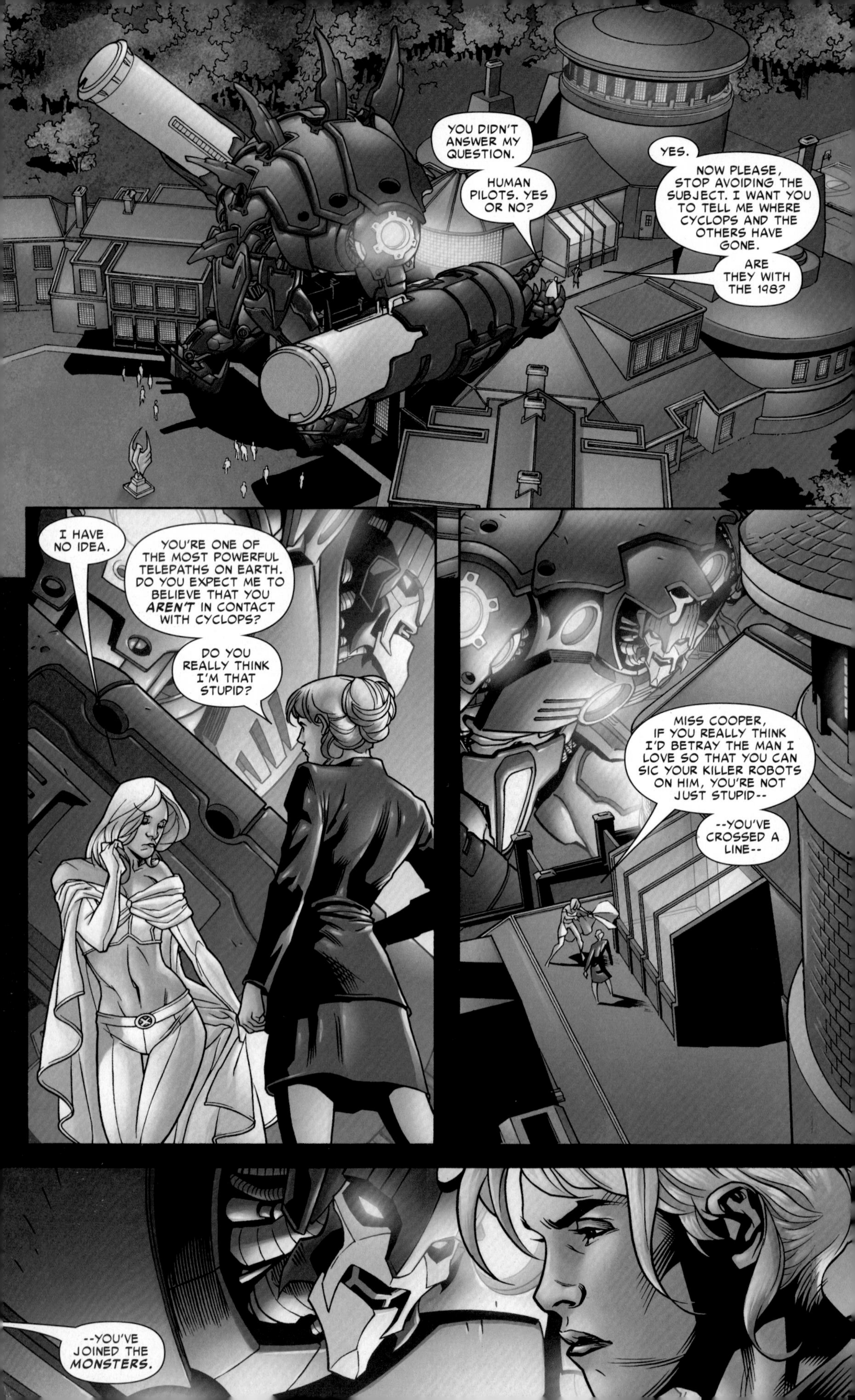
YOU DIDN'T ANSWER MY QUESTION.
HUMAN PILOTS. YES OR NO?
YES.
NOW PLEASE, STOP AVOIDING THE SUBJECT. I WANT YOU TO TELL ME WHERE CYCLOPS AND THE OTHERS HAVE GONE.
ARE THEY WITH THE 198?
I HAVE NO IDEA.
YOU'RE ONE OF THE MOST POWERFUL TELEPATHS ON EARTH. DO YOU EXPECT ME TO BELIEVE THAT YOU *AREN'T* IN CONTACT WITH CYCLOPS?
DO YOU REALLY THINK I'M THAT STUPID?
MISS COOPER, IF YOU REALLY THINK I'D BETRAY THE MAN I LOVE SO THAT YOU CAN SIC YOUR KILLER ROBOTS ON HIM, YOU'RE NOT JUST STUPID--
--YOU'VE CROSSED A LINE--
--YOU'VE JOINED THE *MONSTERS*.

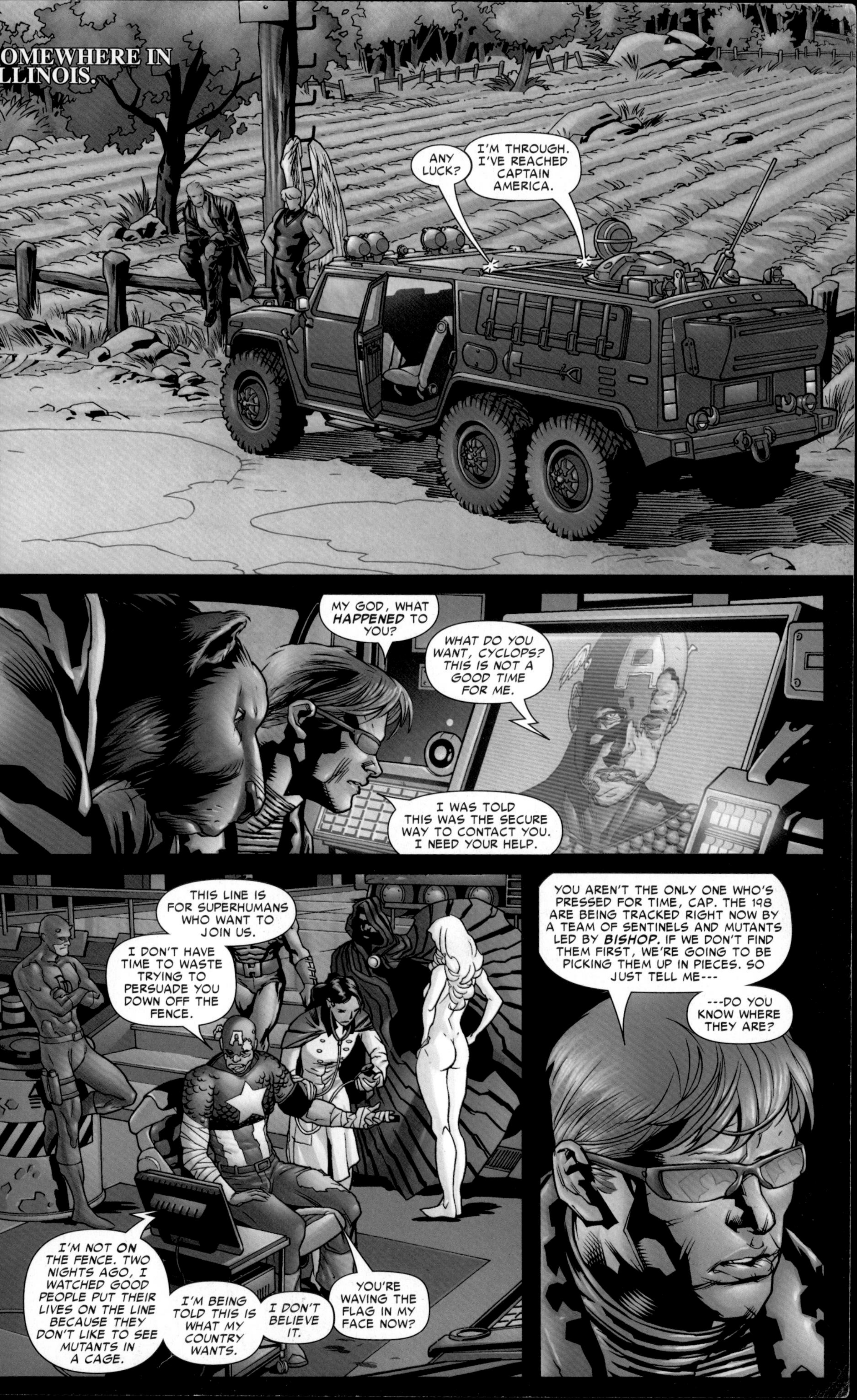
OMEWHERE IN
LLINOIS.
ANY LUCK?
I'M THROUGH. I'VE REACHED CAPTAIN AMERICA.
MY GOD, WHAT HAPPENED TO YOU?
WHAT DO YOU WANT, CYCLOPS? THIS IS NOT A GOOD TIME FOR ME.
I WAS TOLD THIS WAS THE SECURE WAY TO CONTACT YOU. I NEED YOUR HELP.
THIS LINE IS FOR SUPERHUMANS WHO WANT TO JOIN US.
I DON'T HAVE TIME TO WASTE TRYING TO PERSUADE YOU DOWN OFF THE FENCE.
I'M NOT ON THE FENCE. TWO NIGHTS AGO, I WATCHED GOOD PEOPLE PUT THEIR LIVES ON THE LINE BECAUSE THEY DON'T LIKE TO SEE MUTANTS IN A CAGE.
I'M BEING TOLD THIS IS WHAT MY COUNTRY WANTS.
I DON'T BELIEVE IT.
YOU'RE WAVING THE FLAG IN MY FACE NOW?
YOU AREN'T THE ONLY ONE WHO'S PRESSED FOR TIME, CAP. THE 198 ARE BEING TRACKED RIGHT NOW BY A TEAM OF SENTINELS AND MUTANTS LED BY BISHOP. IF WE DON'T FIND THEM FIRST, WE'RE GOING TO BE PICKING THEM UP IN PIECES. SO JUST TELL ME---
---DO YOU KNOW WHERE THEY ARE?

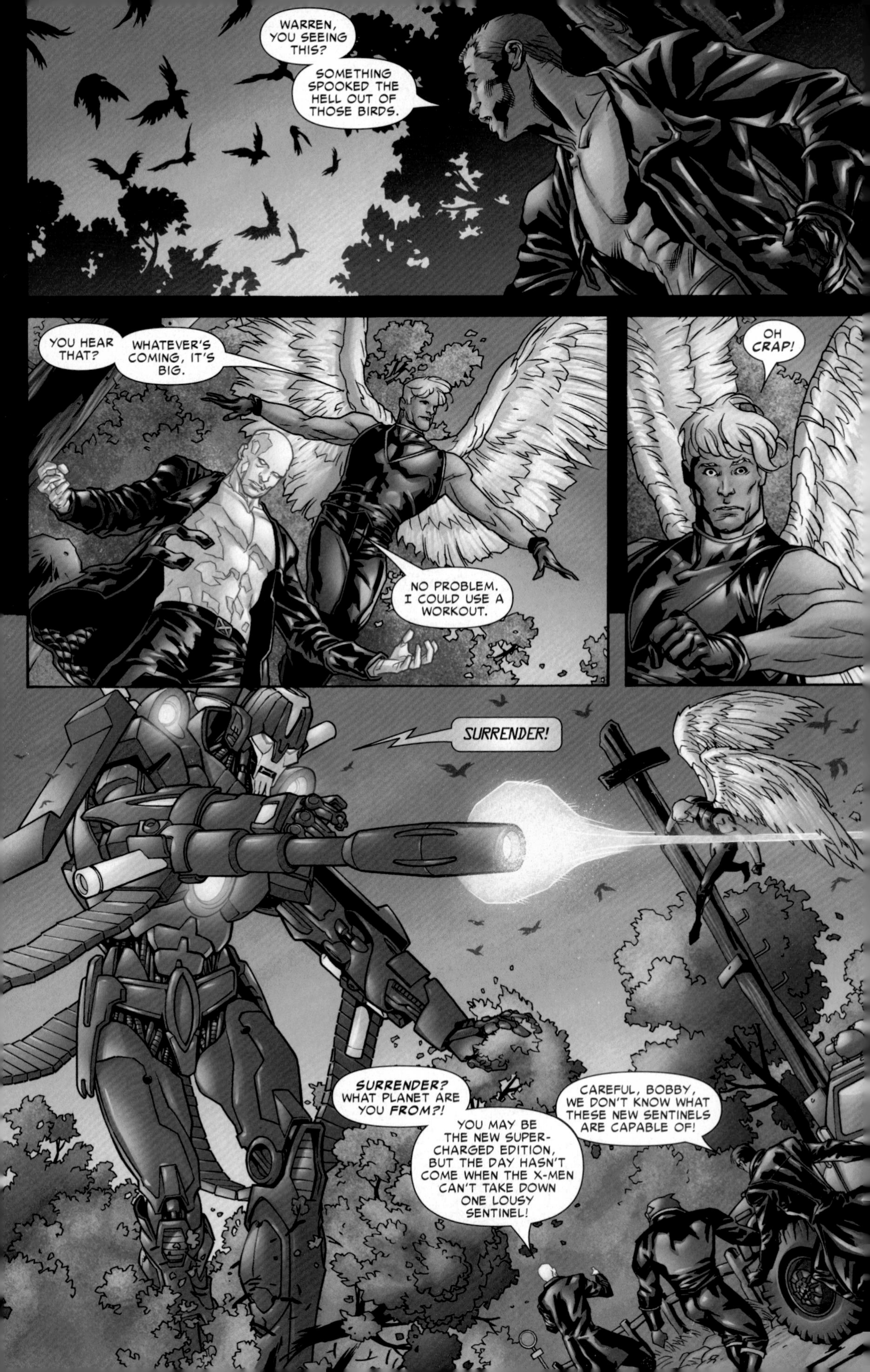
WARREN, YOU SEEING THIS?
SOMETHING SPOOKED THE HELL OUT OF THOSE BIRDS.
YOU HEAR THAT?
WHATEVER'S COMING, IT'S BIG.
NO PROBLEM. I COULD USE A WORKOUT.
OH CRAP!
SURRENDER!
SURRENDER? WHAT PLANET ARE YOU FROM?!
YOU MAY BE THE NEW SUPER-CHARGED EDITION, BUT THE DAY HASN'T COME WHEN THE X-MEN CAN'T TAKE DOWN ONE LOUSY SENTINEL!
CAREFUL, BOBBY, WE DON'T KNOW WHAT THESE NEW SENTINELS ARE CAPABLE OF!

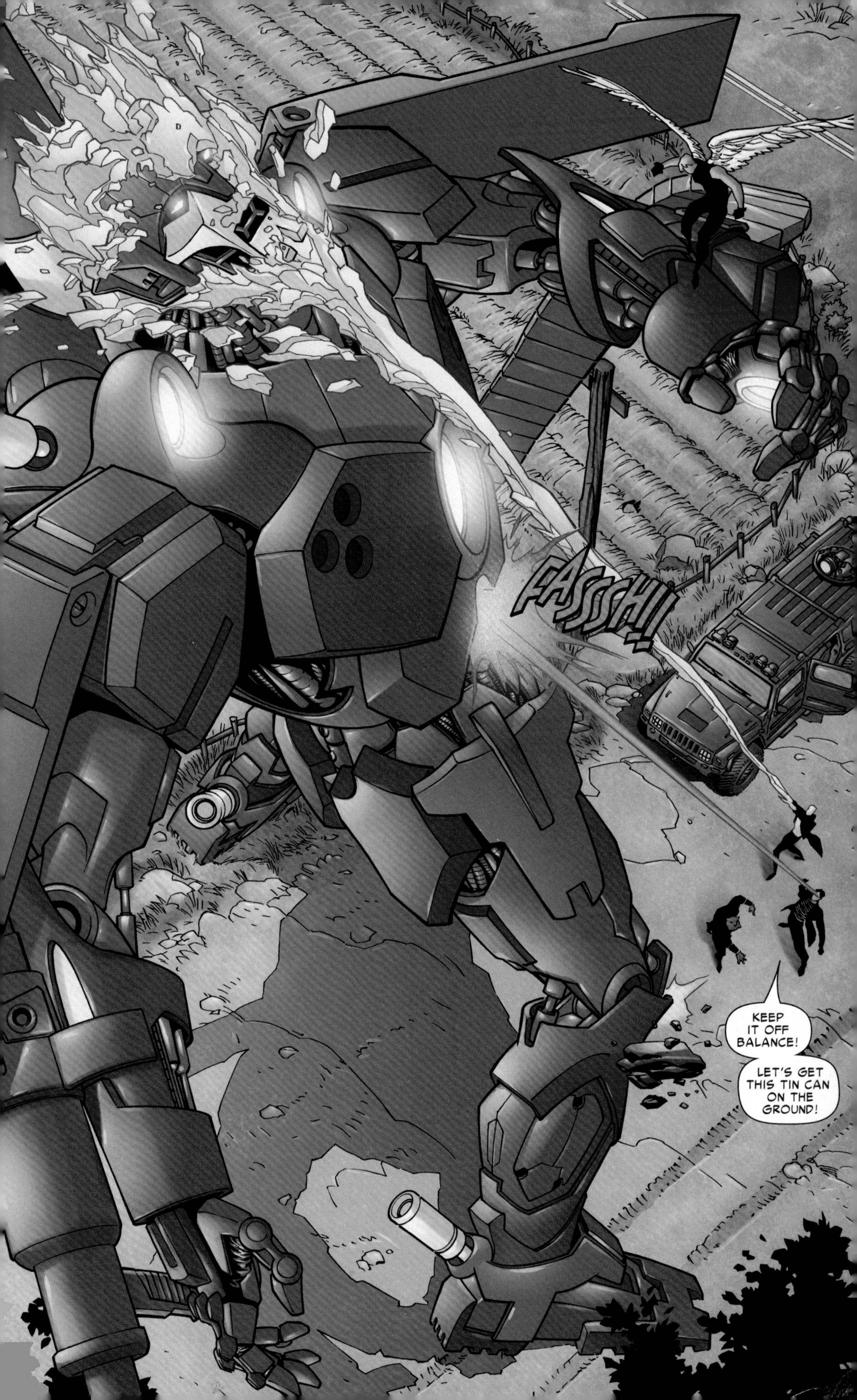
FASSSH!!
KEEP IT OFF BALANCE!
LET'S GET THIS TIN CAN ON THE GROUND!

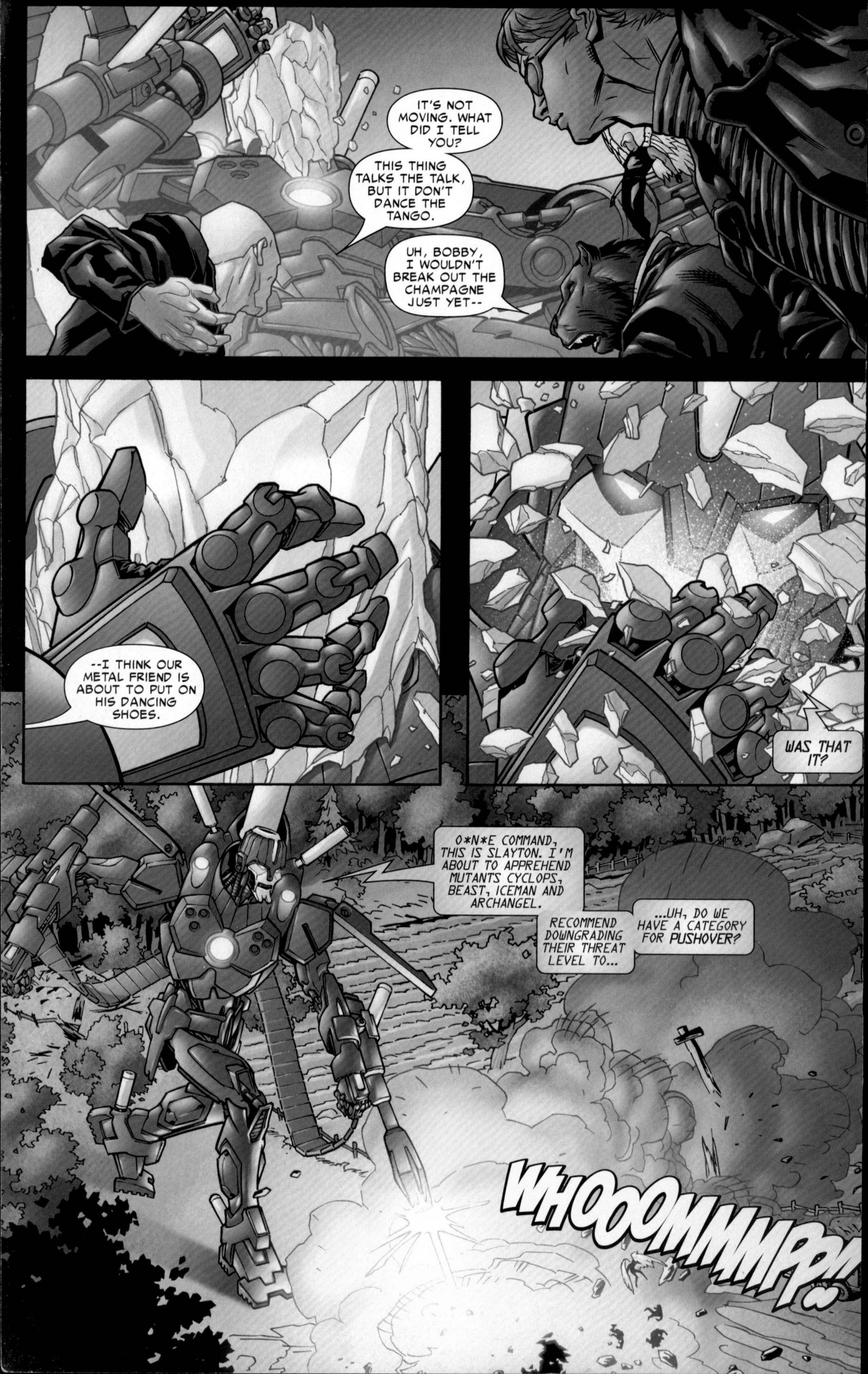
IT'S NOT MOVING. WHAT DID I TELL YOU?
THIS THING TALKS THE TALK, BUT IT DON'T DANCE THE TANGO.
UH, BOBBY, I WOULDN'T BREAK OUT THE CHAMPAGNE JUST YET--
--I THINK OUR METAL FRIEND IS ABOUT TO PUT ON HIS DANCING SHOES.
WAS THAT IT?
O*N*E COMMAND, THIS IS SLAYTON. I'M ABOUT TO APPREHEND MUTANTS CYCLOPS, BEAST, ICEMAN AND ARCHANGEL.
RECOMMEND DOWNGRADING THEIR THREAT LEVEL TO...
...UH, DO WE HAVE A CATEGORY FOR PUSHOVER?
WHOOOMMMPP!

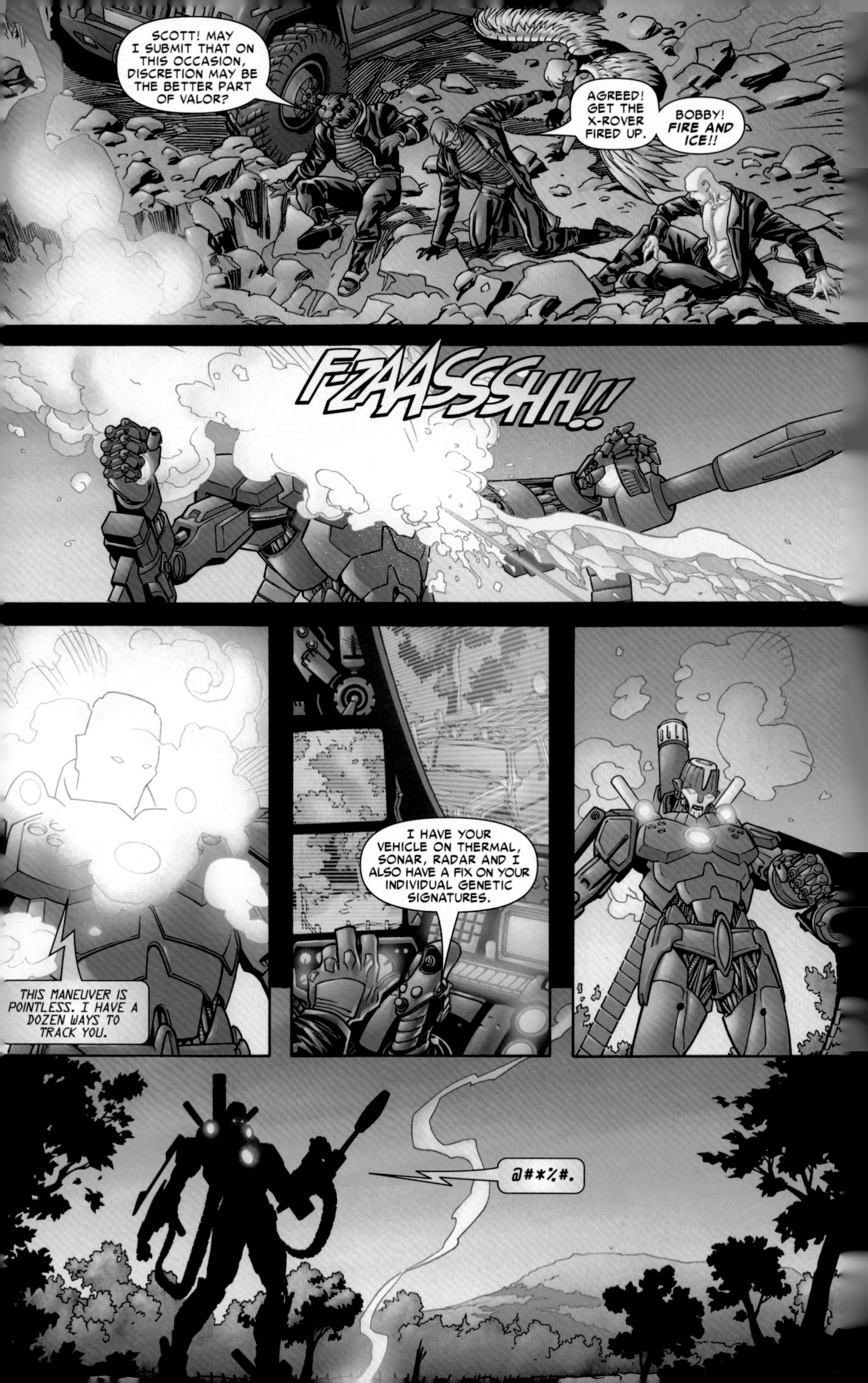
SCOTT! MAY I SUBMIT THAT ON THIS OCCASION, DISCRETION MAY BE THE BETTER PART OF VALOR?
AGREED! GET THE X-ROVER FIRED UP.
BOBBY! FIRE AND ICE!!
FZAASSSHH!!
THIS MANEUVER IS POINTLESS. I HAVE A DOZEN WAYS TO TRACK YOU.
I HAVE YOUR VEHICLE ON THERMAL, SONAR, RADAR AND I ALSO HAVE A FIX ON YOUR INDIVIDUAL GENETIC SIGNATURES.
@#*%#.

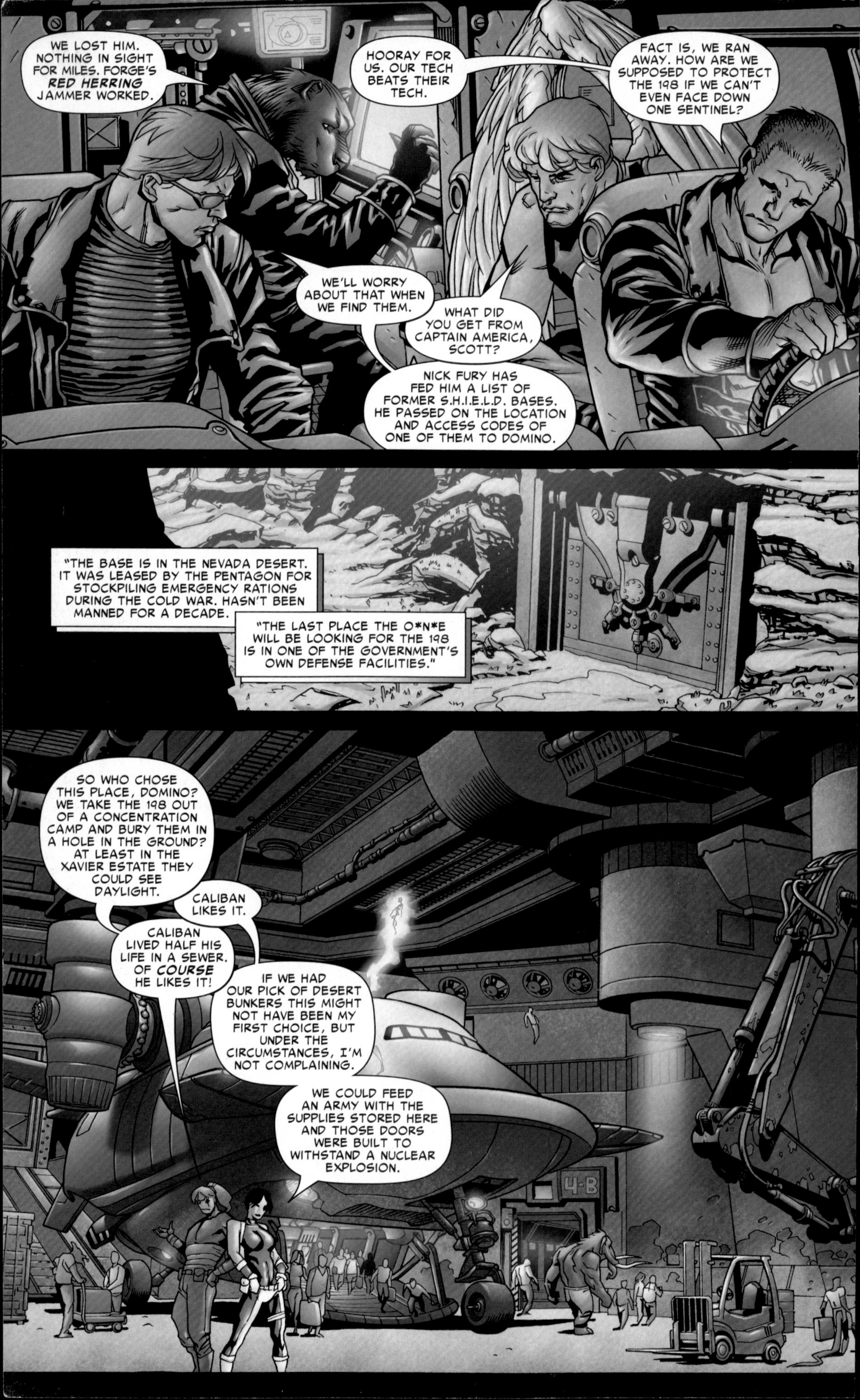

WE LOST HIM. NOTHING IN SIGHT FOR MILES. FORGE'S *RED HERRING* JAMMER WORKED.
HOORAY FOR US. OUR TECH BEATS THEIR TECH.
FACT IS, WE RAN AWAY. HOW ARE WE SUPPOSED TO PROTECT THE 198 IF WE CAN'T EVEN FACE DOWN ONE SENTINEL?
WE'LL WORRY ABOUT THAT WHEN WE FIND THEM.
WHAT DID YOU GET FROM CAPTAIN AMERICA, SCOTT?
NICK FURY HAS FED HIM A LIST OF FORMER S.H.I.E.L.D. BASES. HE PASSED ON THE LOCATION AND ACCESS CODES OF ONE OF THEM TO DOMINO.
"THE BASE IS IN THE NEVADA DESERT. IT WAS LEASED BY THE PENTAGON FOR STOCKPILING EMERGENCY RATIONS DURING THE COLD WAR. HASN'T BEEN MANNED FOR A DECADE.
"THE LAST PLACE THE O*N*E WILL BE LOOKING FOR THE 198 IS IN ONE OF THE GOVERNMENT'S OWN DEFENSE FACILITIES."
SO WHO CHOSE THIS PLACE, DOMINO? WE TAKE THE 198 OUT OF A CONCENTRATION CAMP AND BURY THEM IN A HOLE IN THE GROUND? AT LEAST IN THE XAVIER ESTATE THEY COULD SEE DAYLIGHT.
CALIBAN LIKES IT.
CALIBAN LIVED HALF HIS LIFE IN A SEWER. OF *COURSE* HE LIKES IT!
IF WE HAD OUR PICK OF DESERT BUNKERS THIS MIGHT NOT HAVE BEEN MY FIRST CHOICE, BUT UNDER THE CIRCUMSTANCES, I'M NOT COMPLAINING.
WE COULD FEED AN ARMY WITH THE SUPPLIES STORED HERE AND THOSE DOORS WERE BUILT TO WITHSTAND A NUCLEAR EXPLOSION.
4-B

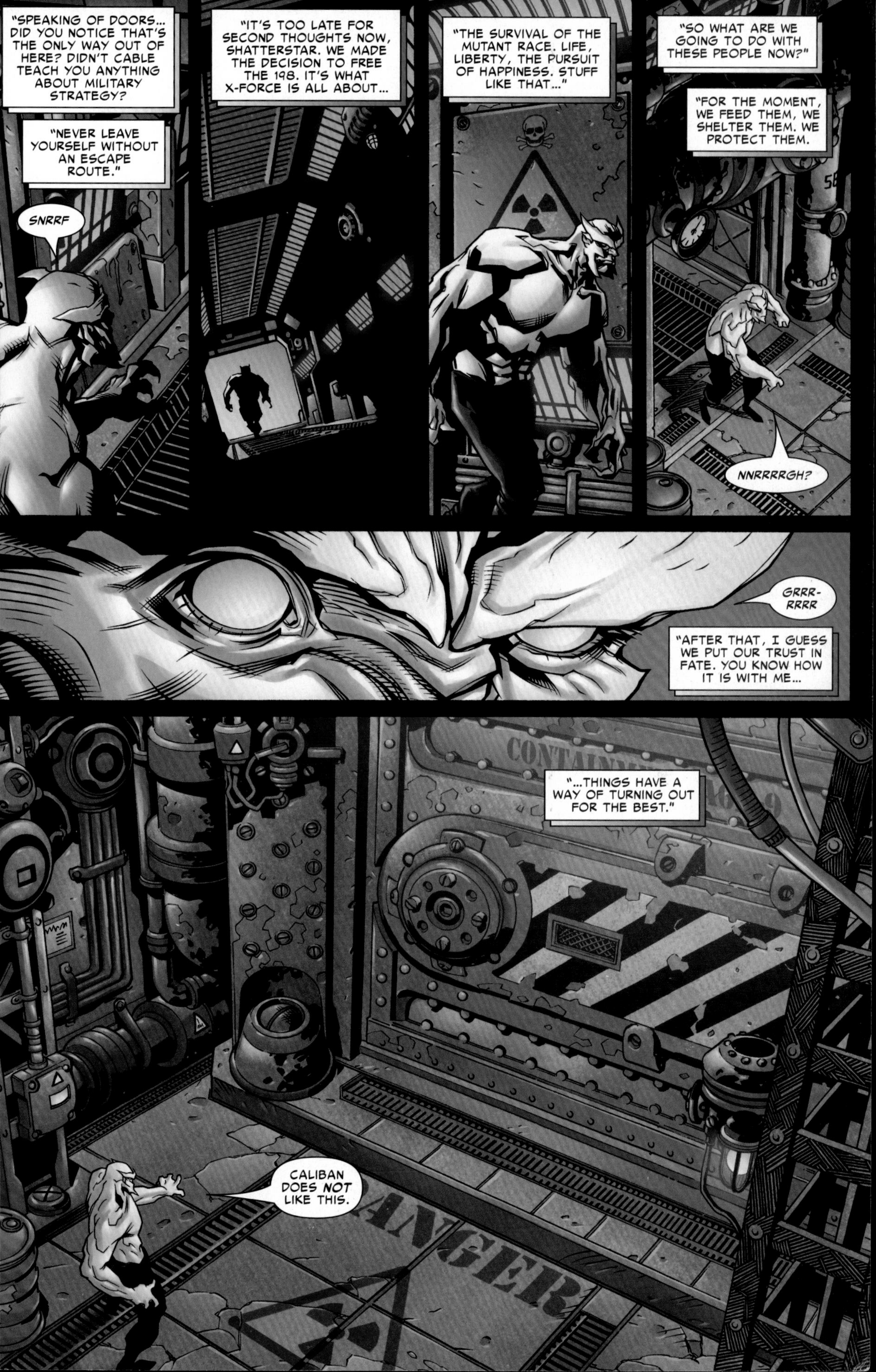
"SPEAKING OF DOORS... DID YOU NOTICE THAT'S THE ONLY WAY OUT OF HERE? DIDN'T CABLE TEACH YOU ANYTHING ABOUT MILITARY STRATEGY?
"NEVER LEAVE YOURSELF WITHOUT AN ESCAPE ROUTE."
SNRRF
"IT'S TOO LATE FOR SECOND THOUGHTS NOW, SHATTERSTAR. WE MADE THE DECISION TO FREE THE 198. IT'S WHAT X-FORCE IS ALL ABOUT...
"THE SURVIVAL OF THE MUTANT RACE. LIFE, LIBERTY, THE PURSUIT OF HAPPINESS. STUFF LIKE THAT..."
"SO WHAT ARE WE GOING TO DO WITH THESE PEOPLE NOW?"
"FOR THE MOMENT, WE FEED THEM, WE SHELTER THEM. WE PROTECT THEM.
NNRRRRGH?
GRRR-RRRR
"AFTER THAT, I GUESS WE PUT OUR TRUST IN FATE. YOU KNOW HOW IT IS WITH ME...
"...THINGS HAVE A WAY OF TURNING OUT FOR THE BEST."
CALIBAN DOES NOT LIKE THIS.

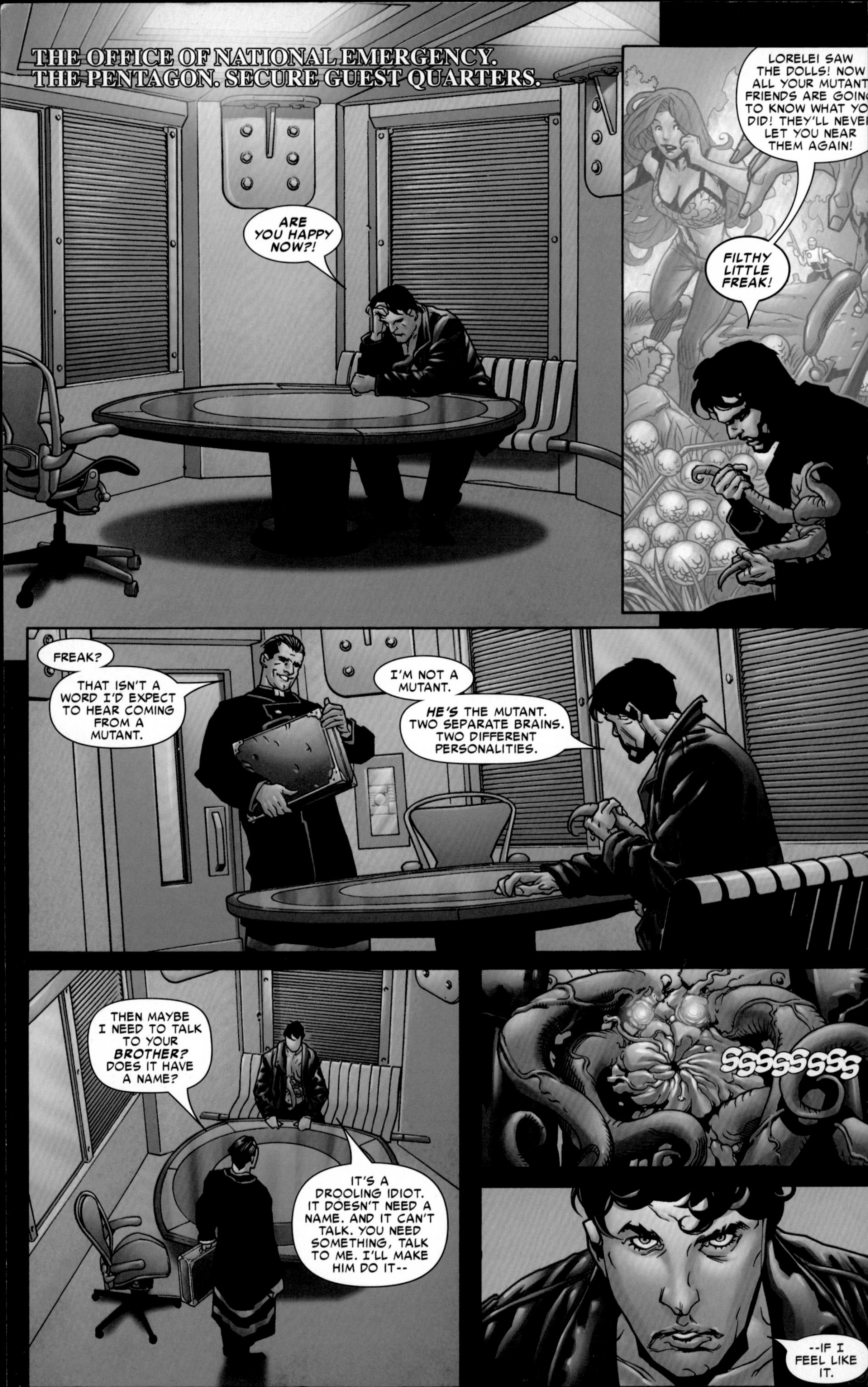
THE OFFICE OF NATIONAL EMERGENCY. THE PENTAGON. SECURE GUEST QUARTERS.
ARE YOU HAPPY NOW?!
LORELEI SAW THE DOLLS! NOW ALL YOUR MUTANT FRIENDS ARE GOING TO KNOW WHAT YOU DID! THEY'LL NEVER LET YOU NEAR THEM AGAIN!
FILTHY LITTLE FREAK!
FREAK?
THAT ISN'T A WORD I'D EXPECT TO HEAR COMING FROM A MUTANT.
I'M NOT A MUTANT.
HE'S THE MUTANT. TWO SEPARATE BRAINS. TWO DIFFERENT PERSONALITIES.
THEN MAYBE I NEED TO TALK TO YOUR BROTHER? DOES IT HAVE A NAME?
IT'S A DROOLING IDIOT. IT DOESN'T NEED A NAME. AND IT CAN'T TALK. YOU NEED SOMETHING, TALK TO ME. I'LL MAKE HIM DO IT--
SSSSSSSS
--IF I FEEL LIKE IT.

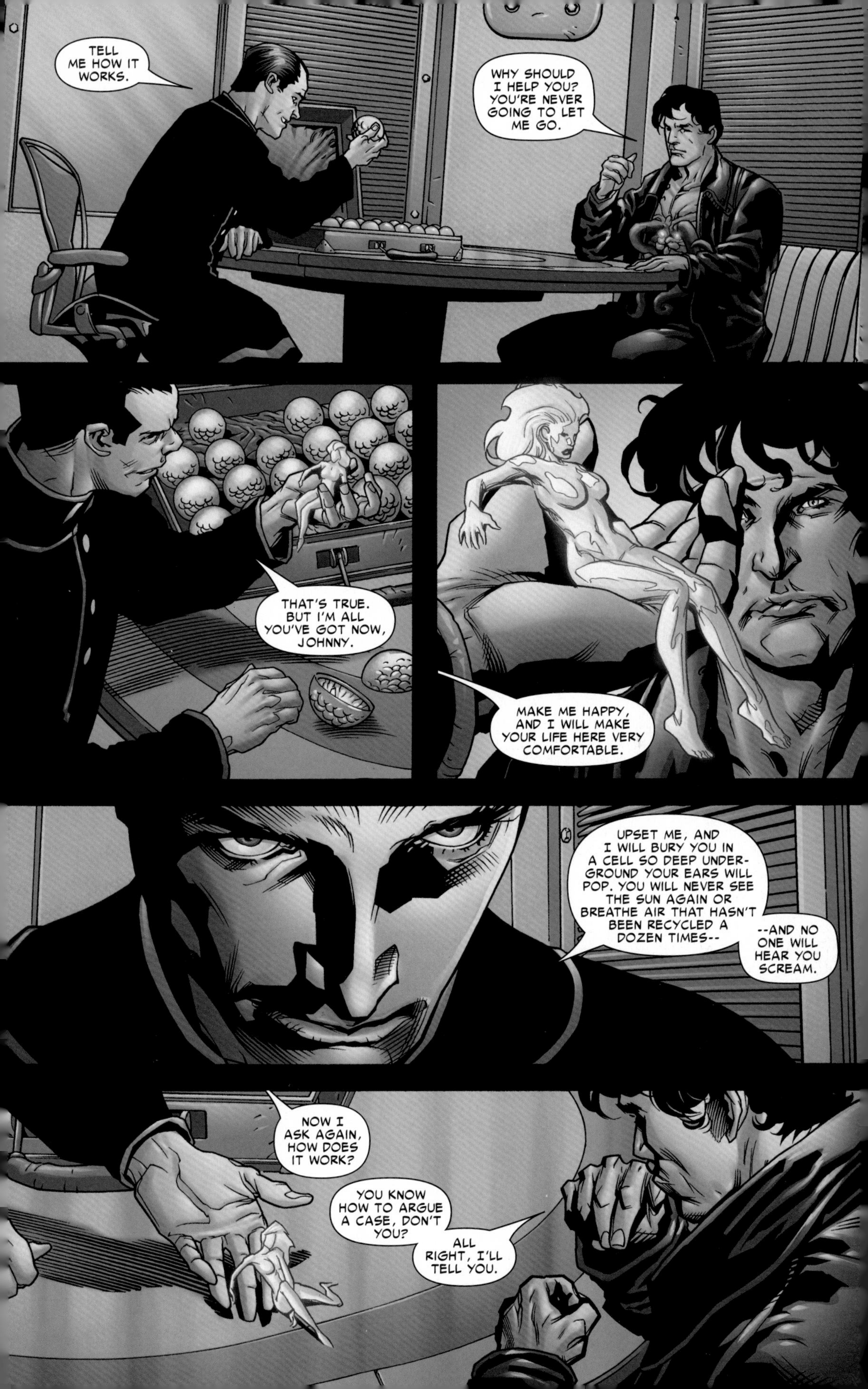
TELL ME HOW IT WORKS.
WHY SHOULD I HELP YOU? YOU'RE NEVER GOING TO LET ME GO.
THAT'S TRUE. BUT I'M ALL YOU'VE GOT NOW, JOHNNY.
MAKE ME HAPPY, AND I WILL MAKE YOUR LIFE HERE VERY COMFORTABLE.
UPSET ME, AND I WILL BURY YOU IN A CELL SO DEEP UNDER-GROUND YOUR EARS WILL POP. YOU WILL NEVER SEE THE SUN AGAIN OR BREATHE AIR THAT HASN'T BEEN RECYCLED A DOZEN TIMES--
--AND NO ONE WILL HEAR YOU SCREAM.
NOW I ASK AGAIN, HOW DOES IT WORK?
YOU KNOW HOW TO ARGUE A CASE, DON'T YOU?
ALL RIGHT, I'LL TELL YOU.

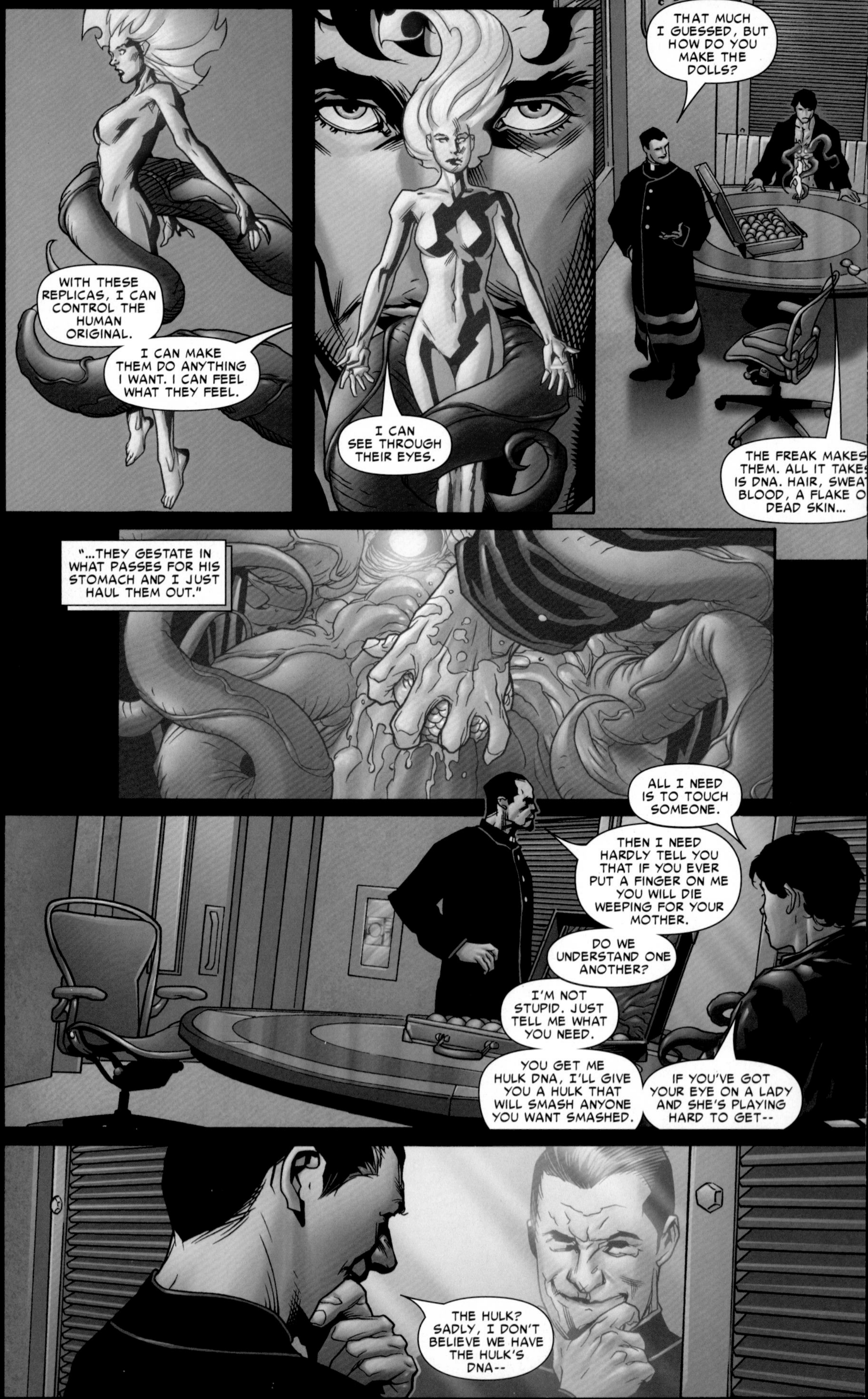
WITH THESE REPLICAS, I CAN CONTROL THE HUMAN ORIGINAL.
I CAN MAKE THEM DO ANYTHING I WANT. I CAN FEEL WHAT THEY FEEL.
I CAN SEE THROUGH THEIR EYES.
THAT MUCH I GUESSED, BUT HOW DO YOU MAKE THE DOLLS?
THE FREAK MAKES THEM. ALL IT TAKES IS DNA. HAIR, SWEAT BLOOD, A FLAKE OF DEAD SKIN...
"...THEY GESTATE IN WHAT PASSES FOR HIS STOMACH AND I JUST HAUL THEM OUT."
ALL I NEED IS TO TOUCH SOMEONE.
THEN I NEED HARDLY TELL YOU THAT IF YOU EVER PUT A FINGER ON ME YOU WILL DIE WEEPING FOR YOUR MOTHER.
DO WE UNDERSTAND ONE ANOTHER?
I'M NOT STUPID. JUST TELL ME WHAT YOU NEED.
YOU GET ME HULK DNA, I'LL GIVE YOU A HULK THAT WILL SMASH ANYONE YOU WANT SMASHED.
IF YOU'VE GOT YOUR EYE ON A LADY AND SHE'S PLAYING HARD TO GET--
THE HULK? SADLY, I DON'T BELIEVE WE HAVE THE HULK'S DNA--

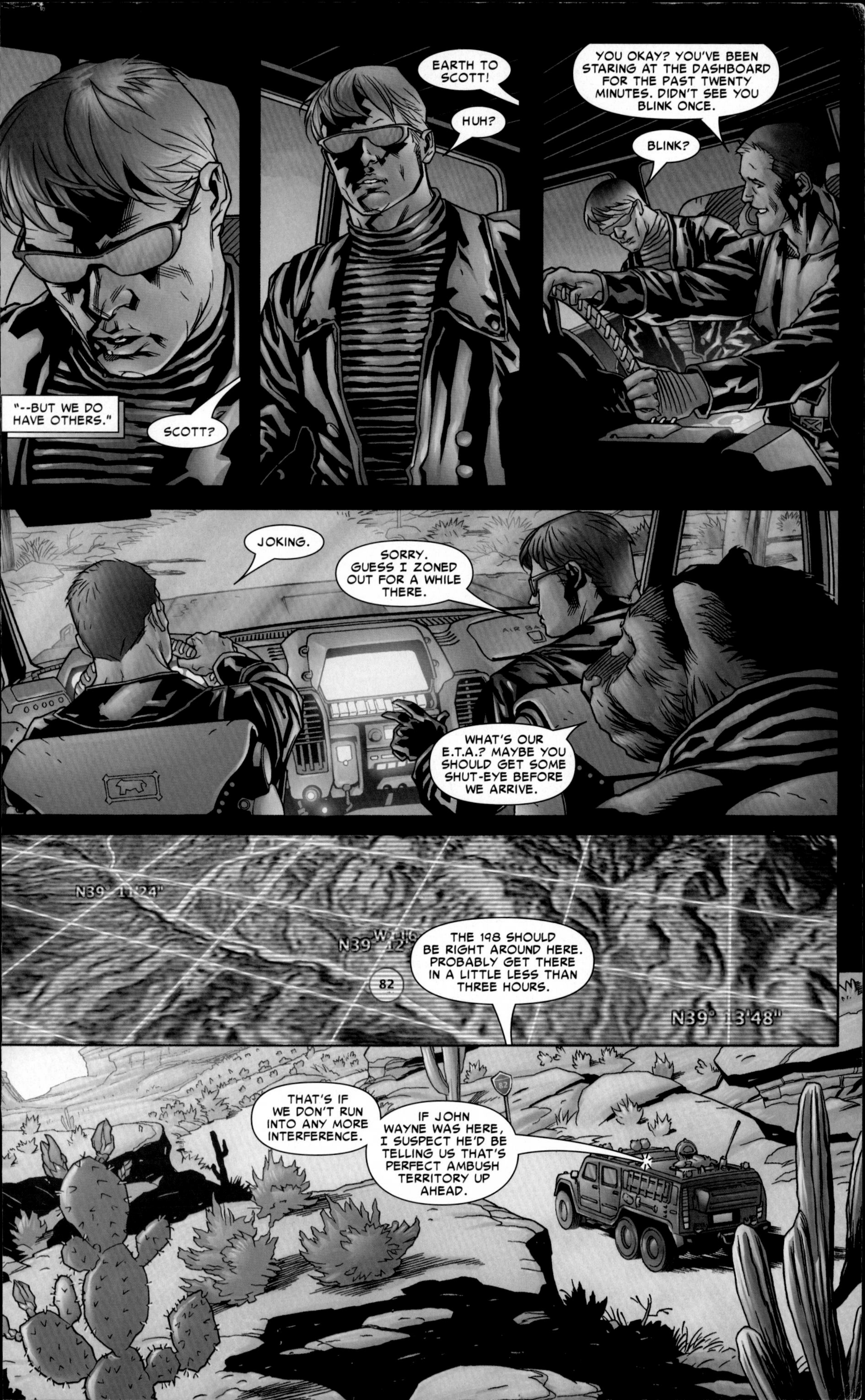
"--BUT WE DO HAVE OTHERS."
SCOTT?
EARTH TO SCOTT!
HUH?
YOU OKAY? YOU'VE BEEN STARING AT THE DASHBOARD FOR THE PAST TWENTY MINUTES. DIDN'T SEE YOU BLINK ONCE.
BLINK?
JOKING.
SORRY. GUESS I ZONED OUT FOR A WHILE THERE.
AIR BAG
WHAT'S OUR E.T.A.? MAYBE YOU SHOULD GET SOME SHUT-EYE BEFORE WE ARRIVE.
N39° 11'24"
THE 198 SHOULD BE RIGHT AROUND HERE. PROBABLY GET THERE IN A LITTLE LESS THAN THREE HOURS.
82
N39° 13'48"
82
THAT'S IF WE DON'T RUN INTO ANY MORE INTERFERENCE.
IF JOHN WAYNE WAS HERE, I SUSPECT HE'D BE TELLING US THAT'S PERFECT AMBUSH TERRITORY UP AHEAD.

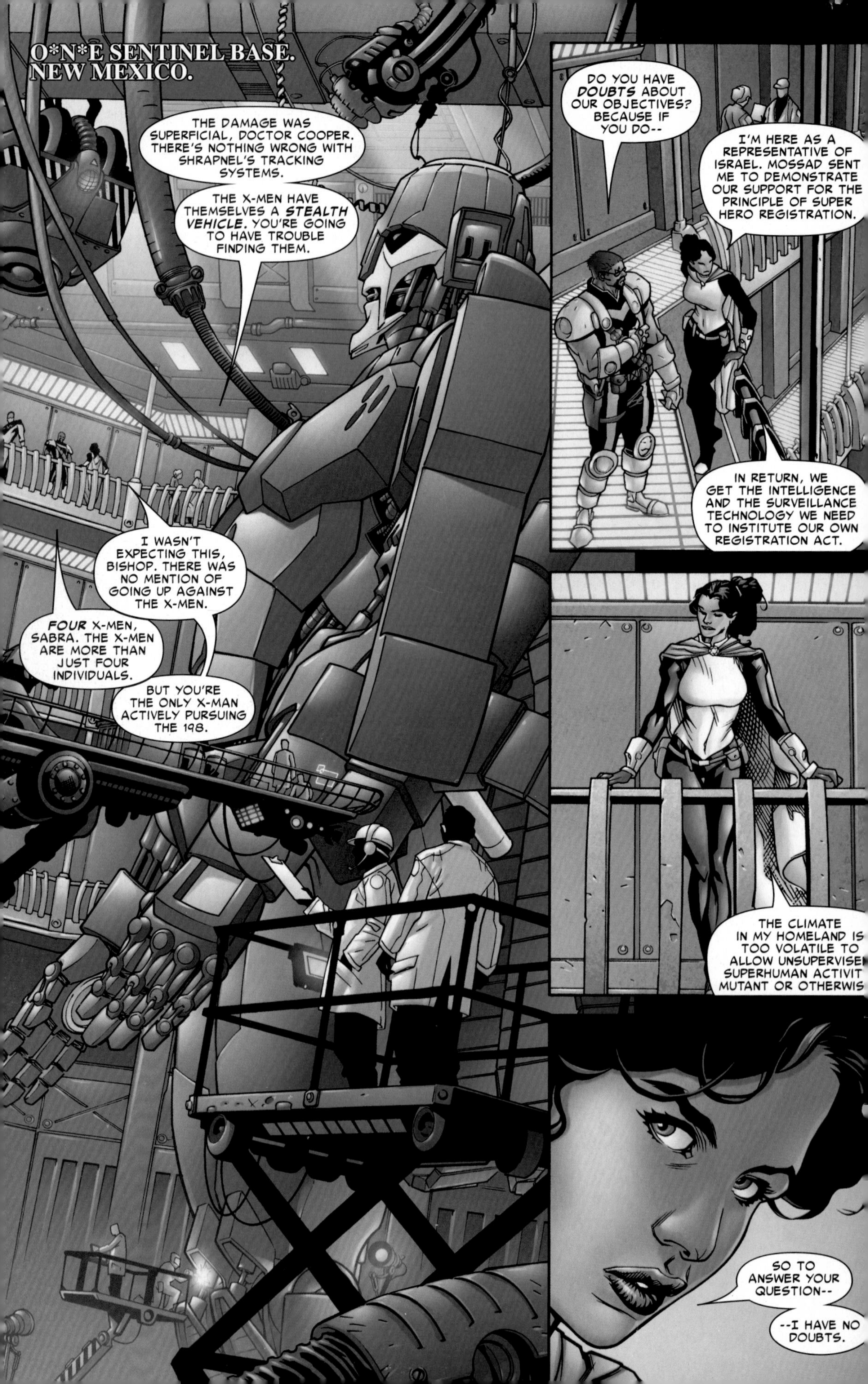
O*N*E SENTINEL BASE. NEW MEXICO.
THE DAMAGE WAS SUPERFICIAL, DOCTOR COOPER. THERE'S NOTHING WRONG WITH SHRAPNEL'S TRACKING SYSTEMS.
THE X-MEN HAVE THEMSELVES A STEALTH VEHICLE. YOU'RE GOING TO HAVE TROUBLE FINDING THEM.
I WASN'T EXPECTING THIS, BISHOP. THERE WAS NO MENTION OF GOING UP AGAINST THE X-MEN.
FOUR X-MEN, SABRA. THE X-MEN ARE MORE THAN JUST FOUR INDIVIDUALS.
BUT YOU'RE THE ONLY X-MAN ACTIVELY PURSUING THE 198.
DO YOU HAVE DOUBTS ABOUT OUR OBJECTIVES? BECAUSE IF YOU DO--
I'M HERE AS A REPRESENTATIVE OF ISRAEL. MOSSAD SENT ME TO DEMONSTRATE OUR SUPPORT FOR THE PRINCIPLE OF SUPER HERO REGISTRATION.
IN RETURN, WE GET THE INTELLIGENCE AND THE SURVEILLANCE TECHNOLOGY WE NEED TO INSTITUTE OUR OWN REGISTRATION ACT.
THE CLIMATE IN MY HOMELAND IS TOO VOLATILE TO ALLOW UNSUPERVISE SUPERHUMAN ACTIVIT MUTANT OR OTHERWIS
SO TO ANSWER YOUR QUESTION--
--I HAVE NO DOUBTS.

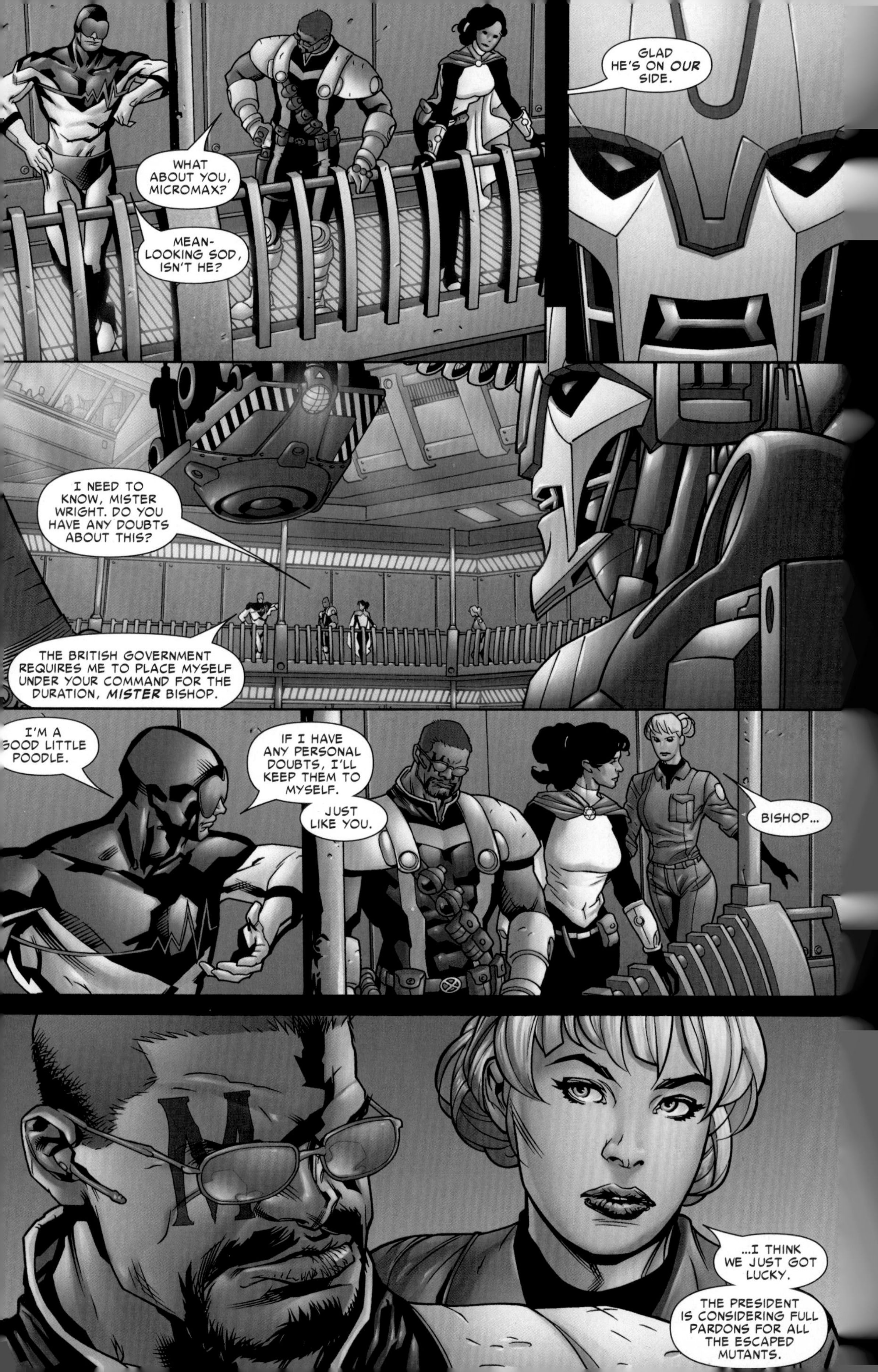
WHAT ABOUT YOU, MICROMAX?
MEAN-LOOKING SOD, ISN'T HE?
GLAD HE'S ON OUR SIDE.
I NEED TO KNOW, MISTER WRIGHT. DO YOU HAVE ANY DOUBTS ABOUT THIS?
THE BRITISH GOVERNMENT REQUIRES ME TO PLACE MYSELF UNDER YOUR COMMAND FOR THE DURATION, MISTER BISHOP.
I'M A GOOD LITTLE POODLE.
IF I HAVE ANY PERSONAL DOUBTS, I'LL KEEP THEM TO MYSELF.
JUST LIKE YOU.
BISHOP...
...I THINK WE JUST GOT LUCKY.
THE PRESIDENT IS CONSIDERING FULL PARDONS FOR ALL THE ESCAPED MUTANTS.

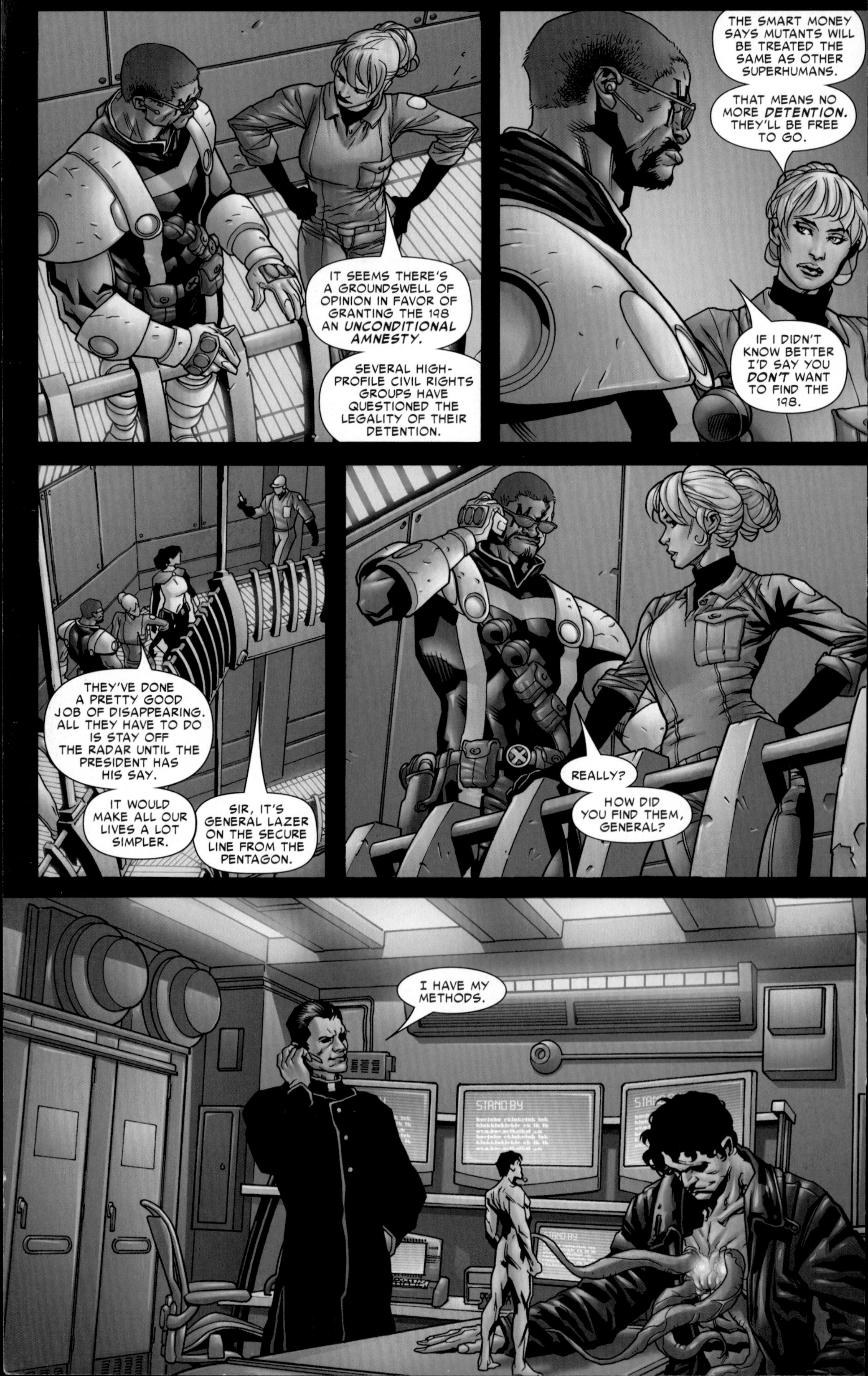
IT SEEMS THERE'S A GROUNDSWELL OF OPINION IN FAVOR OF GRANTING THE 198 AN *UNCONDITIONAL AMNESTY.*
SEVERAL HIGH-PROFILE CIVIL RIGHTS GROUPS HAVE QUESTIONED THE LEGALITY OF THEIR DETENTION.
THE SMART MONEY SAYS MUTANTS WILL BE TREATED THE SAME AS OTHER SUPERHUMANS.
THAT MEANS NO MORE *DETENTION.* THEY'LL BE FREE TO GO.
IF I DIDN'T KNOW BETTER I'D SAY YOU *DON'T* WANT TO FIND THE 198.
THEY'VE DONE A PRETTY GOOD JOB OF DISAPPEARING. ALL THEY HAVE TO DO IS STAY OFF THE RADAR UNTIL THE PRESIDENT HAS HIS SAY.
IT WOULD MAKE ALL OUR LIVES A LOT SIMPLER.
SIR, IT'S GENERAL LAZER ON THE SECURE LINE FROM THE PENTAGON.
REALLY?
HOW DID YOU FIND THEM, GENERAL?
I HAVE MY METHODS.
STAND BY

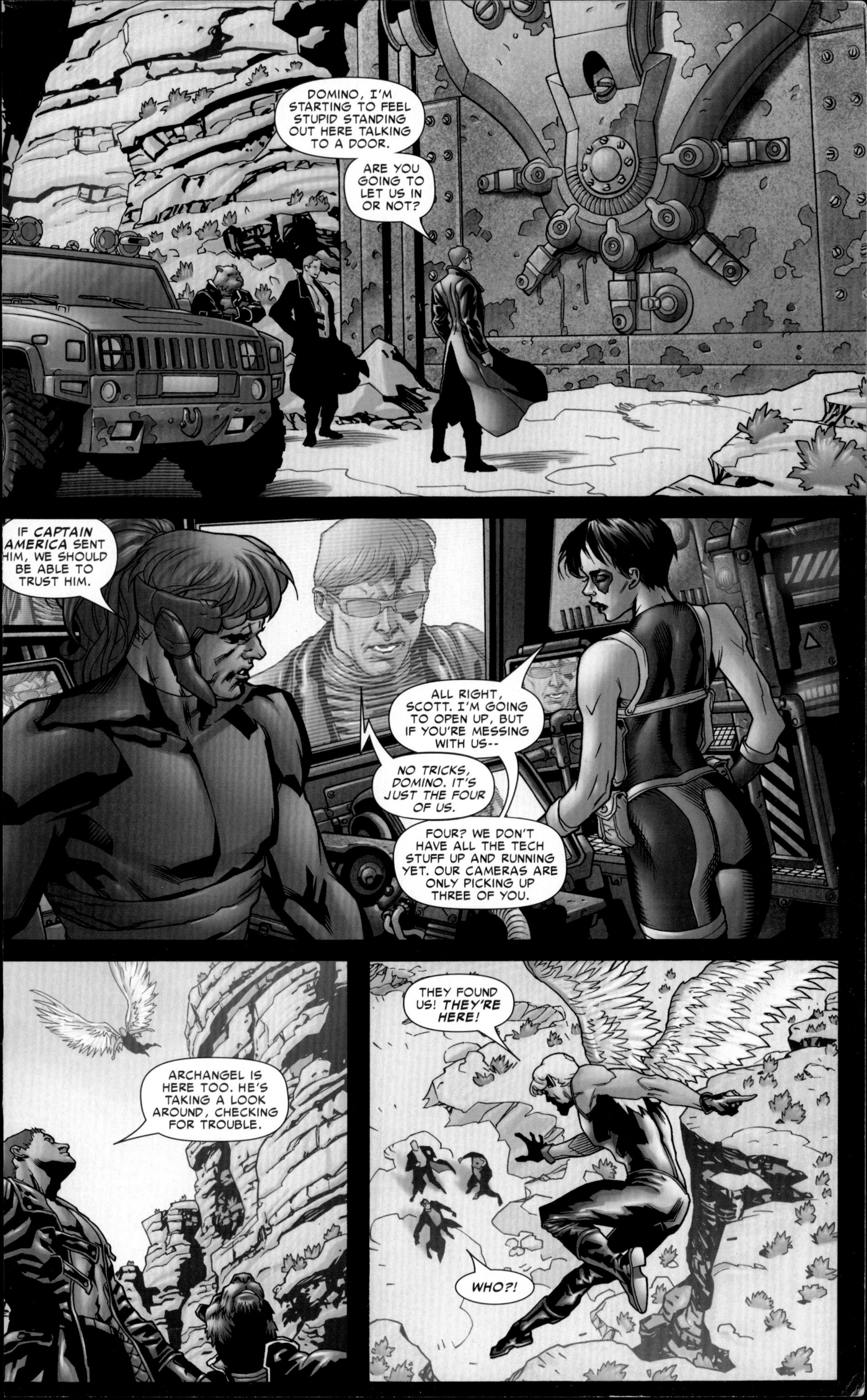
DOMINO, I'M STARTING TO FEEL STUPID STANDING OUT HERE TALKING TO A DOOR.
ARE YOU GOING TO LET US IN OR NOT?
IF *CAPTAIN AMERICA* SENT HIM, WE SHOULD BE ABLE TO TRUST HIM.
ALL RIGHT, SCOTT. I'M GOING TO OPEN UP, BUT IF YOU'RE MESSING WITH US--
NO TRICKS, DOMINO. IT'S JUST THE FOUR OF US.
FOUR? WE DON'T HAVE ALL THE TECH STUFF UP AND RUNNING YET. OUR CAMERAS ARE ONLY PICKING UP THREE OF YOU.
ARCHANGEL IS HERE TOO. HE'S TAKING A LOOK AROUND, CHECKING FOR TROUBLE.
THEY FOUND US! *THEY'RE HERE!*
WHO?!

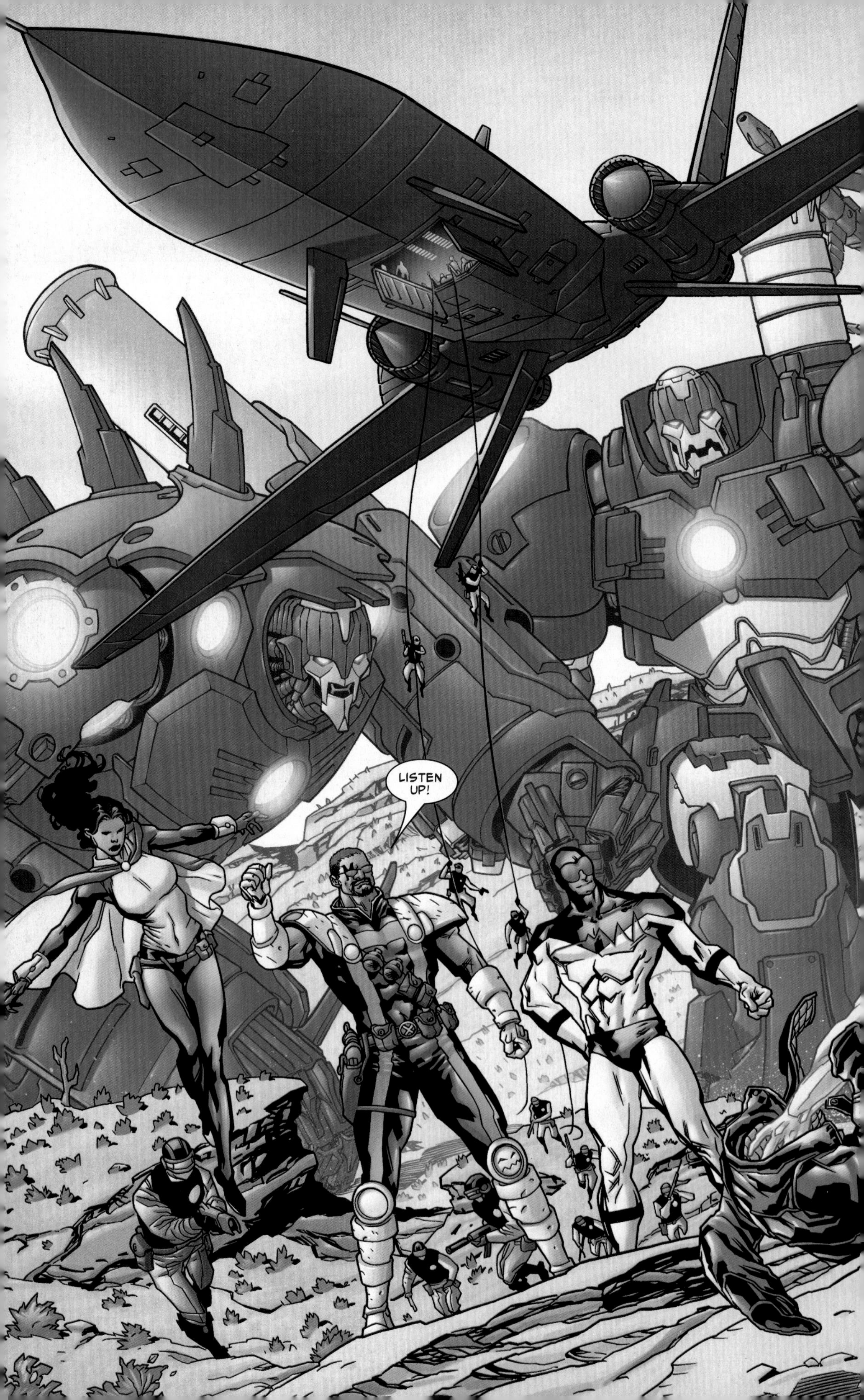
LISTEN UP!

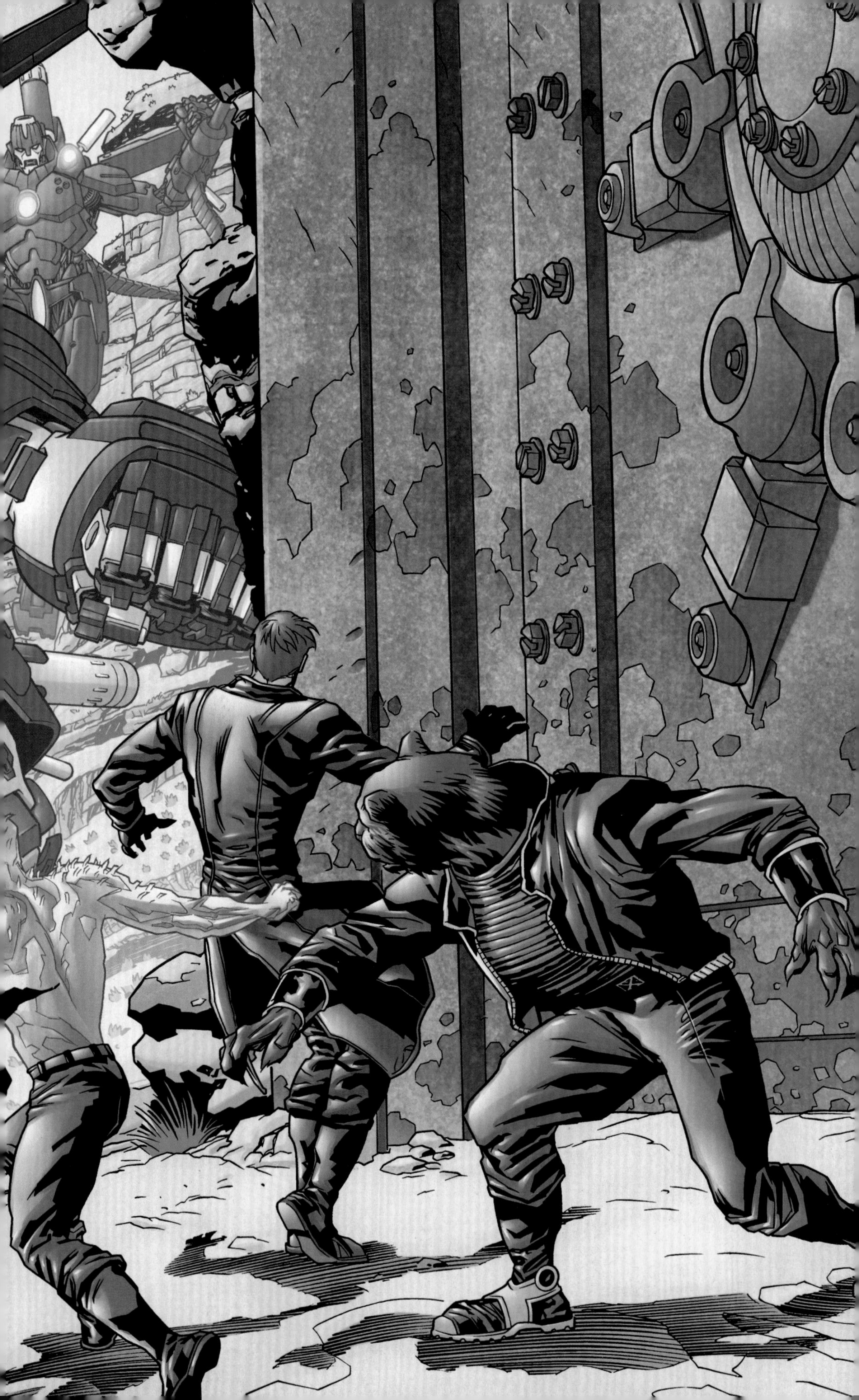

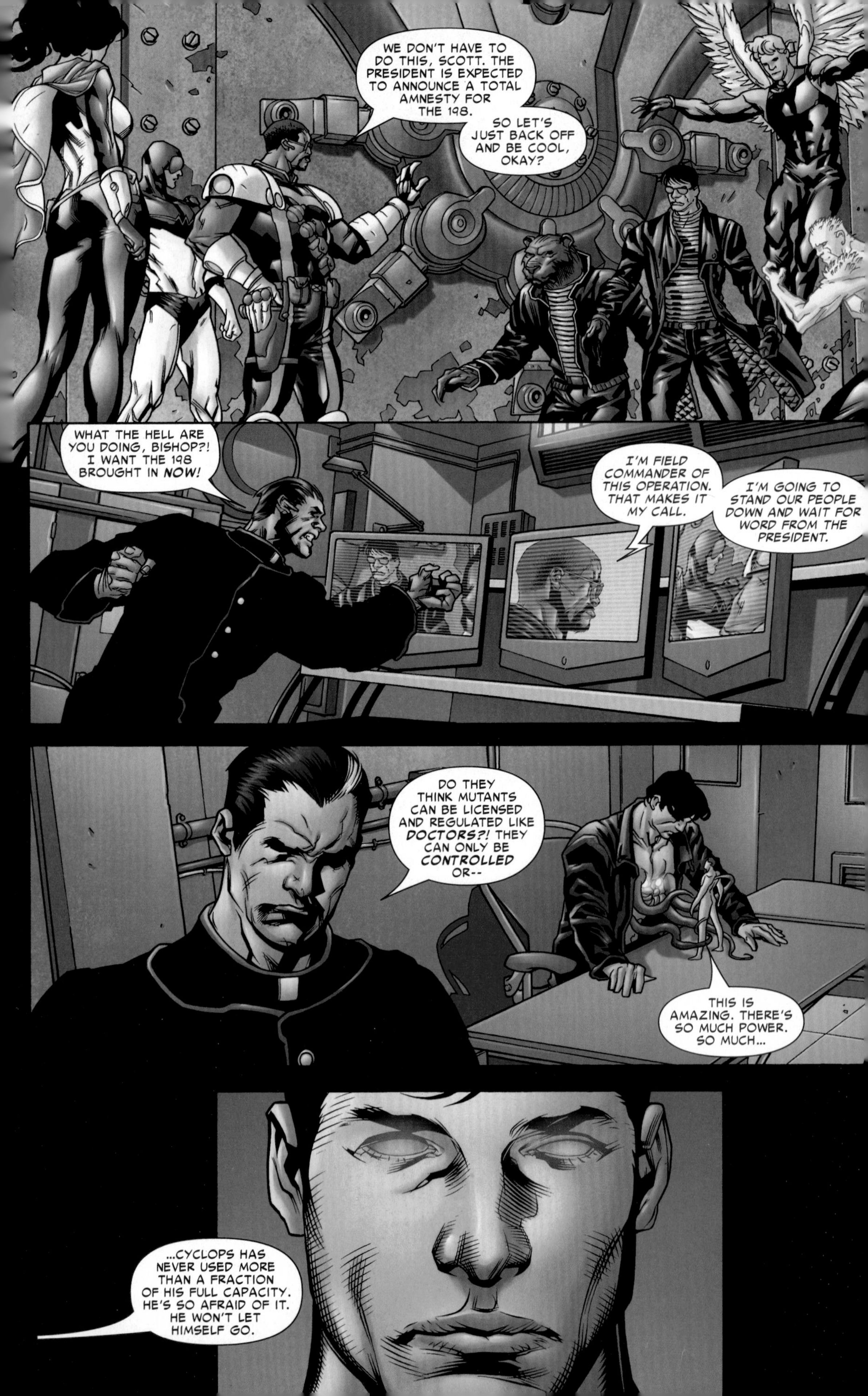
WE DON'T HAVE TO DO THIS, SCOTT. THE PRESIDENT IS EXPECTED TO ANNOUNCE A TOTAL AMNESTY FOR THE 198.
SO LET'S JUST BACK OFF AND BE COOL, OKAY?
WHAT THE HELL ARE YOU DOING, BISHOP?! I WANT THE 198 BROUGHT IN NOW!
I'M FIELD COMMANDER OF THIS OPERATION. THAT MAKES IT MY CALL.
I'M GOING TO STAND OUR PEOPLE DOWN AND WAIT FOR WORD FROM THE PRESIDENT.
DO THEY THINK MUTANTS CAN BE LICENSED AND REGULATED LIKE DOCTORS?! THEY CAN ONLY BE CONTROLLED OR--
THIS IS AMAZING. THERE'S SO MUCH POWER. SO MUCH...
...CYCLOPS HAS NEVER USED MORE THAN A FRACTION OF HIS FULL CAPACITY. HE'S SO AFRAID OF IT. HE WON'T LET HIMSELF GO.

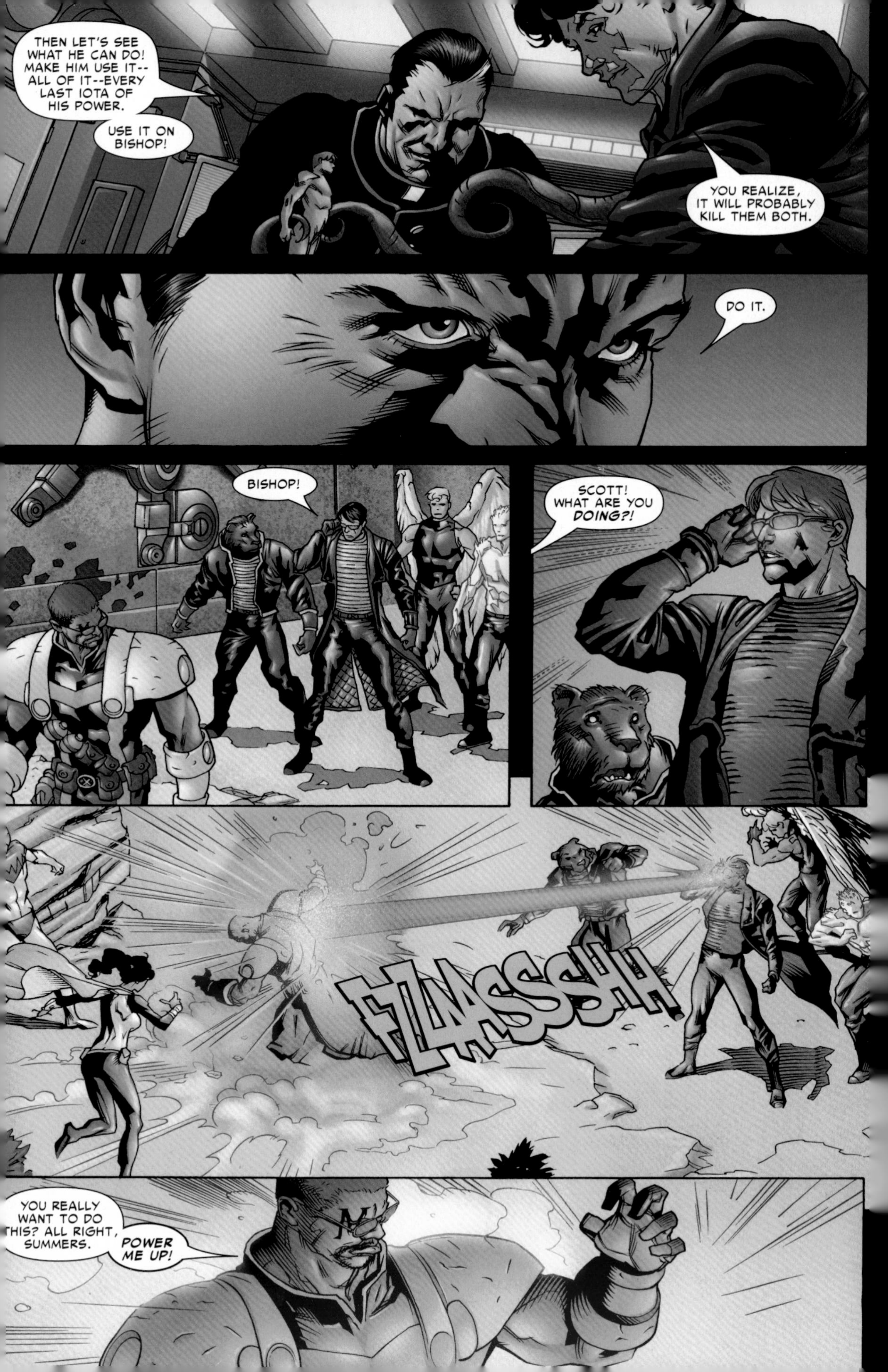
THEN LET'S SEE WHAT HE CAN DO! MAKE HIM USE IT--ALL OF IT--EVERY LAST IOTA OF HIS POWER.
USE IT ON BISHOP!
YOU REALIZE, IT WILL PROBABLY KILL THEM BOTH.
DO IT.
BISHOP!
SCOTT! WHAT ARE YOU *DOING?!*
FZZASSSH
YOU REALLY WANT TO DO THIS? ALL RIGHT, SUMMERS.
POWER ME UP!

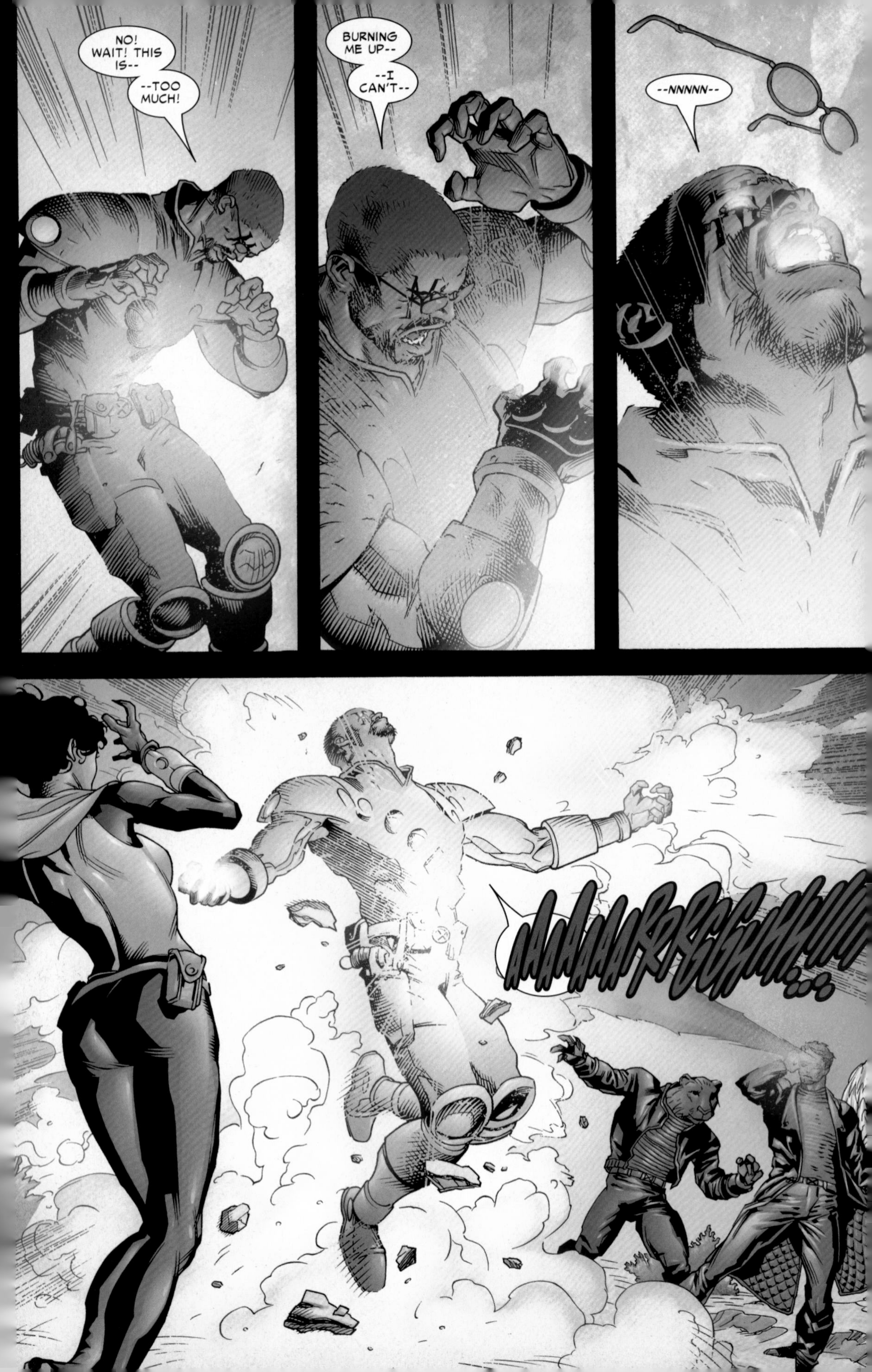
NO! WAIT! THIS IS--
--TOO MUCH!
BURNING ME UP--
--I CAN'T--
--NNNNN--
AAAAAAAARRGGHHHH!...

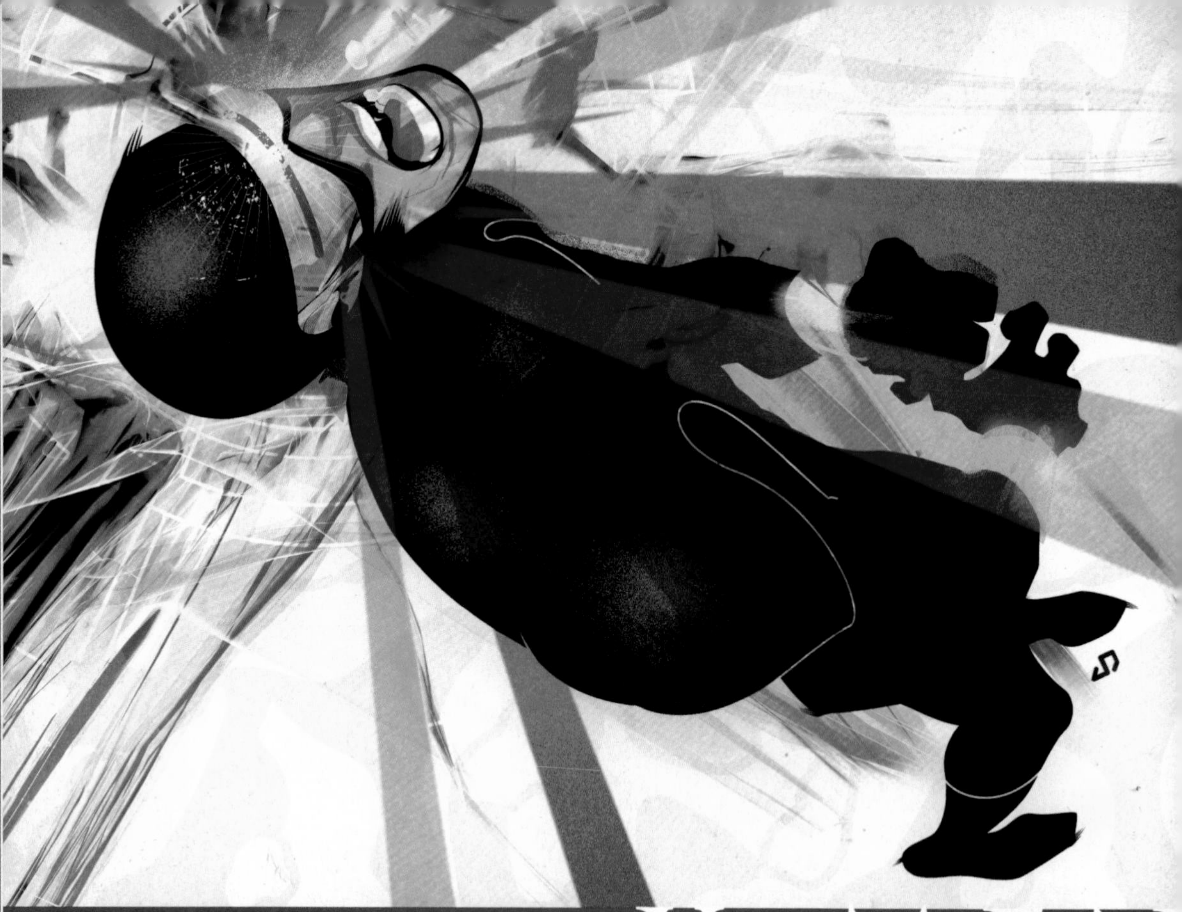

X-MEN

A MARVEL COMICS EVENT

CIVIL WAR

CIVIL WAR: X-MEN #3

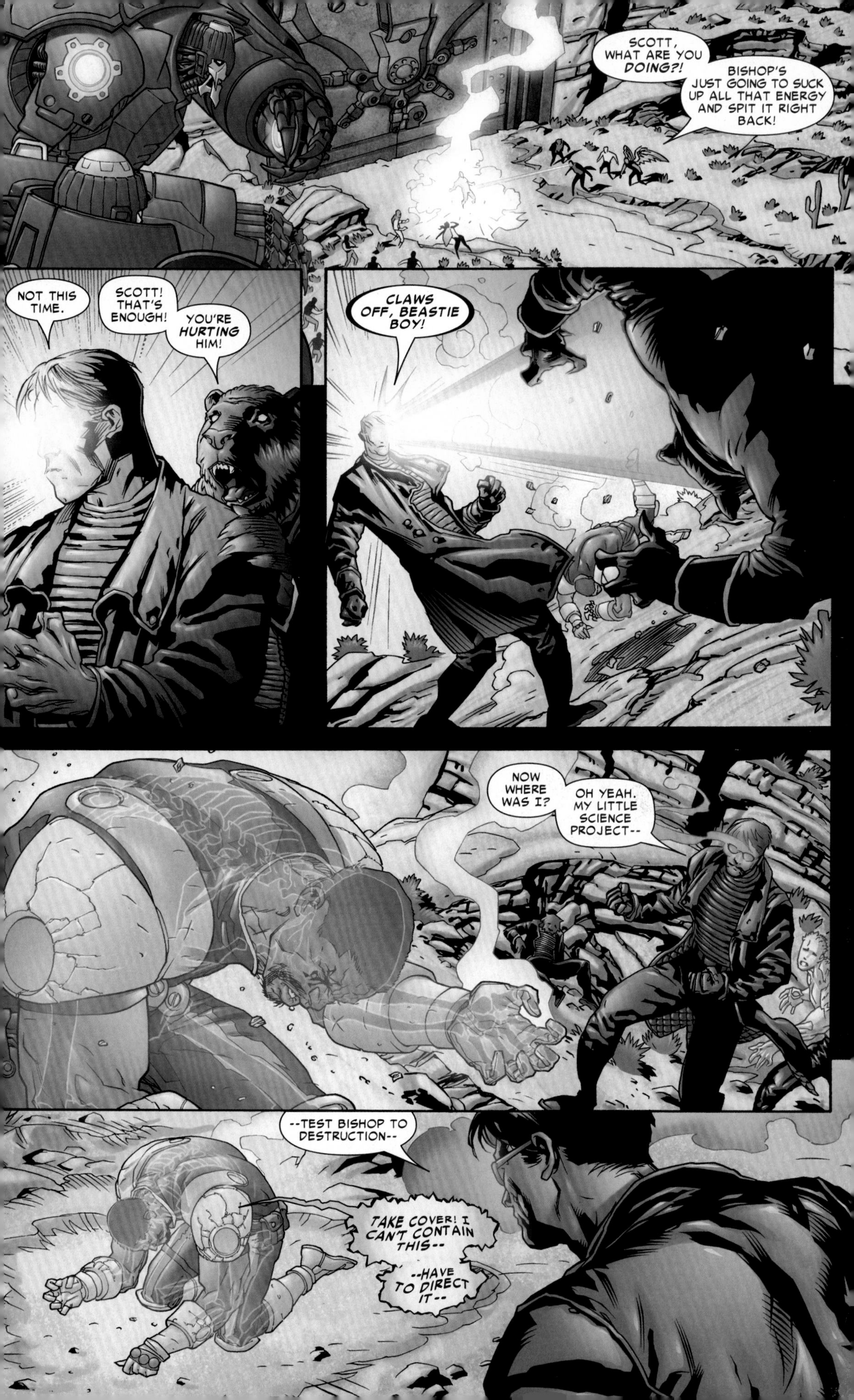
SCOTT, WHAT ARE YOU DOING?!
BISHOP'S JUST GOING TO SUCK UP ALL THAT ENERGY AND SPIT IT RIGHT BACK!
NOT THIS TIME.
SCOTT! THAT'S ENOUGH!
YOU'RE HURTING HIM!
CLAWS OFF, BEASTIE BOY!
NOW WHERE WAS I?
OH YEAH. MY LITTLE SCIENCE PROJECT--
--TEST BISHOP TO DESTRUCTION--
TAKE COVER! I CAN'T CONTAIN THIS--
--HAVE TO DIRECT IT--

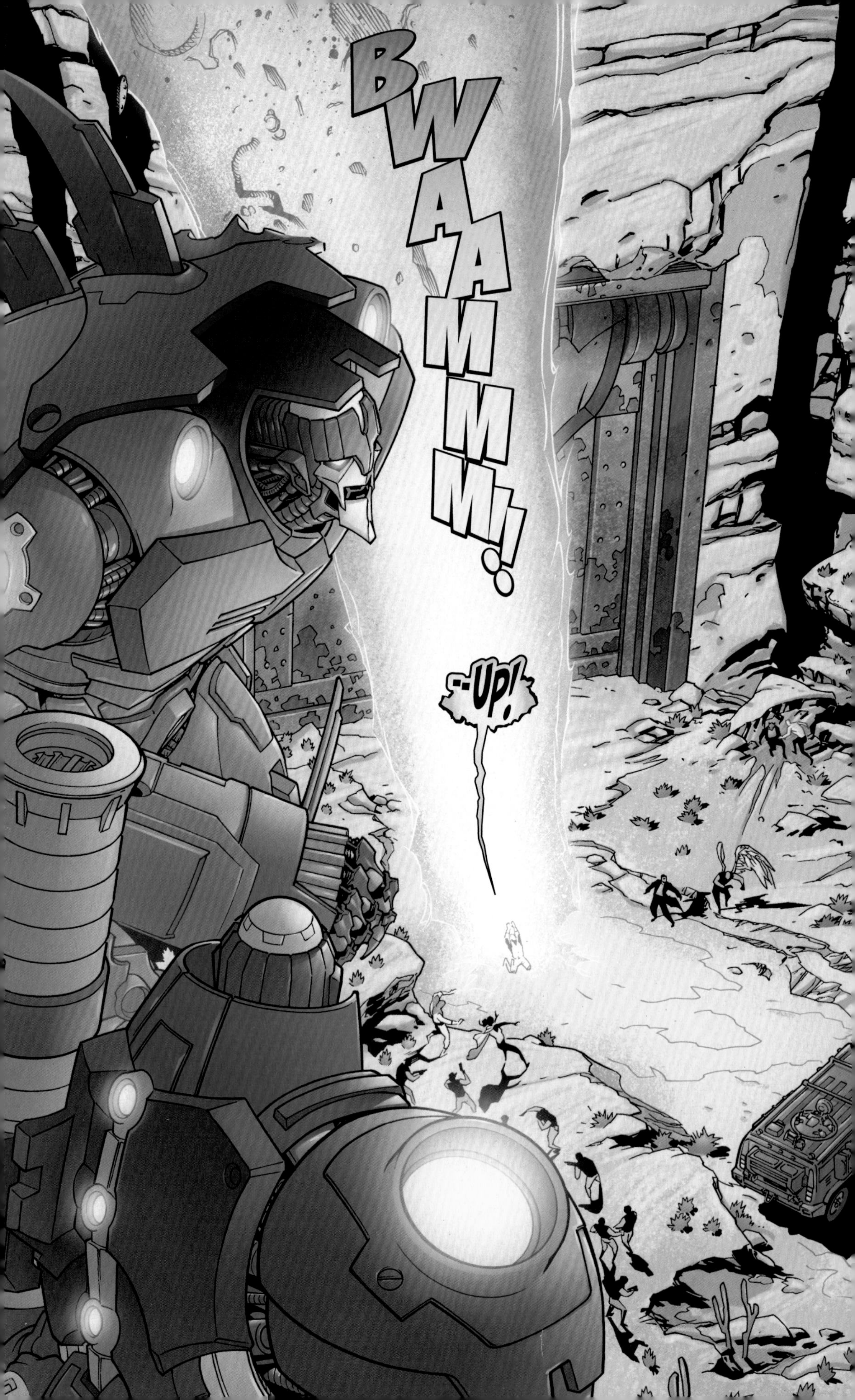
BWAAMMM!!
--UP!

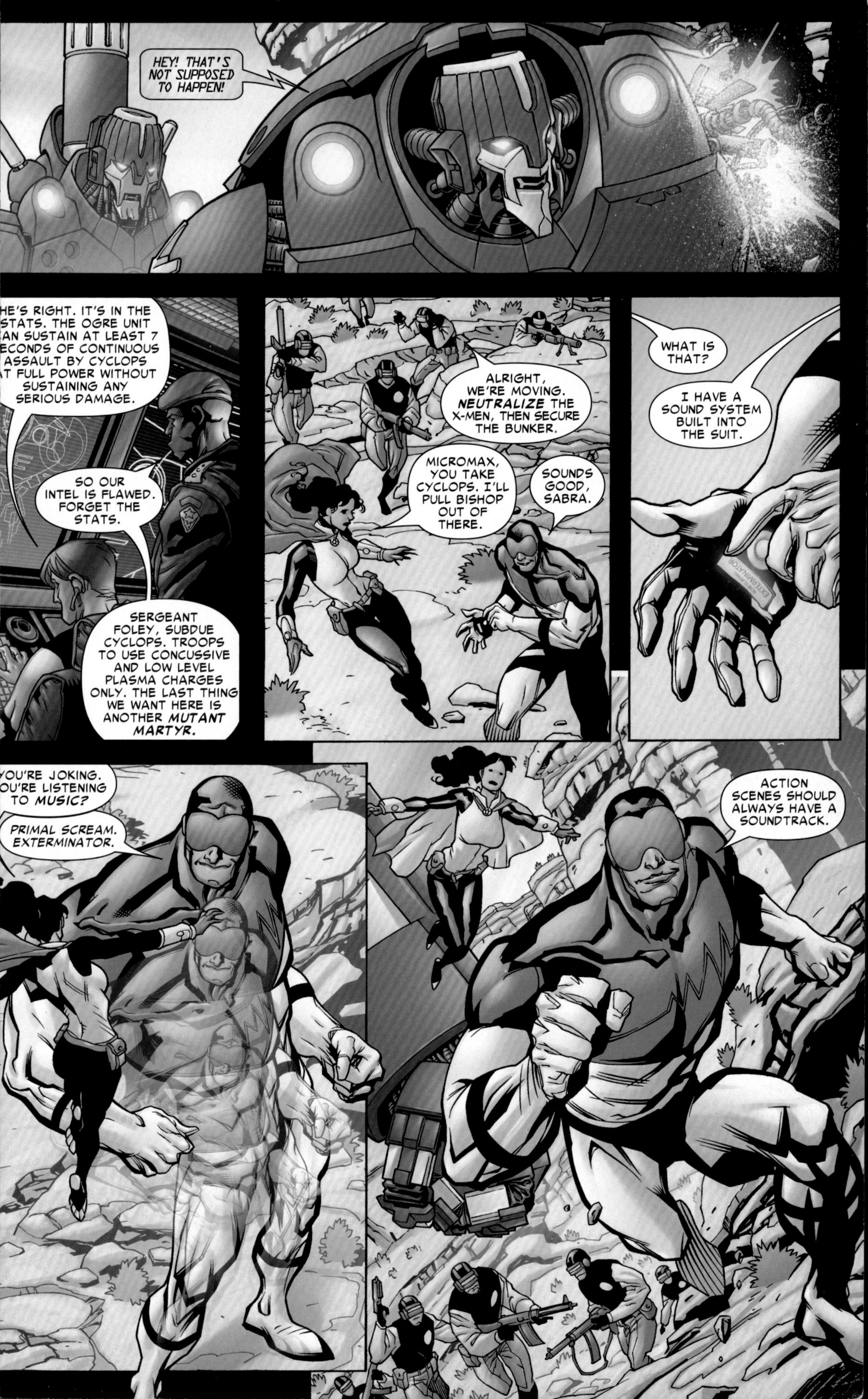
HEY! THAT'S NOT SUPPOSED TO HAPPEN!
HE'S RIGHT. IT'S IN THE STATS. THE OGRE UNIT CAN SUSTAIN AT LEAST 7 SECONDS OF CONTINUOUS ASSAULT BY CYCLOPS AT FULL POWER WITHOUT SUSTAINING ANY SERIOUS DAMAGE.
SO OUR INTEL IS FLAWED. FORGET THE STATS.
SERGEANT FOLEY, SUBDUE CYCLOPS. TROOPS TO USE CONCUSSIVE AND LOW LEVEL PLASMA CHARGES ONLY. THE LAST THING WE WANT HERE IS ANOTHER MUTANT MARTYR.
ALRIGHT, WE'RE MOVING. NEUTRALIZE THE X-MEN, THEN SECURE THE BUNKER.
MICROMAX, YOU TAKE CYCLOPS. I'LL PULL BISHOP OUT OF THERE.
SOUNDS GOOD, SABRA.
WHAT IS THAT?
I HAVE A SOUND SYSTEM BUILT INTO THE SUIT.
EXTERMINATOR
YOU'RE JOKING. YOU'RE LISTENING TO MUSIC?
PRIMAL SCREAM. EXTERMINATOR.
ACTION SCENES SHOULD ALWAYS HAVE A SOUNDTRACK.

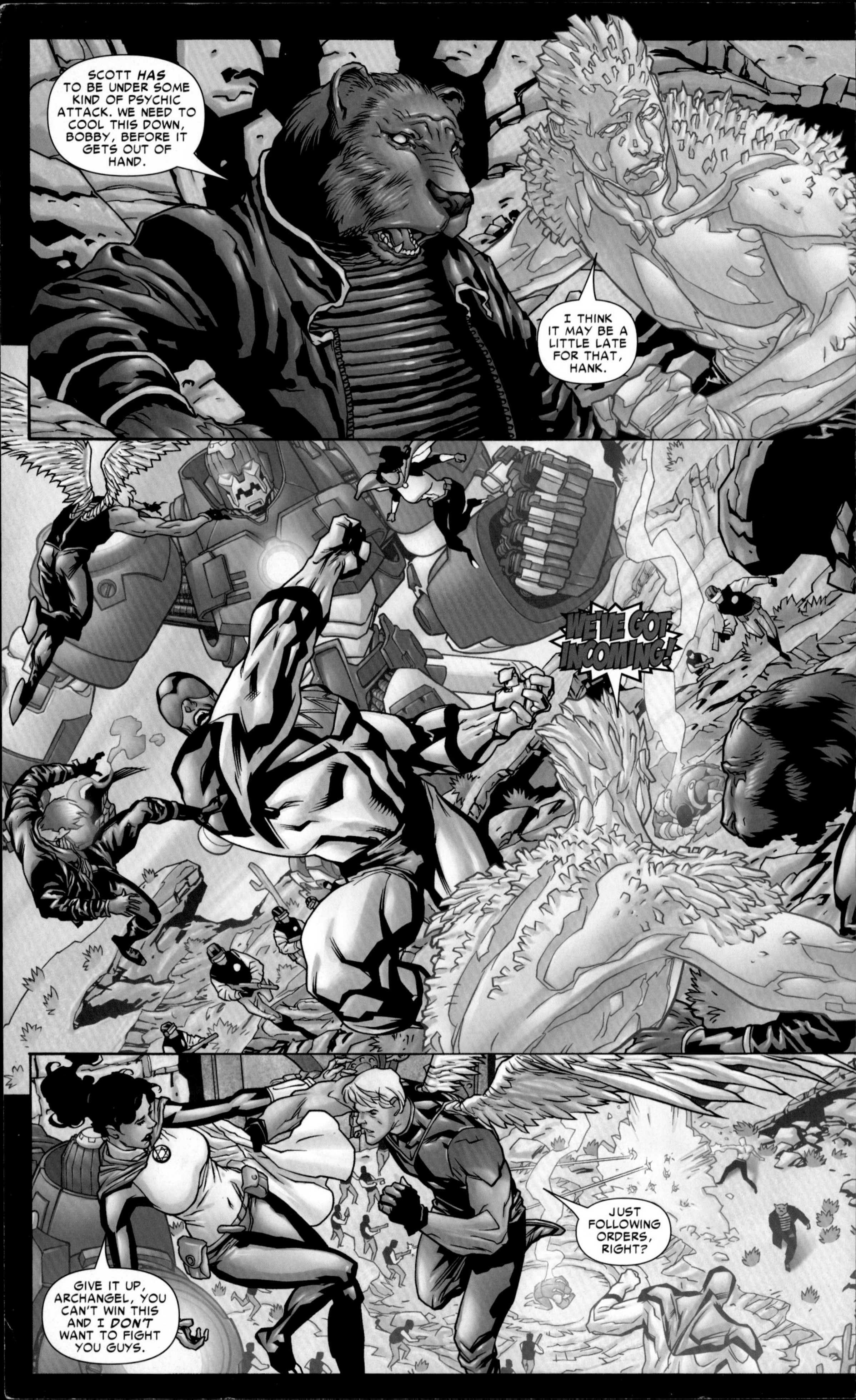
SCOTT HAS TO BE UNDER SOME KIND OF PSYCHIC ATTACK. WE NEED TO COOL THIS DOWN, BOBBY, BEFORE IT GETS OUT OF HAND.
I THINK IT MAY BE A LITTLE LATE FOR THAT, HANK.
WE'VE GOT INCOMING!
GIVE IT UP, ARCHANGEL, YOU CAN'T WIN THIS AND I DON'T WANT TO FIGHT YOU GUYS.
JUST FOLLOWING ORDERS, RIGHT?

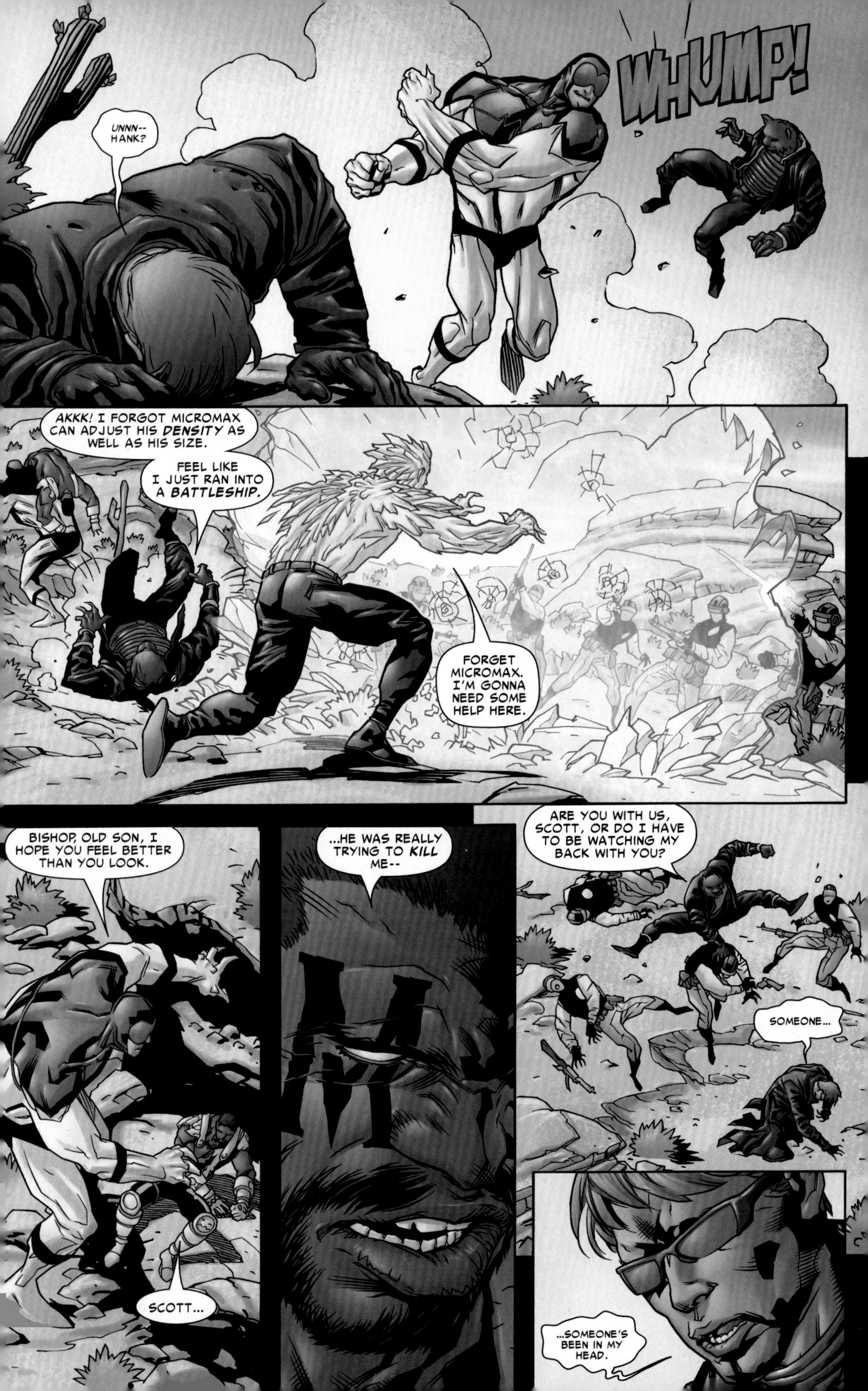
UNNN-- HANK?
WHUMP!
AKKK! I FORGOT MICROMAX CAN ADJUST HIS DENSITY AS WELL AS HIS SIZE.
FEEL LIKE I JUST RAN INTO A BATTLESHIP.
FORGET MICROMAX. I'M GONNA NEED SOME HELP HERE.
BISHOP, OLD SON, I HOPE YOU FEEL BETTER THAN YOU LOOK.
SCOTT...
...HE WAS REALLY TRYING TO KILL ME--
ARE YOU WITH US, SCOTT, OR DO I HAVE TO BE WATCHING MY BACK WITH YOU?
SOMEONE...
...SOMEONE'S BEEN IN MY HEAD.

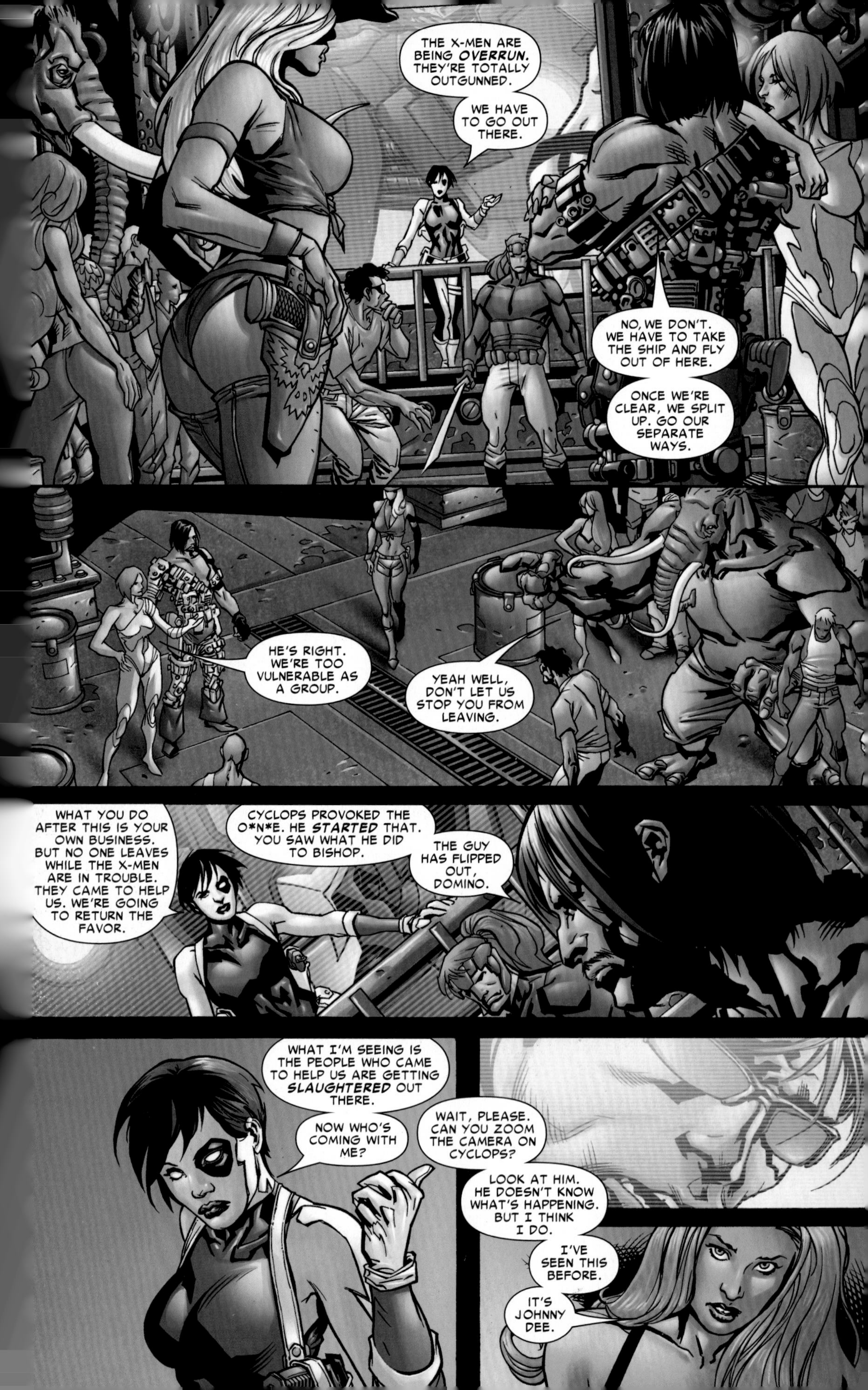
THE X-MEN ARE BEING OVERRUN. THEY'RE TOTALLY OUTGUNNED.
WE HAVE TO GO OUT THERE.
NO, WE DON'T. WE HAVE TO TAKE THE SHIP AND FLY OUT OF HERE.
ONCE WE'RE CLEAR, WE SPLIT UP. GO OUR SEPARATE WAYS.
HE'S RIGHT. WE'RE TOO VULNERABLE AS A GROUP.
YEAH WELL, DON'T LET US STOP YOU FROM LEAVING.
WHAT YOU DO AFTER THIS IS YOUR OWN BUSINESS. BUT NO ONE LEAVES WHILE THE X-MEN ARE IN TROUBLE. THEY CAME TO HELP US. WE'RE GOING TO RETURN THE FAVOR.
CYCLOPS PROVOKED THE O*N*E. HE STARTED THAT. YOU SAW WHAT HE DID TO BISHOP.
THE GUY HAS FLIPPED OUT, DOMINO.
WHAT I'M SEEING IS THE PEOPLE WHO CAME TO HELP US ARE GETTING SLAUGHTERED OUT THERE.
NOW WHO'S COMING WITH ME?
WAIT, PLEASE. CAN YOU ZOOM THE CAMERA ON CYCLOPS?
LOOK AT HIM. HE DOESN'T KNOW WHAT'S HAPPENING. BUT I THINK I DO.
I'VE SEEN THIS BEFORE.
IT'S JOHNNY DEE.

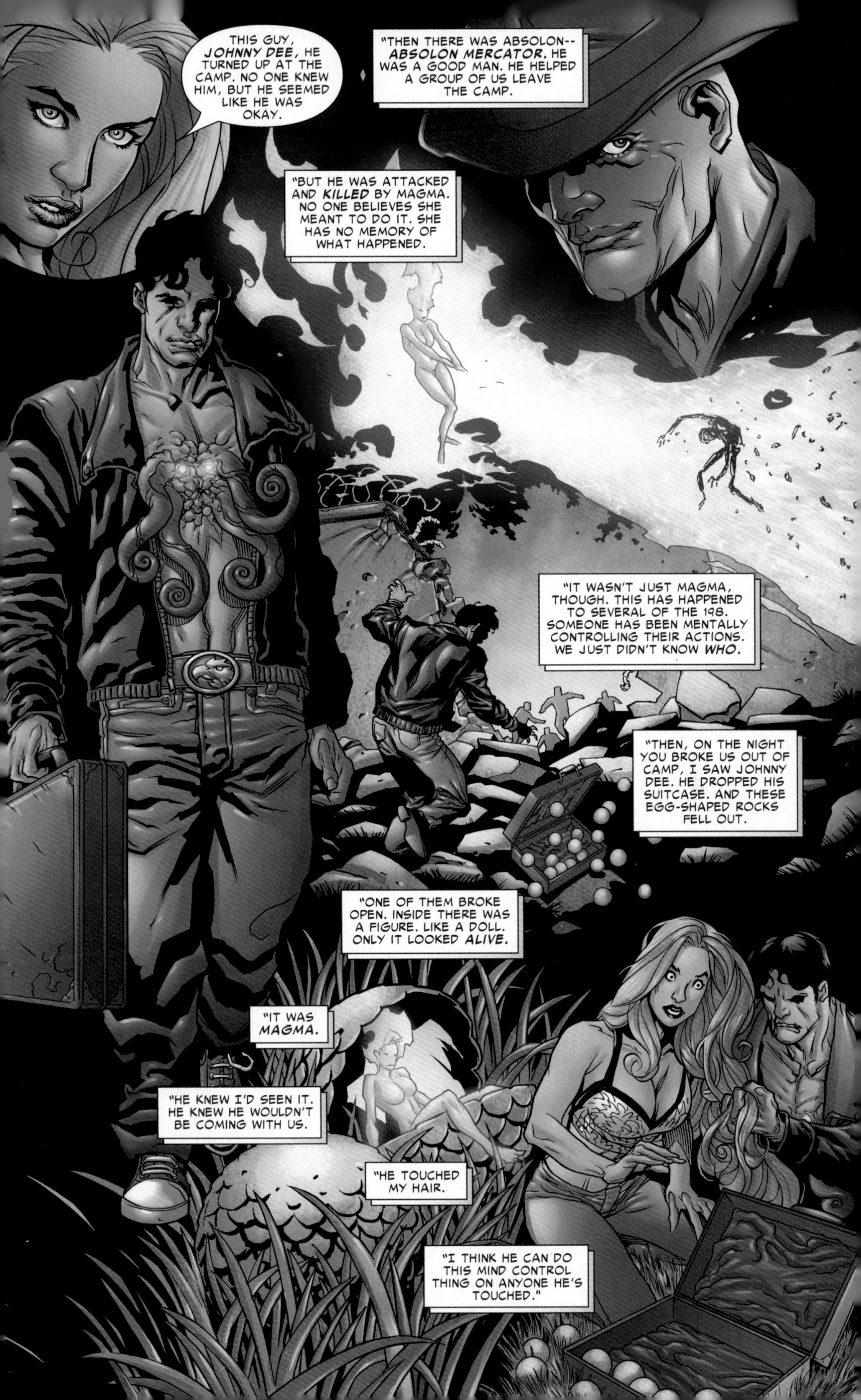

THIS GUY, JOHNNY DEE, HE TURNED UP AT THE CAMP. NO ONE KNEW HIM, BUT HE SEEMED LIKE HE WAS OKAY.
"THEN THERE WAS ABSOLON-- ABSOLON MERCATOR. HE WAS A GOOD MAN. HE HELPED A GROUP OF US LEAVE THE CAMP.
"BUT HE WAS ATTACKED AND KILLED BY MAGMA. NO ONE BELIEVES SHE MEANT TO DO IT. SHE HAS NO MEMORY OF WHAT HAPPENED.
"IT WASN'T JUST MAGMA, THOUGH. THIS HAS HAPPENED TO SEVERAL OF THE 198. SOMEONE HAS BEEN MENTALLY CONTROLLING THEIR ACTIONS. WE JUST DIDN'T KNOW WHO.
"THEN, ON THE NIGHT YOU BROKE US OUT OF CAMP, I SAW JOHNNY DEE. HE DROPPED HIS SUITCASE. AND THESE EGG-SHAPED ROCKS FELL OUT.
"ONE OF THEM BROKE OPEN. INSIDE THERE WAS A FIGURE. LIKE A DOLL. ONLY IT LOOKED ALIVE.
"IT WAS MAGMA.
"HE KNEW I'D SEEN IT. HE KNEW HE WOULDN'T BE COMING WITH US.
"HE TOUCHED MY HAIR.
"I THINK HE CAN DO THIS MIND CONTROL THING ON ANYONE HE'S TOUCHED."

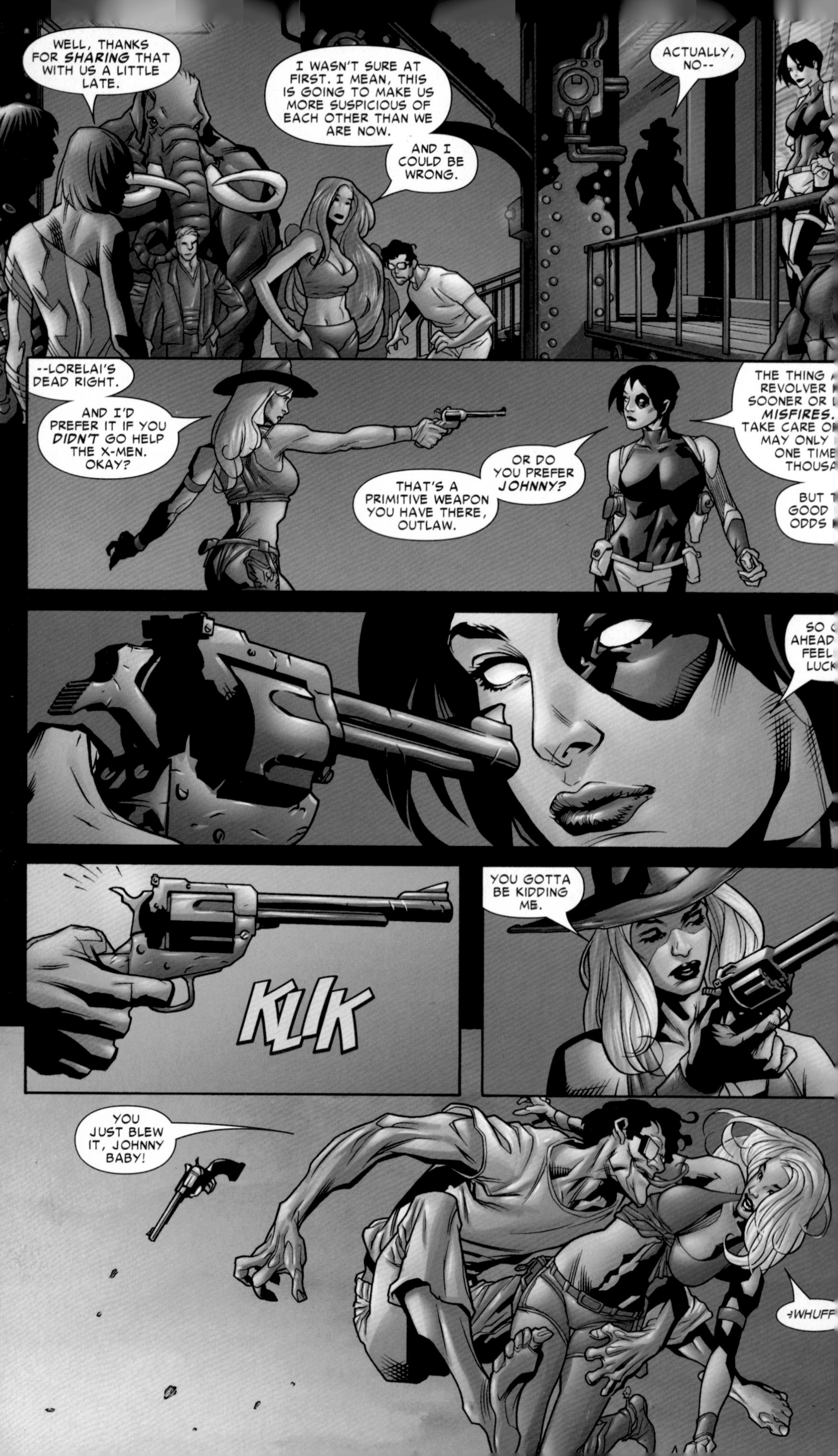

WELL, THANKS FOR SHARING THAT WITH US A LITTLE LATE.
I WASN'T SURE AT FIRST. I MEAN, THIS IS GOING TO MAKE US MORE SUSPICIOUS OF EACH OTHER THAN WE ARE NOW.
AND I COULD BE WRONG.
ACTUALLY, NO--
--LORELAI'S DEAD RIGHT.
AND I'D PREFER IT IF YOU DIDN'T GO HELP THE X-MEN. OKAY?
THAT'S A PRIMITIVE WEAPON YOU HAVE THERE, OUTLAW.
OR DO YOU PREFER JOHNNY?
THE THING REVOLVER SOONER OR MISFIRES. TAKE CARE MAY ONLY ONE
BUT GOOD ODDS
AHEAD FEEL
KLIK
YOU GOTTA BE KIDDING ME.
YOU JUST BLEW IT, JOHNNY BABY!

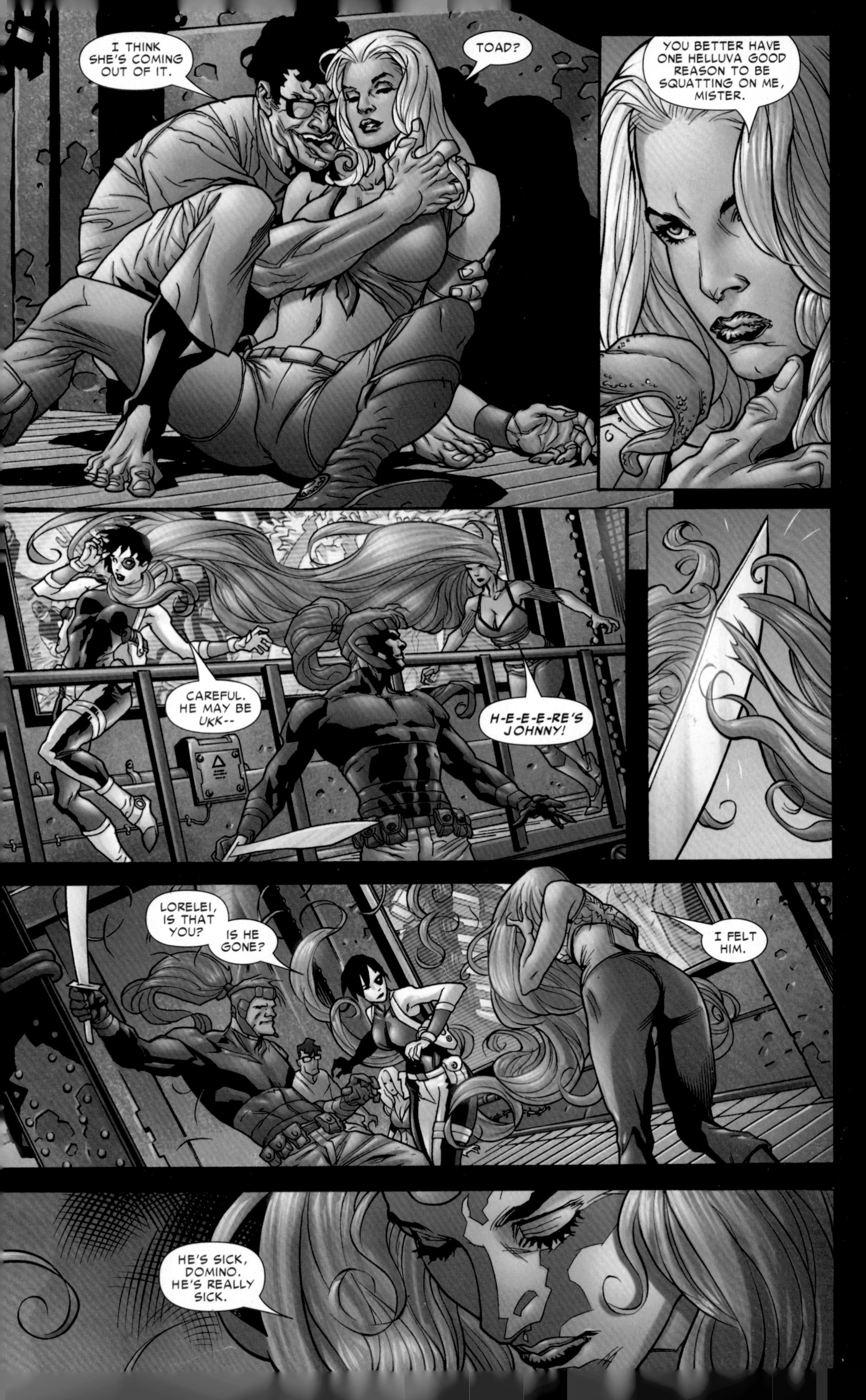
I THINK SHE'S COMING OUT OF IT.
TOAD?
YOU BETTER HAVE ONE HELLUVA GOOD REASON TO BE SQUATTING ON ME, MISTER.
CAREFUL. HE MAY BE UKK--
H-E-E-E-RE'S JOHNNY!
LORELEI, IS THAT YOU?
IS HE GONE?
I FELT HIM.
HE'S SICK, DOMINO. HE'S REALLY SICK.

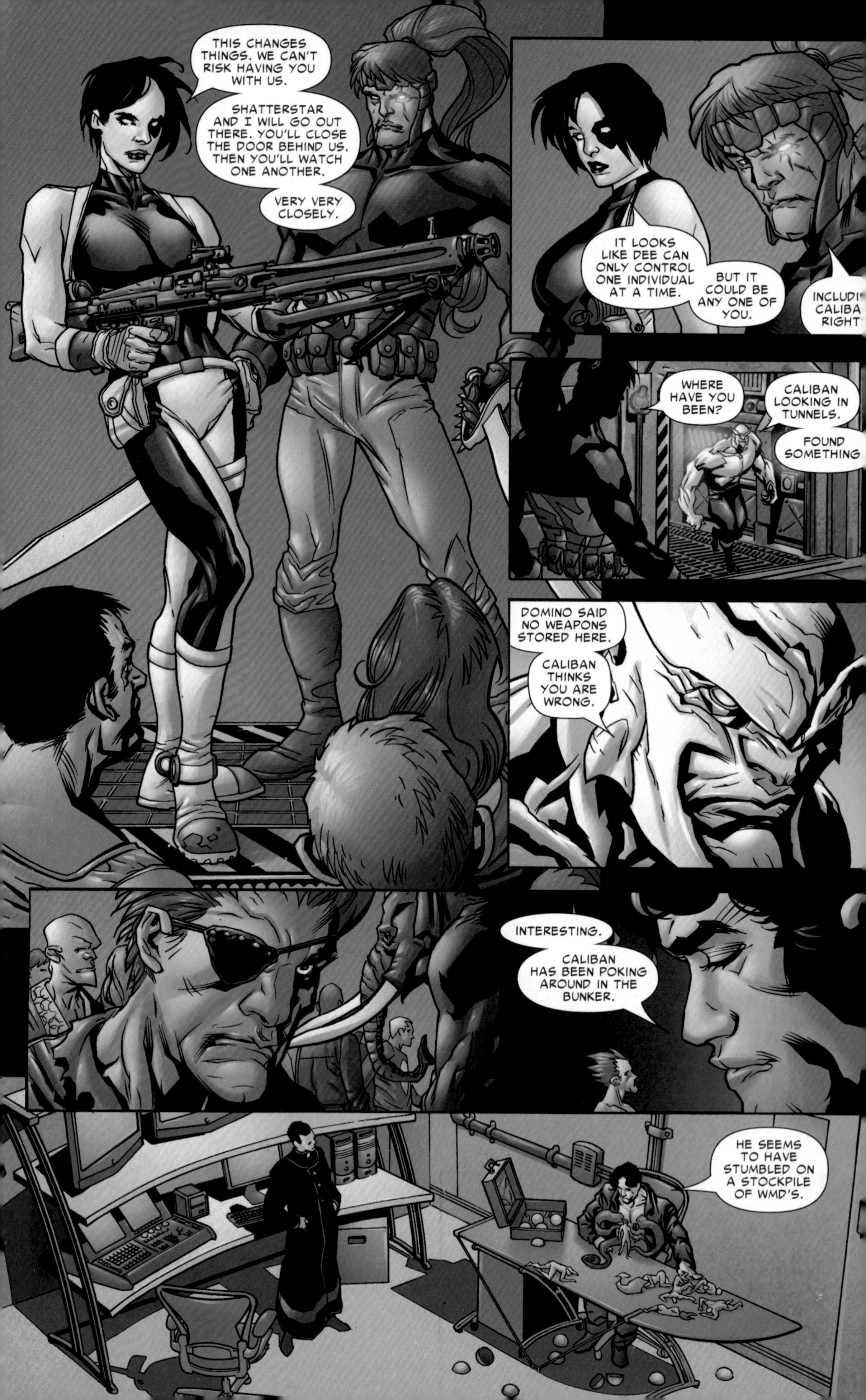

THIS CHANGES THINGS. WE CAN'T RISK HAVING YOU WITH US.
SHATTERSTAR AND I WILL GO OUT THERE. YOU'LL CLOSE THE DOOR BEHIND US. THEN YOU'LL WATCH ONE ANOTHER.
VERY VERY CLOSELY.
IT LOOKS LIKE DEE CAN ONLY CONTROL ONE INDIVIDUAL AT A TIME.
BUT IT COULD BE ANY ONE OF YOU.
INCLUDI CALIBA RIGHT
WHERE HAVE YOU BEEN?
CALIBAN LOOKING IN TUNNELS.
FOUND SOMETHING
DOMINO SAID NO WEAPONS STORED HERE.
CALIBAN THINKS YOU ARE WRONG.
INTERESTING.
CALIBAN HAS BEEN POKING AROUND IN THE BUNKER.
HE SEEMS TO HAVE STUMBLED ON A STOCKPILE OF WMD'S.

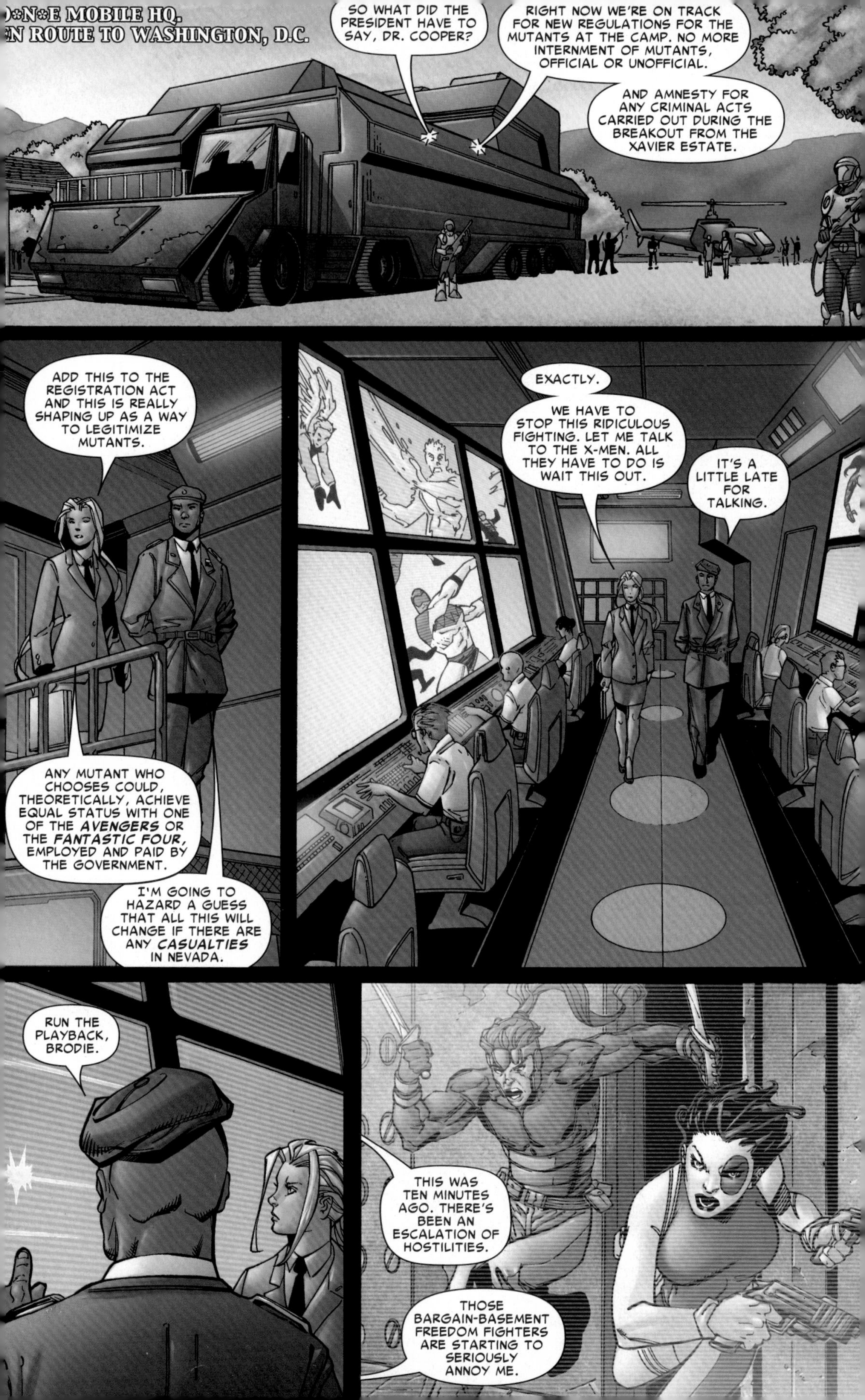
O*N*E MOBILE HQ. EN ROUTE TO WASHINGTON, D.C.
SO WHAT DID THE PRESIDENT HAVE TO SAY, DR. COOPER?
RIGHT NOW WE'RE ON TRACK FOR NEW REGULATIONS FOR THE MUTANTS AT THE CAMP. NO MORE INTERNMENT OF MUTANTS, OFFICIAL OR UNOFFICIAL.
AND AMNESTY FOR ANY CRIMINAL ACTS CARRIED OUT DURING THE BREAKOUT FROM THE XAVIER ESTATE.
ADD THIS TO THE REGISTRATION ACT AND THIS IS REALLY SHAPING UP AS A WAY TO LEGITIMIZE MUTANTS.
ANY MUTANT WHO CHOOSES COULD, THEORETICALLY, ACHIEVE EQUAL STATUS WITH ONE OF THE *AVENGERS* OR THE *FANTASTIC FOUR*, EMPLOYED AND PAID BY THE GOVERNMENT.
I'M GOING TO HAZARD A GUESS THAT ALL THIS WILL CHANGE IF THERE ARE ANY *CASUALTIES* IN NEVADA.
EXACTLY.
WE HAVE TO STOP THIS RIDICULOUS FIGHTING. LET ME TALK TO THE X-MEN. ALL THEY HAVE TO DO IS WAIT THIS OUT.
IT'S A LITTLE LATE FOR TALKING.
RUN THE PLAYBACK, BRODIE.
THIS WAS TEN MINUTES AGO. THERE'S BEEN AN ESCALATION OF HOSTILITIES.
THOSE BARGAIN-BASEMENT FREEDOM FIGHTERS ARE STARTING TO SERIOUSLY ANNOY ME.

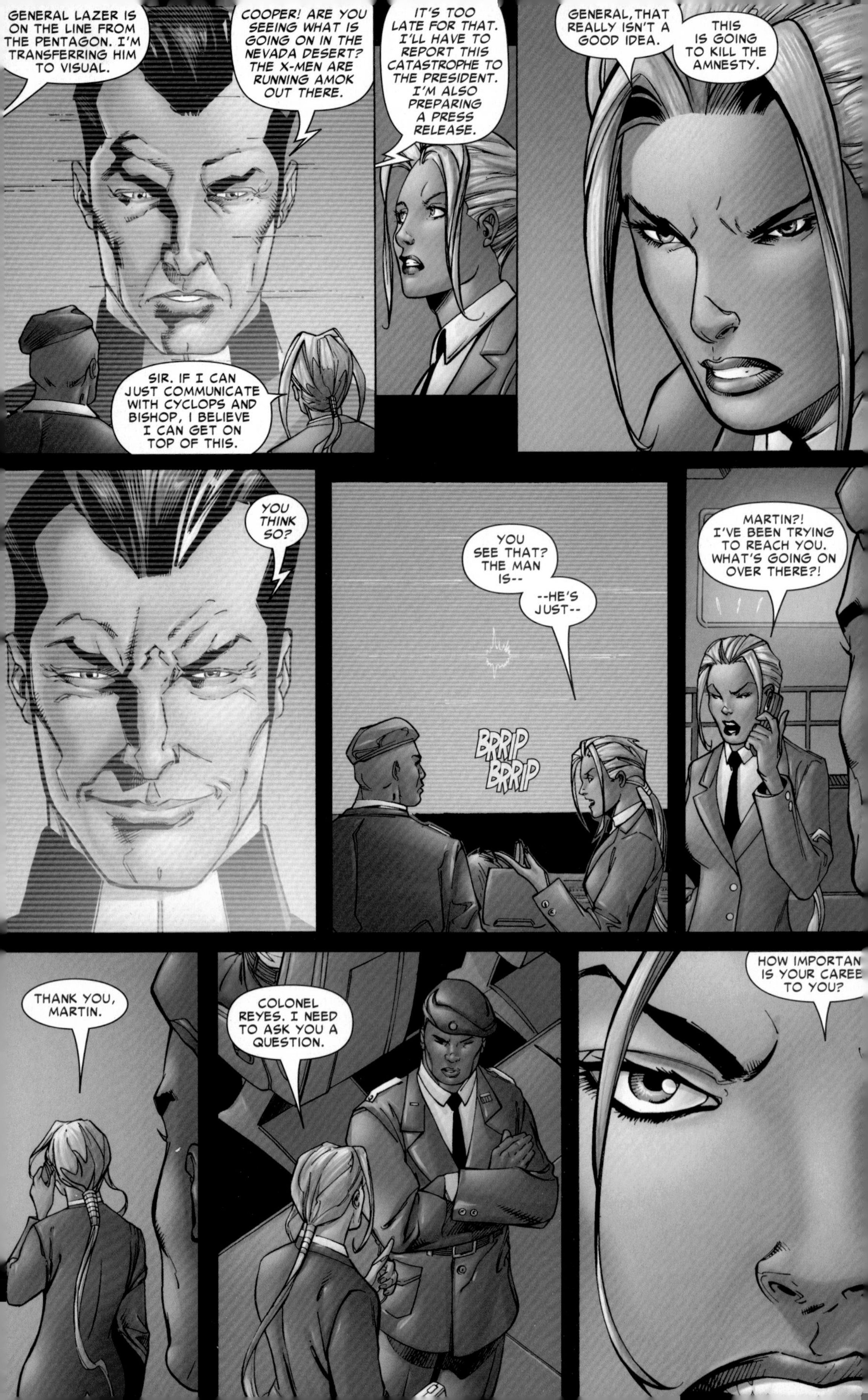
GENERAL LAZER IS ON THE LINE FROM THE PENTAGON. I'M TRANSFERRING HIM TO VISUAL.
COOPER! ARE YOU SEEING WHAT IS GOING ON IN THE NEVADA DESERT? THE X-MEN ARE RUNNING AMOK OUT THERE.
SIR. IF I CAN JUST COMMUNICATE WITH CYCLOPS AND BISHOP, I BELIEVE I CAN GET ON TOP OF THIS.
IT'S TOO LATE FOR THAT. I'LL HAVE TO REPORT THIS CATASTROPHE TO THE PRESIDENT. I'M ALSO PREPARING A PRESS RELEASE.
GENERAL, THAT REALLY ISN'T A GOOD IDEA.
THIS IS GOING TO KILL THE AMNESTY.
YOU THINK SO?
YOU SEE THAT? THE MAN IS--
--HE'S JUST--
BRRIP
BRRIP
MARTIN?! I'VE BEEN TRYING TO REACH YOU. WHAT'S GOING ON OVER THERE?!
THANK YOU, MARTIN.
COLONEL REYES. I NEED TO ASK YOU A QUESTION.
HOW IMPORTAN
IS YOUR CAREE
TO YOU?

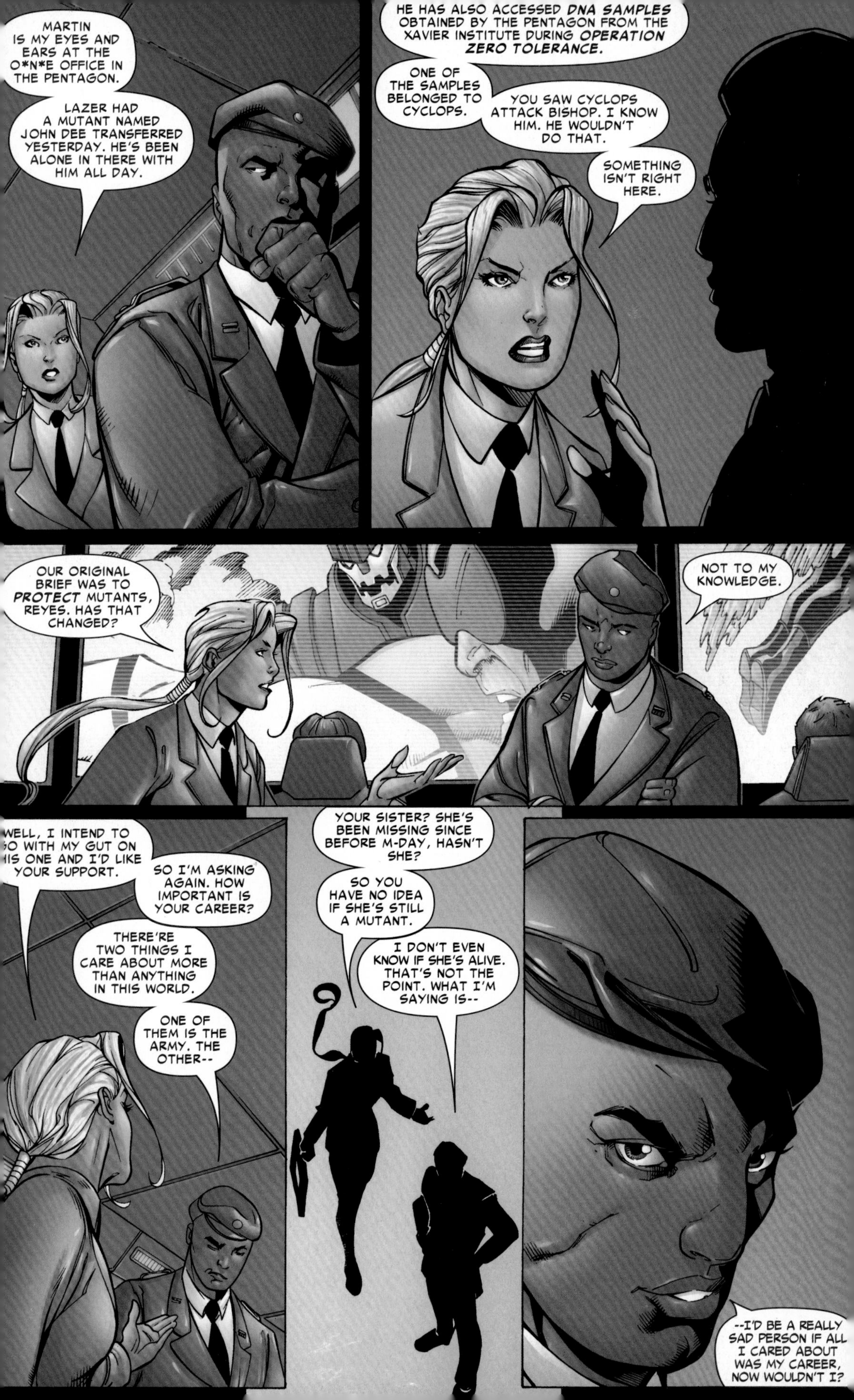
MARTIN IS MY EYES AND EARS AT THE O*N*E OFFICE IN THE PENTAGON.
LAZER HAD A MUTANT NAMED JOHN DEE TRANSFERRED YESTERDAY. HE'S BEEN ALONE IN THERE WITH HIM ALL DAY.
HE HAS ALSO ACCESSED DNA SAMPLES OBTAINED BY THE PENTAGON FROM THE XAVIER INSTITUTE DURING OPERATION ZERO TOLERANCE.
ONE OF THE SAMPLES BELONGED TO CYCLOPS.
YOU SAW CYCLOPS ATTACK BISHOP. I KNOW HIM. HE WOULDN'T DO THAT.
SOMETHING ISN'T RIGHT HERE.
OUR ORIGINAL BRIEF WAS TO PROTECT MUTANTS, REYES. HAS THAT CHANGED?
NOT TO MY KNOWLEDGE.
WELL, I INTEND TO GO WITH MY GUT ON THIS ONE AND I'D LIKE YOUR SUPPORT.
SO I'M ASKING AGAIN. HOW IMPORTANT IS YOUR CAREER?
THERE'RE TWO THINGS I CARE ABOUT MORE THAN ANYTHING IN THIS WORLD.
ONE OF THEM IS THE ARMY. THE OTHER--
YOUR SISTER? SHE'S BEEN MISSING SINCE BEFORE M-DAY, HASN'T SHE?
SO YOU HAVE NO IDEA IF SHE'S STILL A MUTANT.
I DON'T EVEN KNOW IF SHE'S ALIVE. THAT'S NOT THE POINT. WHAT I'M SAYING IS--
--I'D BE A REALLY SAD PERSON IF ALL I CARED ABOUT WAS MY CAREER, NOW WOULDN'T I?

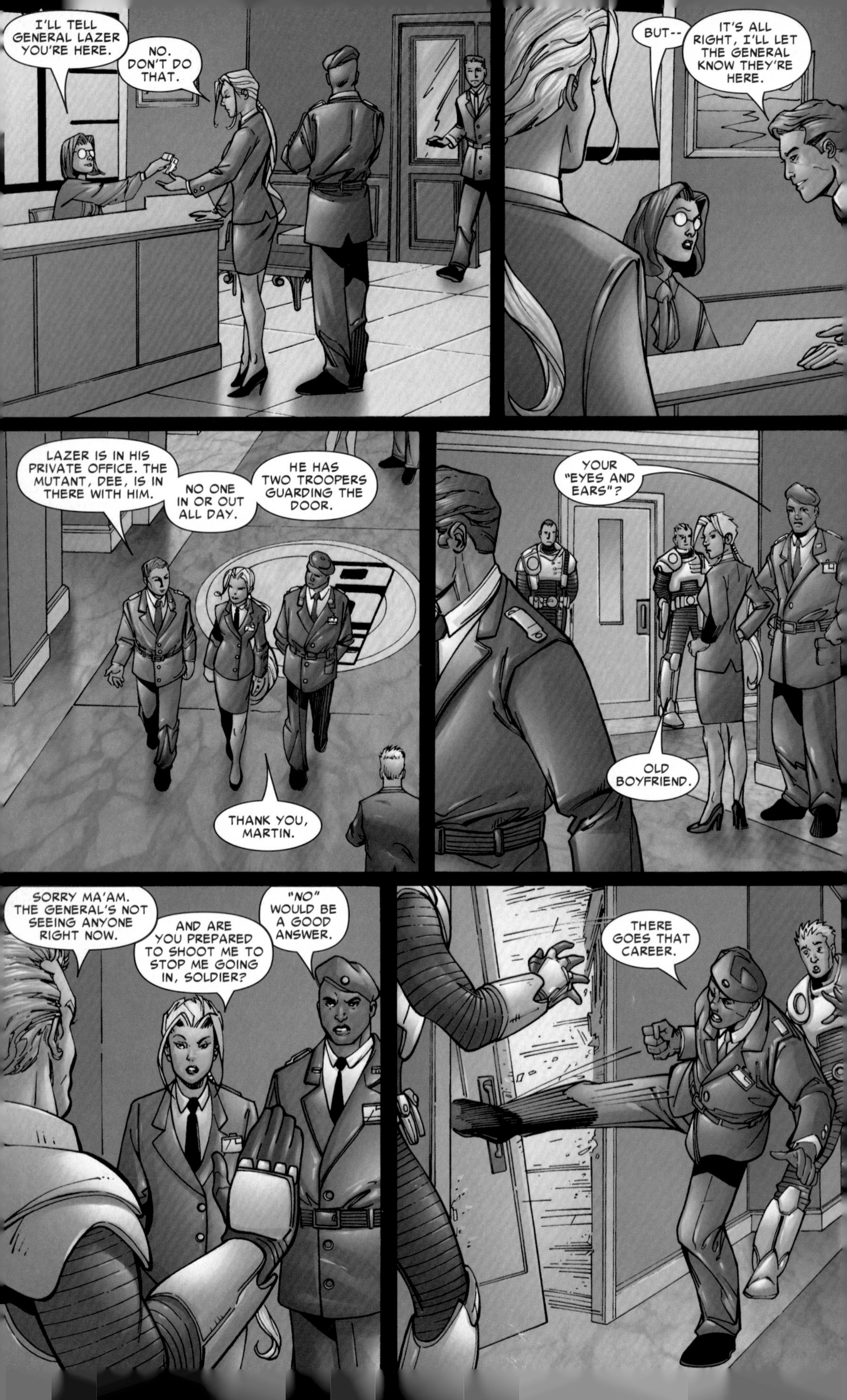
I'LL TELL GENERAL LAZER YOU'RE HERE.
NO. DON'T DO THAT.
BUT--
IT'S ALL RIGHT, I'LL LET THE GENERAL KNOW THEY'RE HERE.
LAZER IS IN HIS PRIVATE OFFICE. THE MUTANT, DEE, IS IN THERE WITH HIM.
NO ONE IN OR OUT ALL DAY.
HE HAS TWO TROOPERS GUARDING THE DOOR.
THANK YOU, MARTIN.
YOUR "EYES AND EARS"?
OLD BOYFRIEND.
SORRY MA'AM. THE GENERAL'S NOT SEEING ANYONE RIGHT NOW.
AND ARE YOU PREPARED TO SHOOT ME TO STOP ME GOING IN, SOLDIER?
"NO" WOULD BE A GOOD ANSWER.
THERE GOES THAT CAREER.

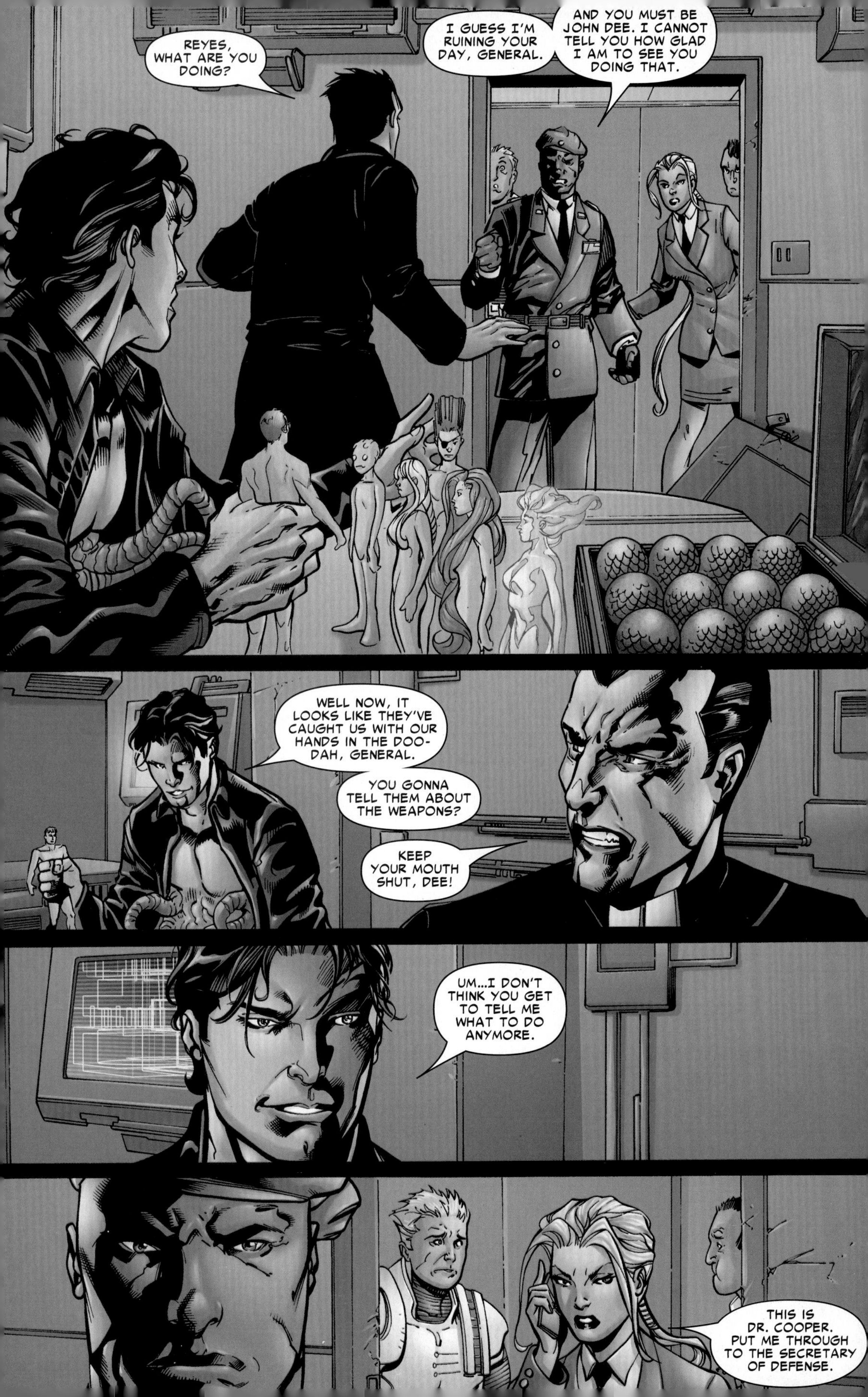
REYES, WHAT ARE YOU DOING?
I GUESS I'M RUINING YOUR DAY, GENERAL.
AND YOU MUST BE JOHN DEE. I CANNOT TELL YOU HOW GLAD I AM TO SEE YOU DOING THAT.
WELL NOW, IT LOOKS LIKE THEY'VE CAUGHT US WITH OUR HANDS IN THE DOO-DAH, GENERAL.
YOU GONNA TELL THEM ABOUT THE WEAPONS?
KEEP YOUR MOUTH SHUT, DEE!
UM...I DON'T THINK YOU GET TO TELL ME WHAT TO DO ANYMORE.
THIS IS DR. COOPER. PUT ME THROUGH TO THE SECRETARY OF DEFENSE.

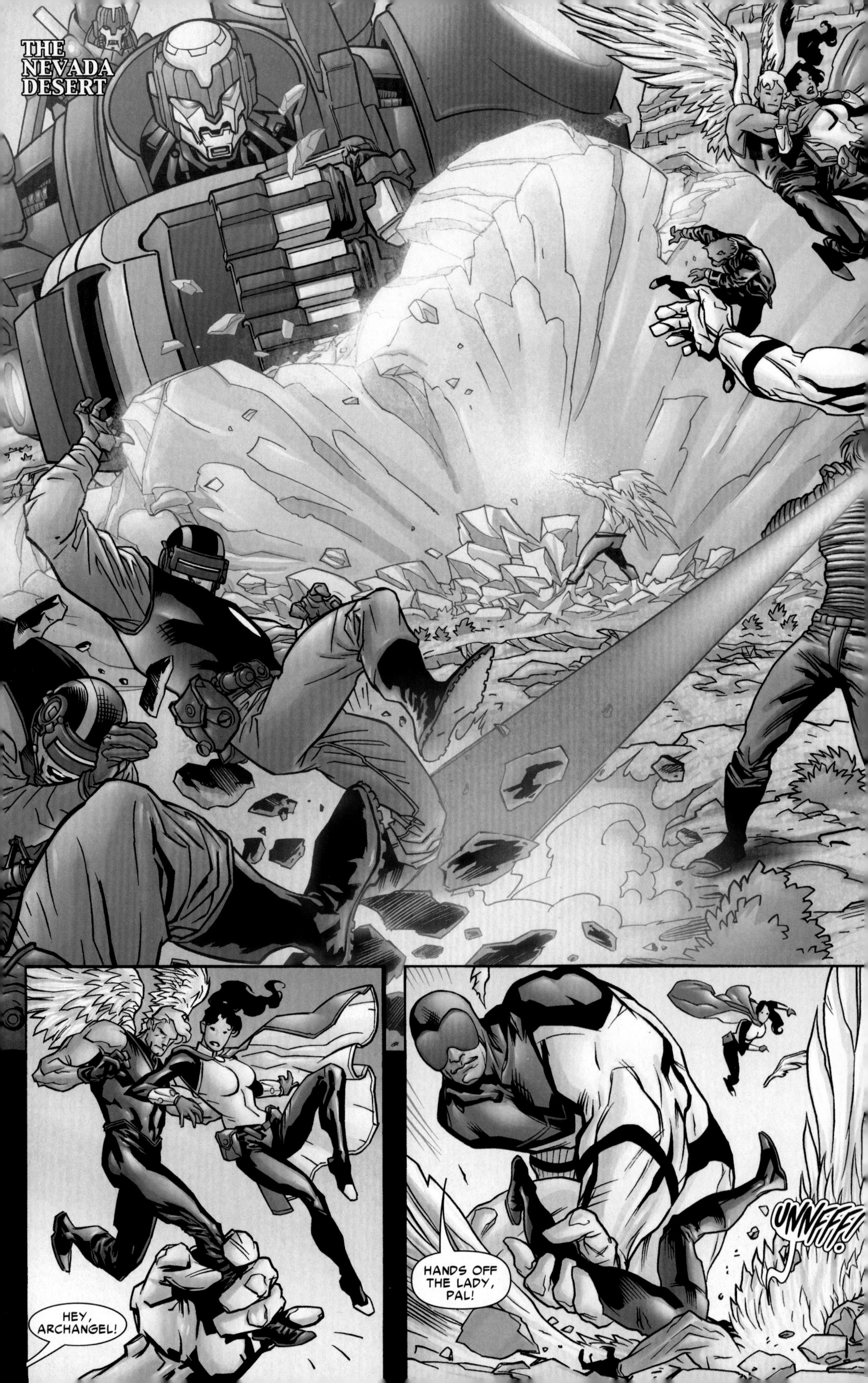
THE NEVADA DESERT
HEY, ARCHANGEL!
HANDS OFF THE LADY, PAL!
UNNFFF!

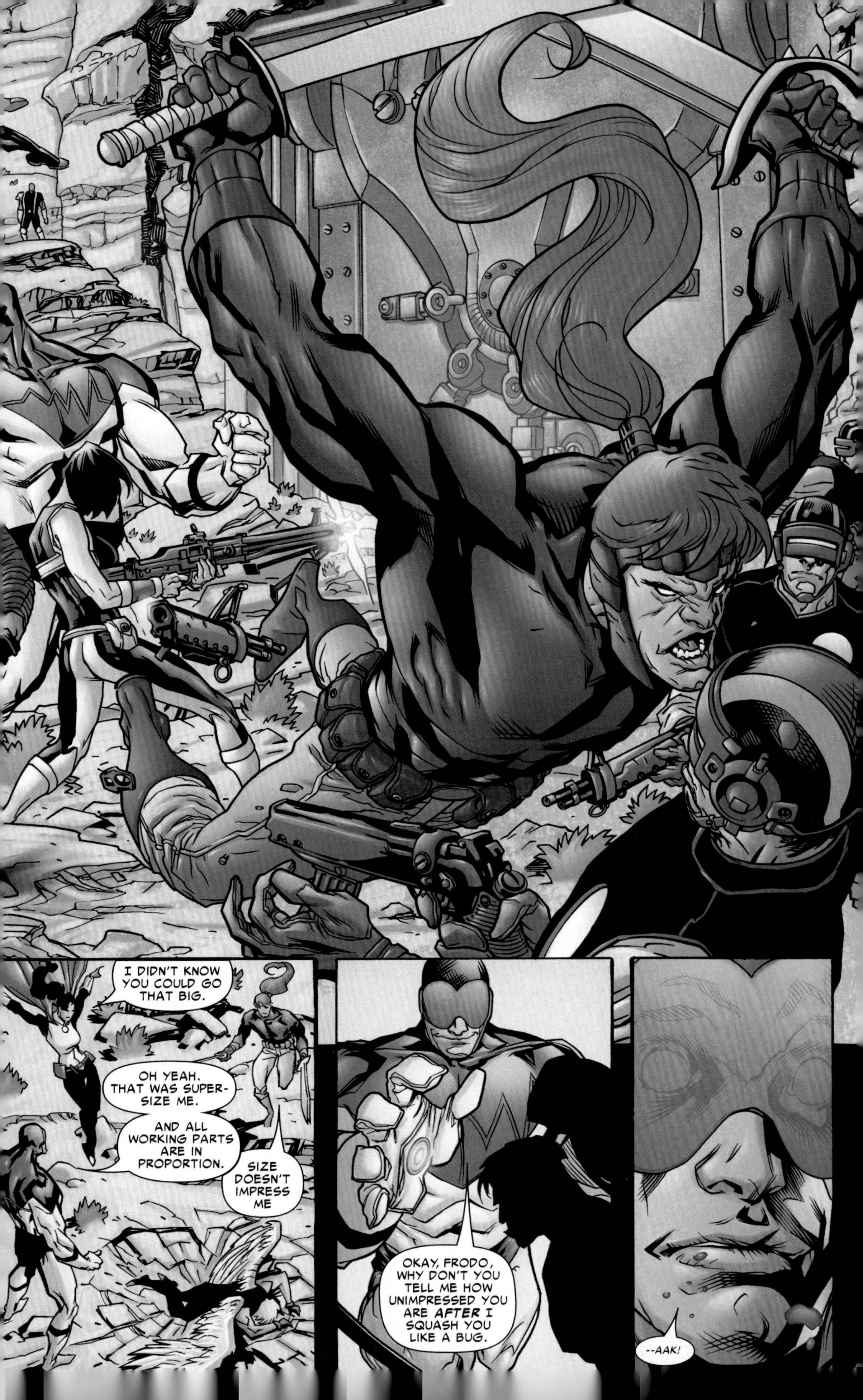
I DIDN'T KNOW YOU COULD GO THAT BIG.
OH YEAH. THAT WAS SUPER-SIZE ME.
AND ALL WORKING PARTS ARE IN PROPORTION.
SIZE DOESN'T IMPRESS ME
OKAY, FRODO, WHY DON'T YOU TELL ME HOW UNIMPRESSED YOU ARE AFTER I SQUASH YOU LIKE A BUG.
--AAK!

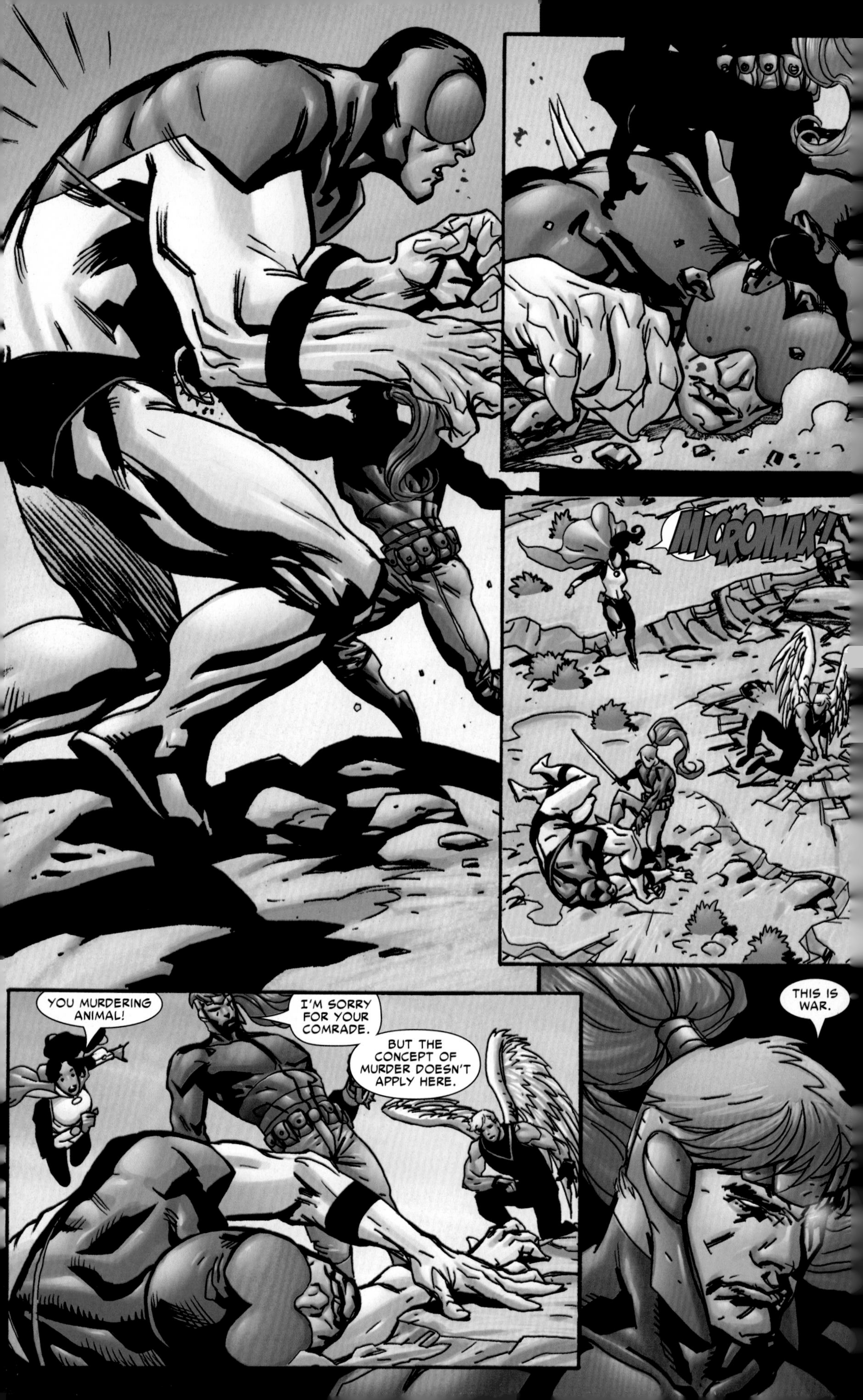
MICROMAX!
YOU MURDERING ANIMAL!
I'M SORRY FOR YOUR COMRADE.
BUT THE CONCEPT OF MURDER DOESN'T APPLY HERE.
THIS IS WAR.

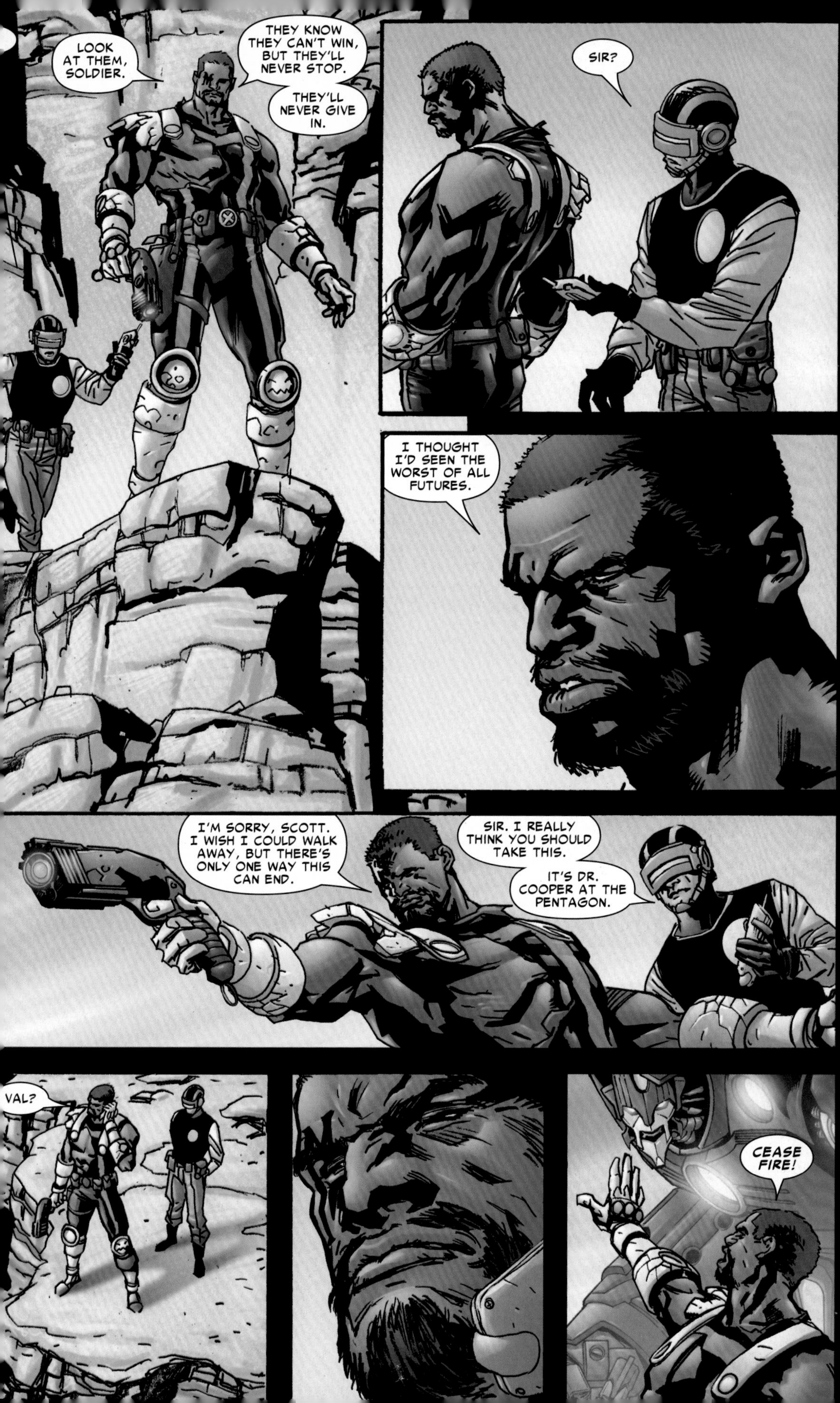
LOOK AT THEM, SOLDIER.
THEY KNOW THEY CAN'T WIN, BUT THEY'LL NEVER STOP.
THEY'LL NEVER GIVE IN.
SIR?
I THOUGHT I'D SEEN THE WORST OF ALL FUTURES.
I'M SORRY, SCOTT. I WISH I COULD WALK AWAY, BUT THERE'S ONLY ONE WAY THIS CAN END.
SIR. I REALLY THINK YOU SHOULD TAKE THIS.
IT'S DR. COOPER AT THE PENTAGON.
VAL?
CEASE FIRE!

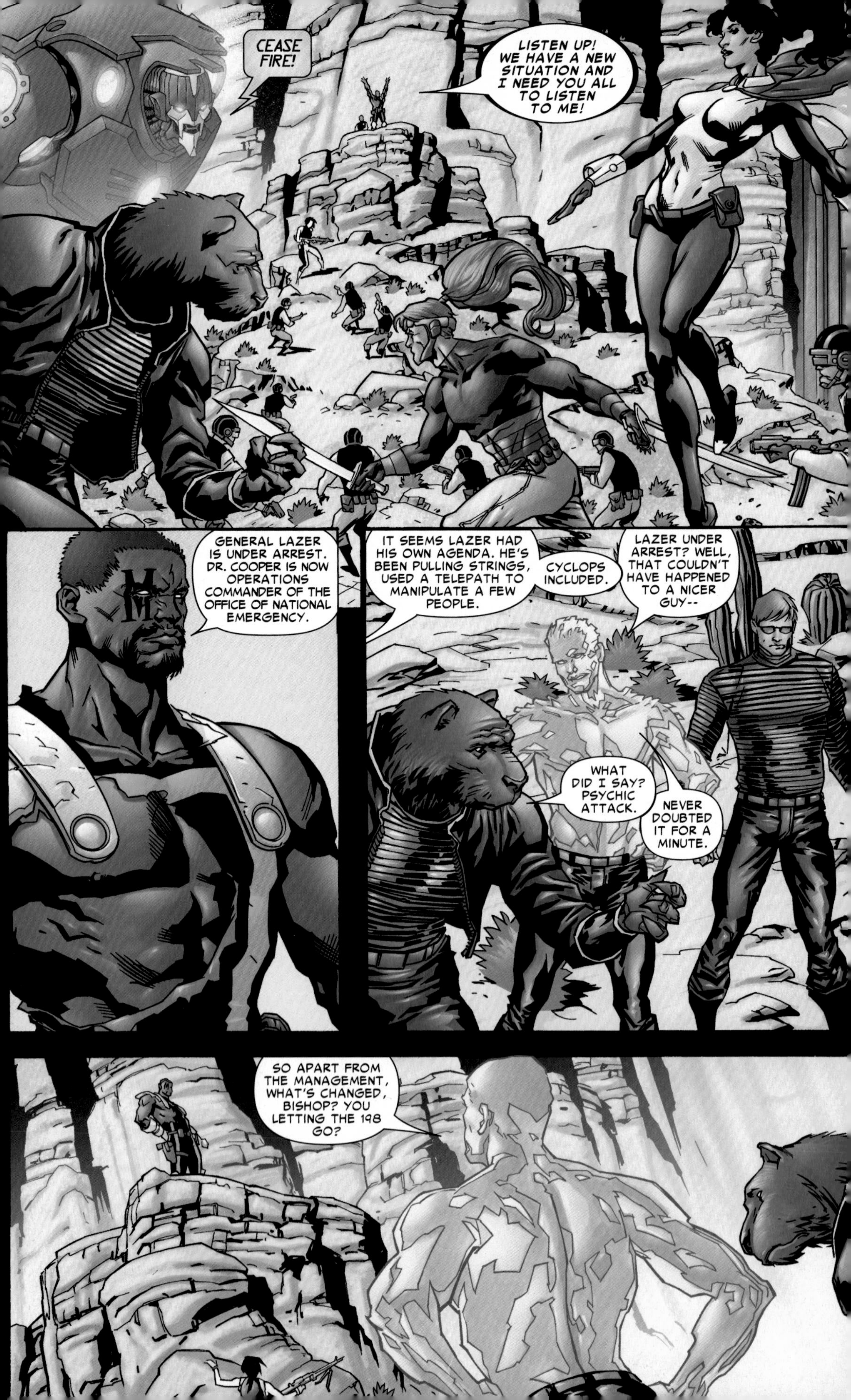
CEASE FIRE!
LISTEN UP! WE HAVE A NEW SITUATION AND I NEED YOU ALL TO LISTEN TO ME!
GENERAL LAZER IS UNDER ARREST. DR. COOPER IS NOW OPERATIONS COMMANDER OF THE OFFICE OF NATIONAL EMERGENCY.
IT SEEMS LAZER HAD HIS OWN AGENDA. HE'S BEEN PULLING STRINGS, USED A TELEPATH TO MANIPULATE A FEW PEOPLE.
CYCLOPS INCLUDED.
LAZER UNDER ARREST? WELL, THAT COULDN'T HAVE HAPPENED TO A NICER GUY--
WHAT DID I SAY? PSYCHIC ATTACK.
NEVER DOUBTED IT FOR A MINUTE.
SO APART FROM THE MANAGEMENT, WHAT'S CHANGED, BISHOP? YOU LETTING THE 198 GO?

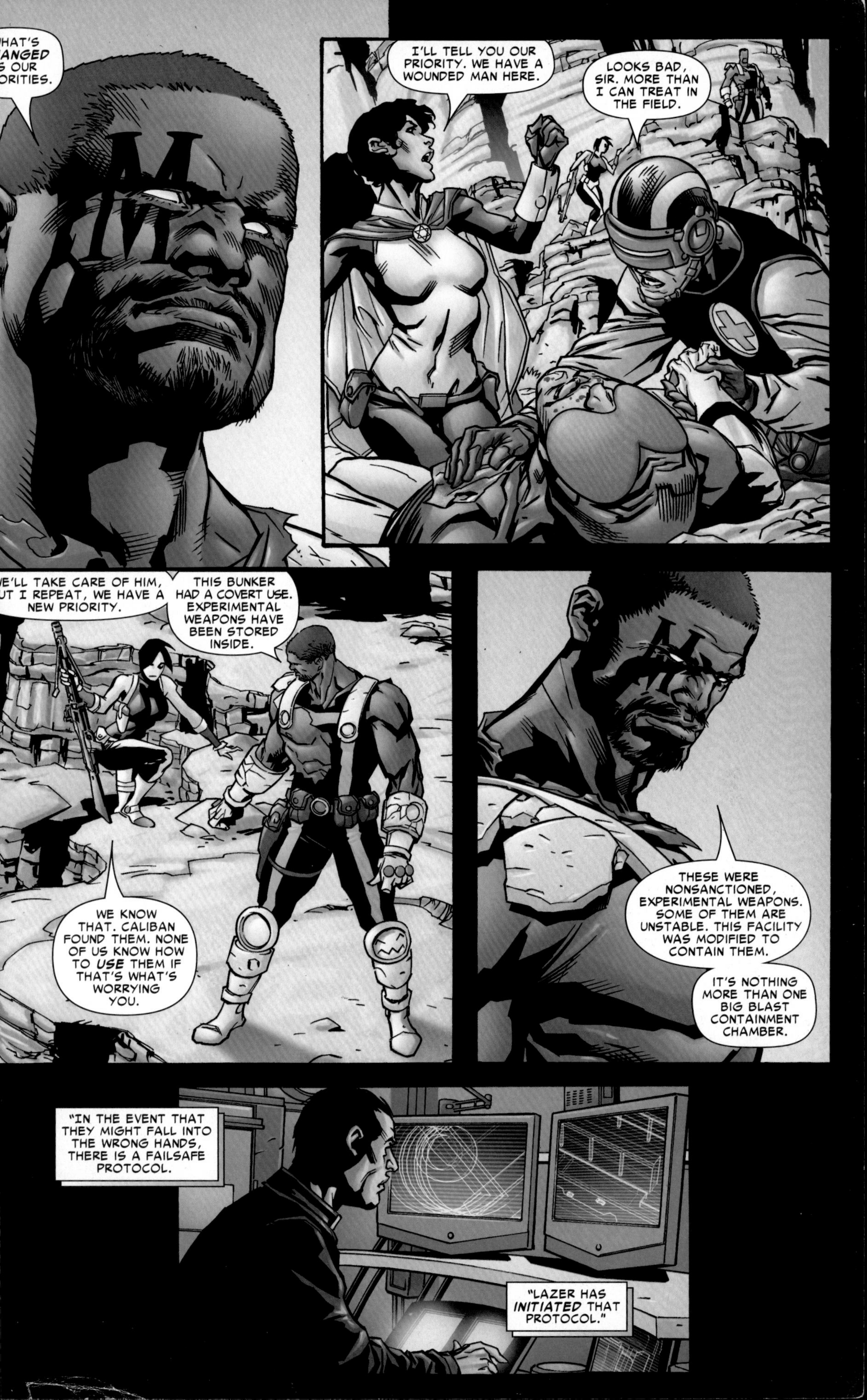
HAT'S ANGED S OUR ORITIES.
I'LL TELL YOU OUR PRIORITY. WE HAVE A WOUNDED MAN HERE.
LOOKS BAD, SIR. MORE THAN I CAN TREAT IN THE FIELD.
E'LL TAKE CARE OF HIM, UT I REPEAT, WE HAVE A NEW PRIORITY.
THIS BUNKER HAD A COVERT USE. EXPERIMENTAL WEAPONS HAVE BEEN STORED INSIDE.
WE KNOW THAT. CALIBAN FOUND THEM. NONE OF US KNOW HOW TO USE THEM IF THAT'S WHAT'S WORRYING YOU.
THESE WERE NONSANCTIONED, EXPERIMENTAL WEAPONS. SOME OF THEM ARE UNSTABLE. THIS FACILITY WAS MODIFIED TO CONTAIN THEM.
IT'S NOTHING MORE THAN ONE BIG BLAST CONTAINMENT CHAMBER.
"IN THE EVENT THAT THEY MIGHT FALL INTO THE WRONG HANDS, THERE IS A FAILSAFE PROTOCOL.
"LAZER HAS INITIATED THAT PROTOCOL."

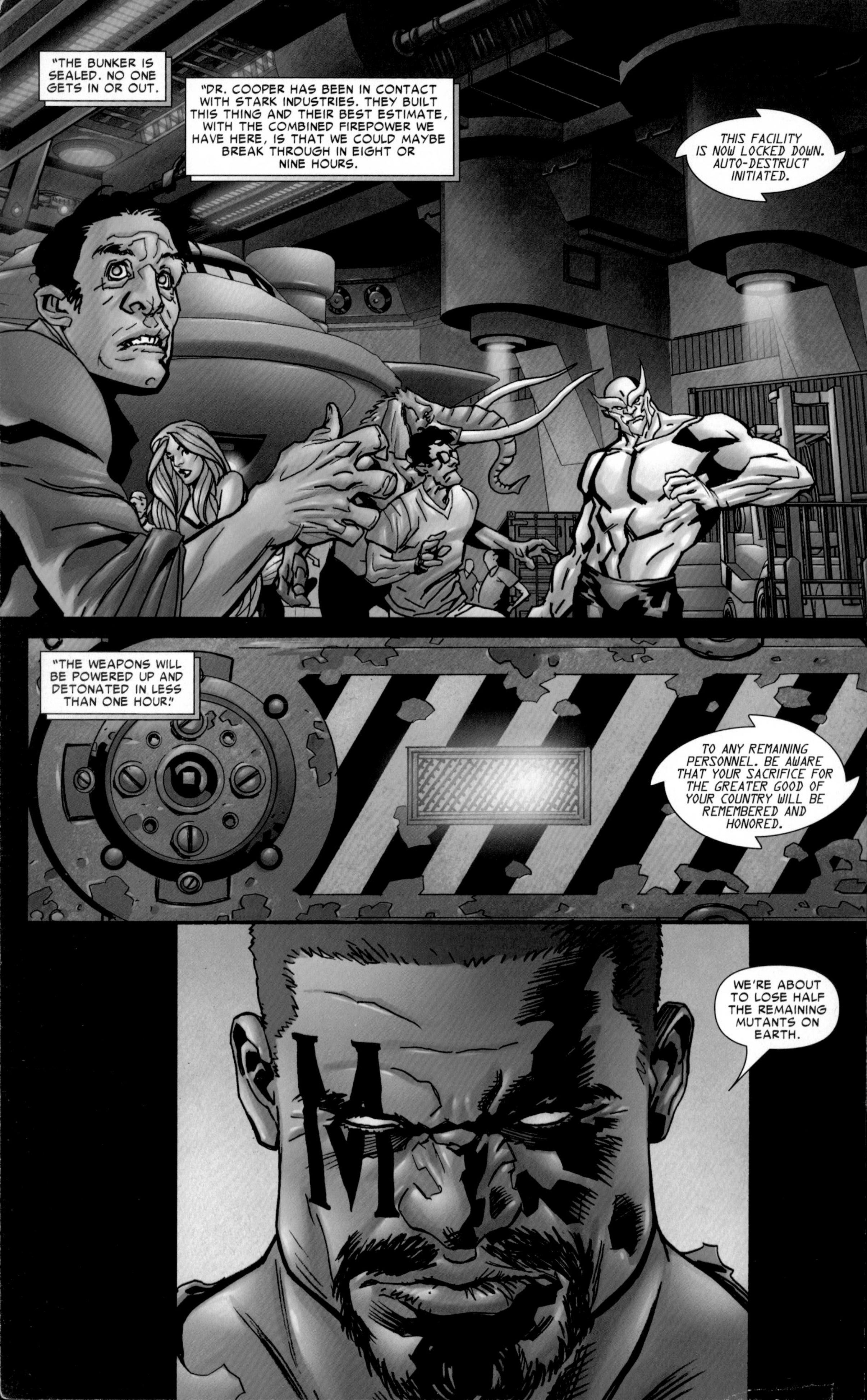
"THE BUNKER IS SEALED. NO ONE GETS IN OR OUT.
"DR. COOPER HAS BEEN IN CONTACT WITH STARK INDUSTRIES. THEY BUILT THIS THING AND THEIR BEST ESTIMATE, WITH THE COMBINED FIREPOWER WE HAVE HERE, IS THAT WE COULD MAYBE BREAK THROUGH IN EIGHT OR NINE HOURS.
THIS FACILITY IS NOW LOCKED DOWN. AUTO-DESTRUCT INITIATED.
"THE WEAPONS WILL BE POWERED UP AND DETONATED IN LESS THAN ONE HOUR."
TO ANY REMAINING PERSONNEL. BE AWARE THAT YOUR SACRIFICE FOR THE GREATER GOOD OF YOUR COUNTRY WILL BE REMEMBERED AND HONORED.
WE'RE ABOUT TO LOSE HALF THE REMAINING MUTANTS ON EARTH.

X-MEN
A MARVEL COMICS EVENT

CIVIL WAR

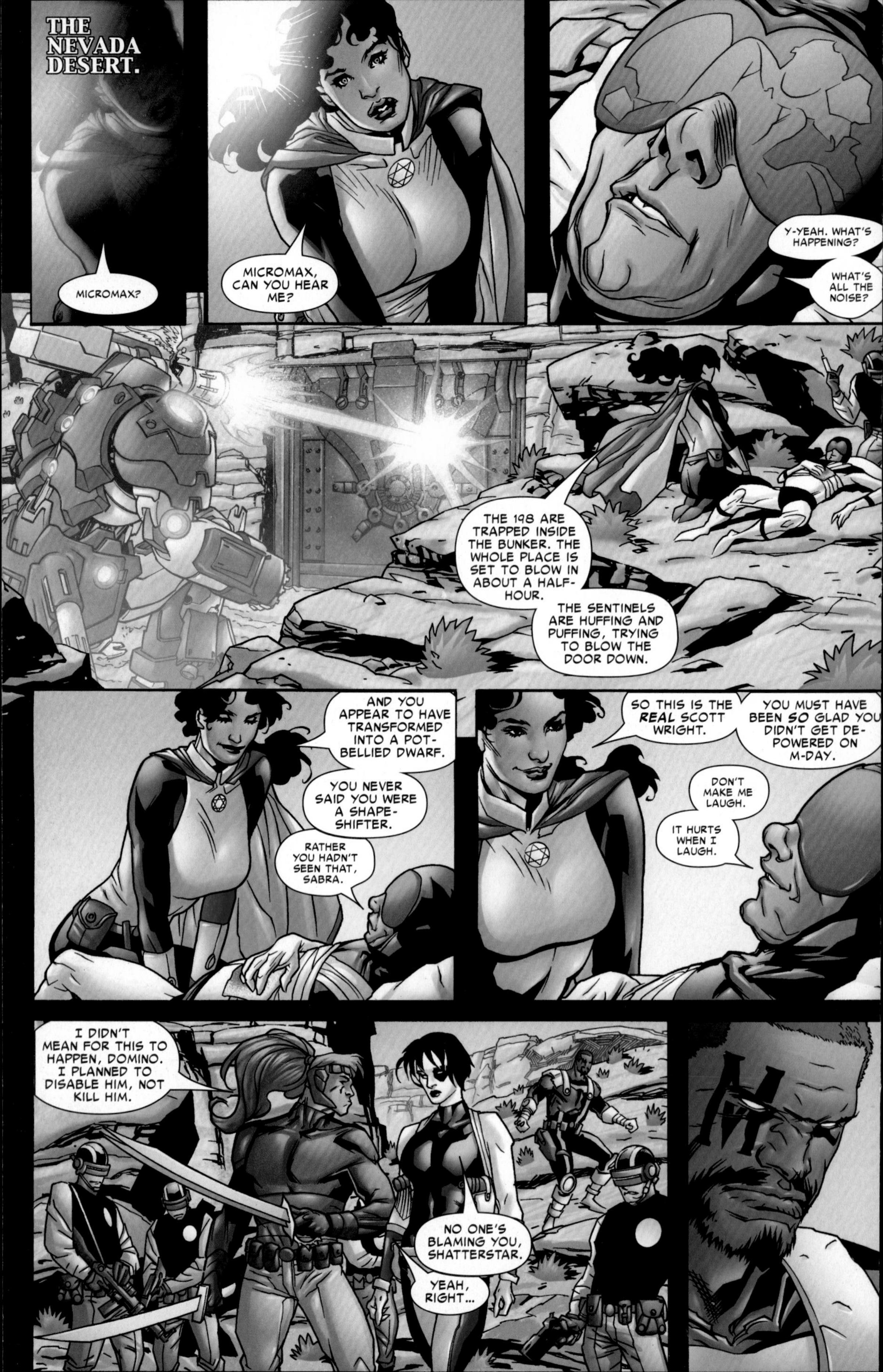
THE NEVADA DESERT.
MICROMAX?
MICROMAX, CAN YOU HEAR ME?
Y-YEAH. WHAT'S HAPPENING?
WHAT'S ALL THE NOISE?
THE 198 ARE TRAPPED INSIDE THE BUNKER. THE WHOLE PLACE IS SET TO BLOW IN ABOUT A HALF-HOUR.
THE SENTINELS ARE HUFFING AND PUFFING, TRYING TO BLOW THE DOOR DOWN.
AND YOU APPEAR TO HAVE TRANSFORMED INTO A POT-BELLIED DWARF.
YOU NEVER SAID YOU WERE A SHAPE-SHIFTER.
RATHER YOU HADN'T SEEN THAT, SABRA.
SO THIS IS THE REAL SCOTT WRIGHT.
YOU MUST HAVE BEEN SO GLAD YOU DIDN'T GET DE-POWERED ON M-DAY.
DON'T MAKE ME LAUGH.
IT HURTS WHEN I LAUGH.
I DIDN'T MEAN FOR THIS TO HAPPEN, DOMINO. I PLANNED TO DISABLE HIM, NOT KILL HIM.
NO ONE'S BLAMING YOU, SHATTERSTAR.
YEAH, RIGHT...

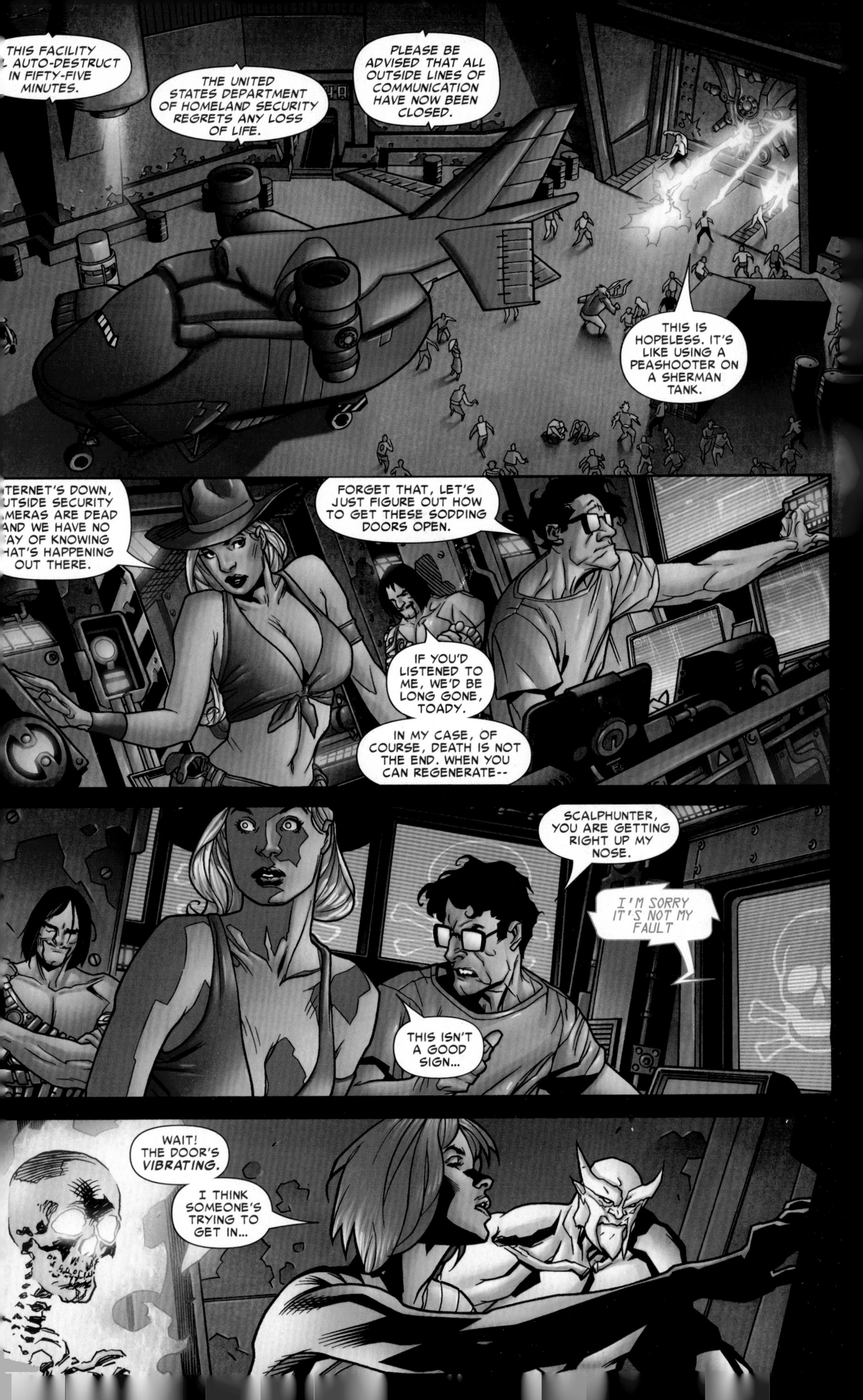
THIS FACILITY
AUTO-DESTRUCT IN FIFTY-FIVE MINUTES.
THE UNITED STATES DEPARTMENT OF HOMELAND SECURITY REGRETS ANY LOSS OF LIFE.
PLEASE BE ADVISED THAT ALL OUTSIDE LINES OF COMMUNICATION HAVE NOW BEEN CLOSED.
THIS IS HOPELESS. IT'S LIKE USING A PEASHOOTER ON A SHERMAN TANK.
TERNET'S DOWN, UTSIDE SECURITY MERAS ARE DEAD AND WE HAVE NO AY OF KNOWING HAT'S HAPPENING OUT THERE.
FORGET THAT, LET'S JUST FIGURE OUT HOW TO GET THESE SODDING DOORS OPEN.
IF YOU'D LISTENED TO ME, WE'D BE LONG GONE, TOADY.
IN MY CASE, OF COURSE, DEATH IS NOT THE END. WHEN YOU CAN REGENERATE--
SCALPHUNTER, YOU ARE GETTING RIGHT UP MY NOSE.
I'M SORRY IT'S NOT MY FAULT
THIS ISN'T A GOOD SIGN...
WAIT! THE DOOR'S VIBRATING.
I THINK SOMEONE'S TRYING TO GET IN...

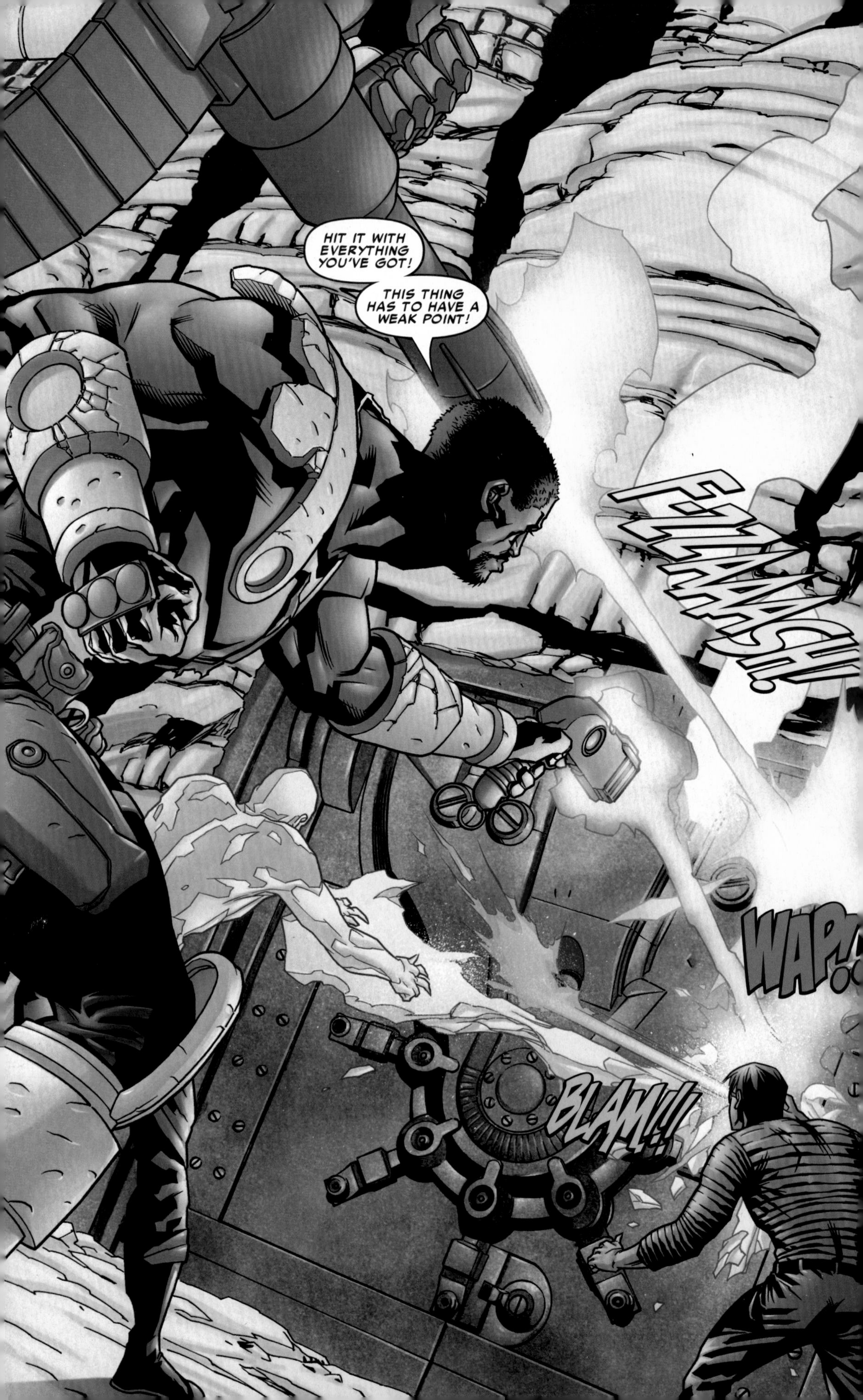
HIT IT WITH EVERYTHING YOU'VE GOT!
THIS THING HAS TO HAVE A WEAK POINT!
FZZAAASH!!
WAP!!
BLAM!!!

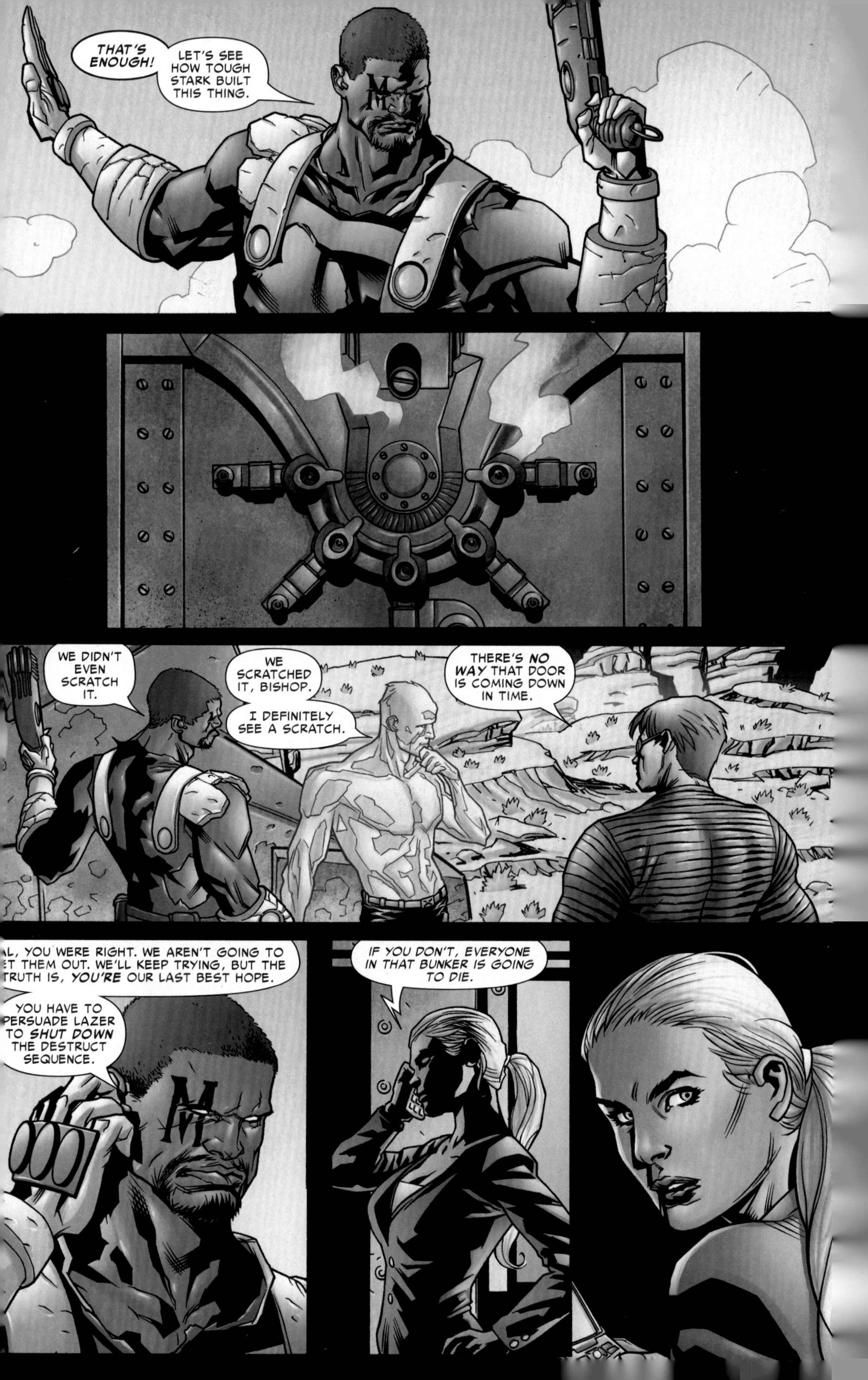
THAT'S ENOUGH!
LET'S SEE HOW TOUGH STARK BUILT THIS THING.
WE DIDN'T EVEN SCRATCH IT.
WE SCRATCHED IT, BISHOP.
I DEFINITELY SEE A SCRATCH.
THERE'S NO WAY THAT DOOR IS COMING DOWN IN TIME.
L, YOU WERE RIGHT. WE AREN'T GOING TO ET THEM OUT. WE'LL KEEP TRYING, BUT THE TRUTH IS, YOU'RE OUR LAST BEST HOPE.
YOU HAVE TO PERSUADE LAZER TO SHUT DOWN THE DESTRUCT SEQUENCE.
IF YOU DON'T, EVERYONE IN THAT BUNKER IS GOING TO DIE.

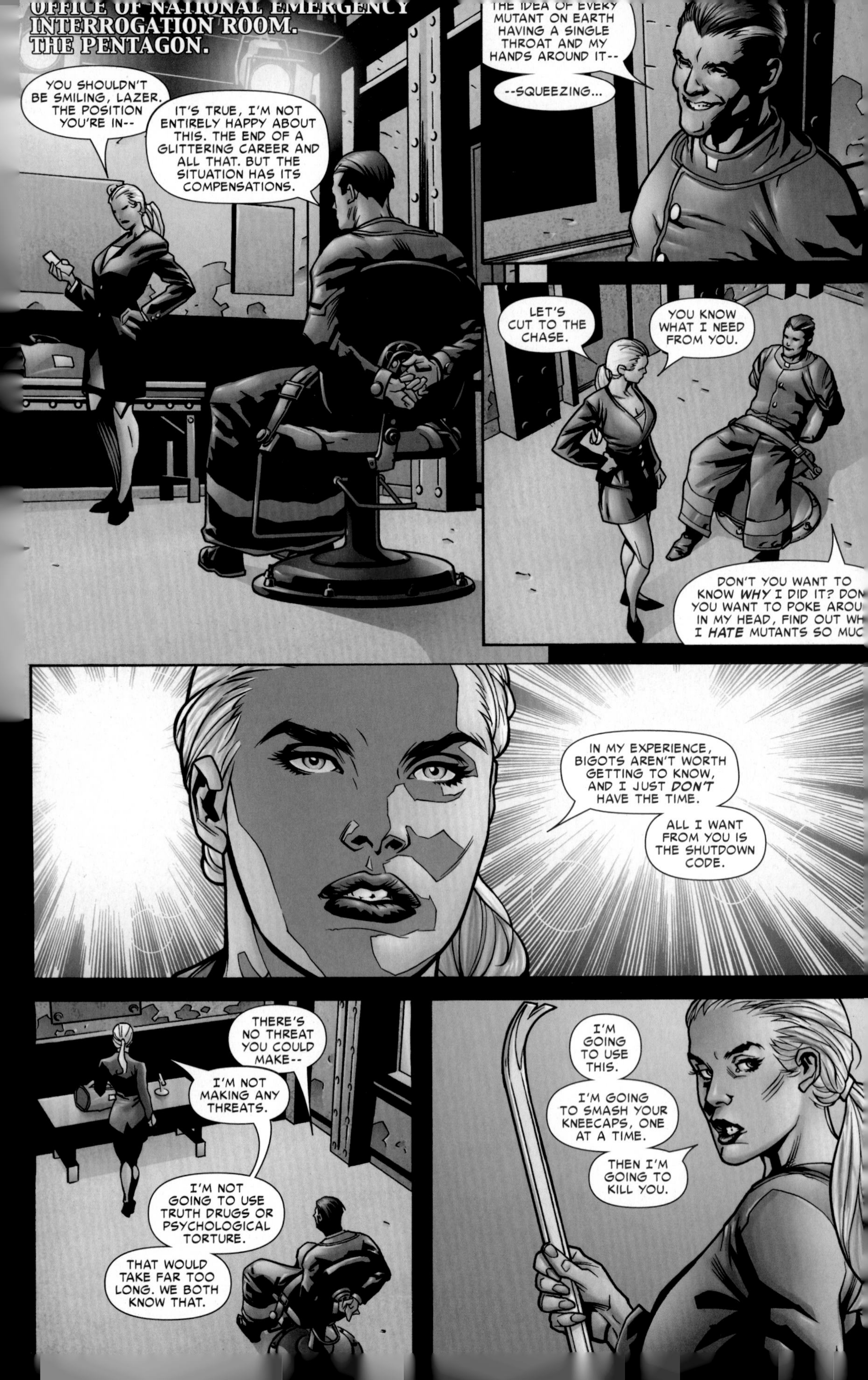
OFFICE OF NATIONAL EMERGENCY
INTERROGATION ROOM. THE PENTAGON.
YOU SHOULDN'T BE SMILING, LAZER. THE POSITION YOU'RE IN--
IT'S TRUE, I'M NOT ENTIRELY HAPPY ABOUT THIS. THE END OF A GLITTERING CAREER AND ALL THAT. BUT THE SITUATION HAS ITS COMPENSATIONS.
THE IDEA OF EVERY MUTANT ON EARTH HAVING A SINGLE THROAT AND MY HANDS AROUND IT--
--SQUEEZING...
LET'S CUT TO THE CHASE.
YOU KNOW WHAT I NEED FROM YOU.
DON'T YOU WANT TO KNOW WHY I DID IT? DON YOU WANT TO POKE AROU IN MY HEAD, FIND OUT WH I HATE MUTANTS SO MUC
IN MY EXPERIENCE, BIGOTS AREN'T WORTH GETTING TO KNOW, AND I JUST DON'T HAVE THE TIME.
ALL I WANT FROM YOU IS THE SHUTDOWN CODE.
THERE'S NO THREAT YOU COULD MAKE--
I'M NOT MAKING ANY THREATS.
I'M NOT GOING TO USE TRUTH DRUGS OR PSYCHOLOGICAL TORTURE.
THAT WOULD TAKE FAR TOO LONG. WE BOTH KNOW THAT.
I'M GOING TO USE THIS.
I'M GOING TO SMASH YOUR KNEECAPS, ONE AT A TIME.
THEN I'M GOING TO KILL YOU.

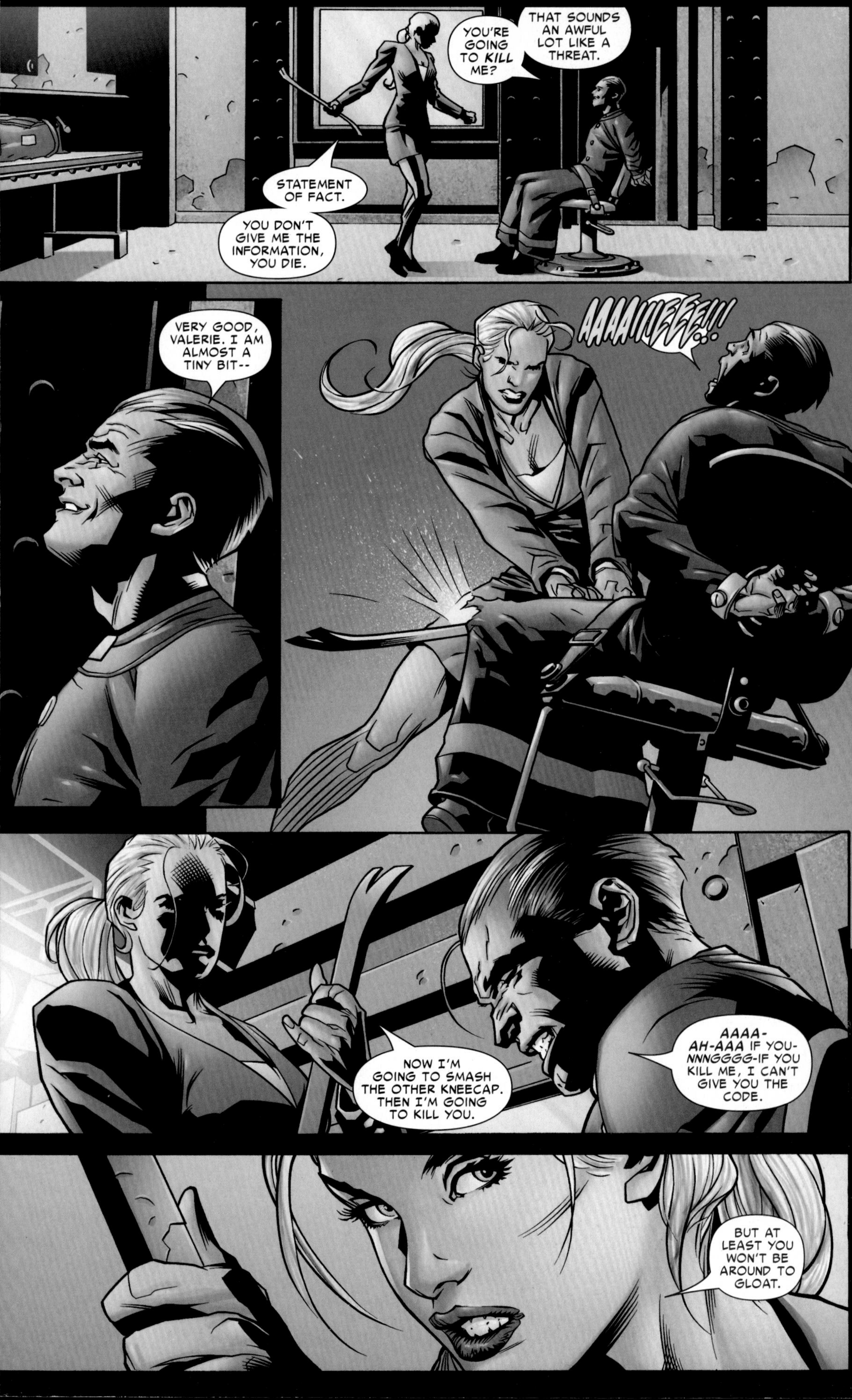
YOU'RE GOING TO KILL ME?
THAT SOUNDS AN AWFUL LOT LIKE A THREAT.
STATEMENT OF FACT.
YOU DON'T GIVE ME THE INFORMATION, YOU DIE.
VERY GOOD, VALERIE. I AM ALMOST A TINY BIT--
AAAAIIIEEE!!!
NOW I'M GOING TO SMASH THE OTHER KNEECAP. THEN I'M GOING TO KILL YOU.
AAAA-AH-AAA IF YOU-NNNGGGG-IF YOU KILL ME, I CAN'T GIVE YOU THE CODE.
BUT AT LEAST YOU WON'T BE AROUND TO GLOAT.

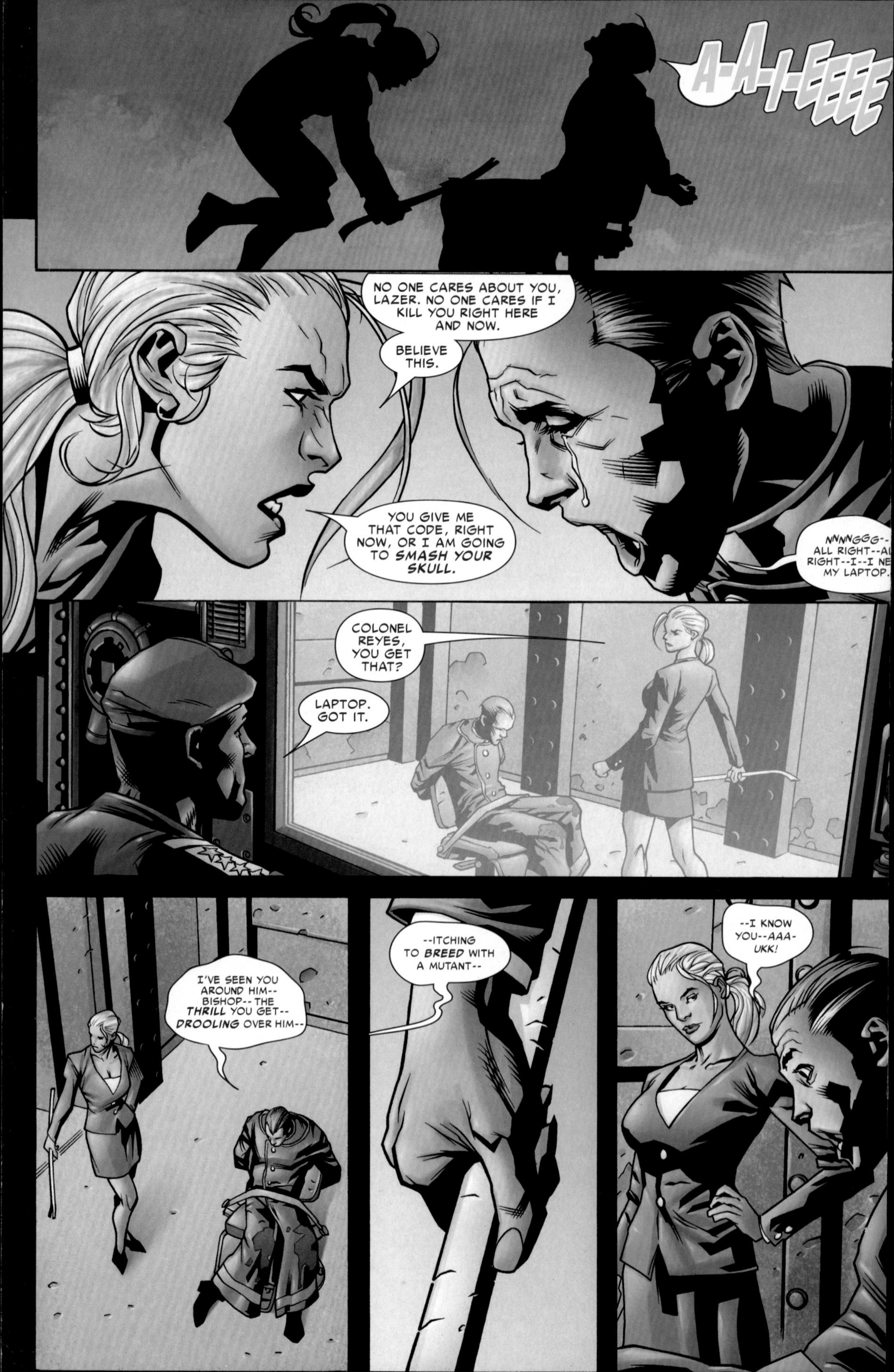
A-A-I-EEEE
NO ONE CARES ABOUT YOU, LAZER. NO ONE CARES IF I KILL YOU RIGHT HERE AND NOW.
BELIEVE THIS.
YOU GIVE ME THAT CODE, RIGHT NOW, OR I AM GOING TO SMASH YOUR SKULL.
NNNNGGG-- ALL RIGHT--AL RIGHT--I--I NE MY LAPTOP.
COLONEL REYES, YOU GET THAT?
LAPTOP. GOT IT.
I'VE SEEN YOU AROUND HIM-- BISHOP-- THE THRILL YOU GET-- DROOLING OVER HIM--
--ITCHING TO BREED WITH A MUTANT--
--I KNOW YOU--AAA-UKK!

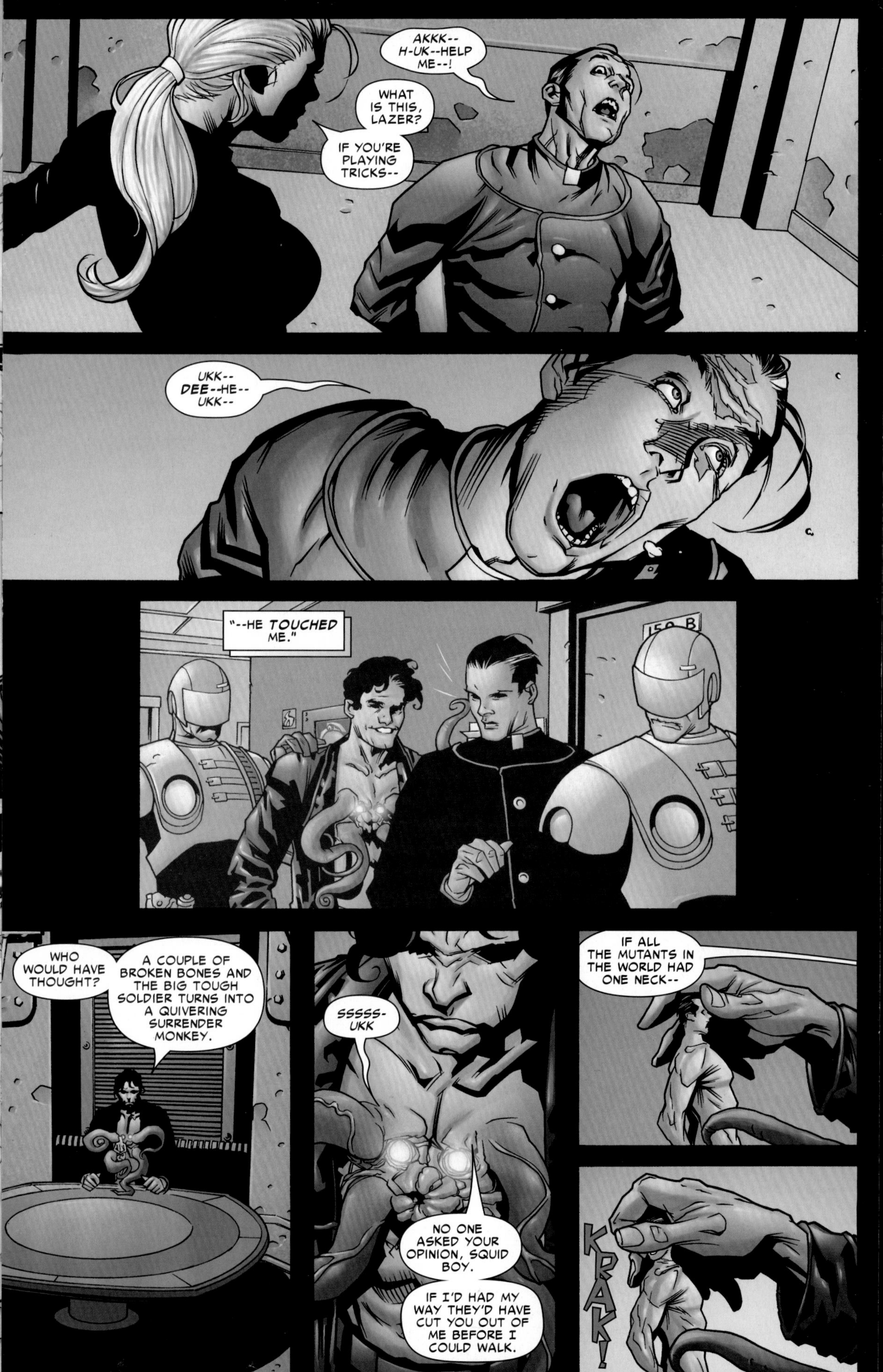

AKKK-- H-UK--HELP ME--!
WHAT IS THIS, LAZER?
IF YOU'RE PLAYING TRICKS--
UKK-- DEE--HE-- UKK--
"--HE TOUCHED ME."
WHO WOULD HAVE THOUGHT?
A COUPLE OF BROKEN BONES AND THE BIG TOUGH SOLDIER TURNS INTO A QUIVERING SURRENDER MONKEY.
SSSSS-UKK
NO ONE ASKED YOUR OPINION, SQUID BOY.
IF I'D HAD MY WAY THEY'D HAVE CUT YOU OUT OF ME BEFORE I COULD WALK.
IF ALL THE MUTANTS IN THE WORLD HAD ONE NECK--
KRAK!

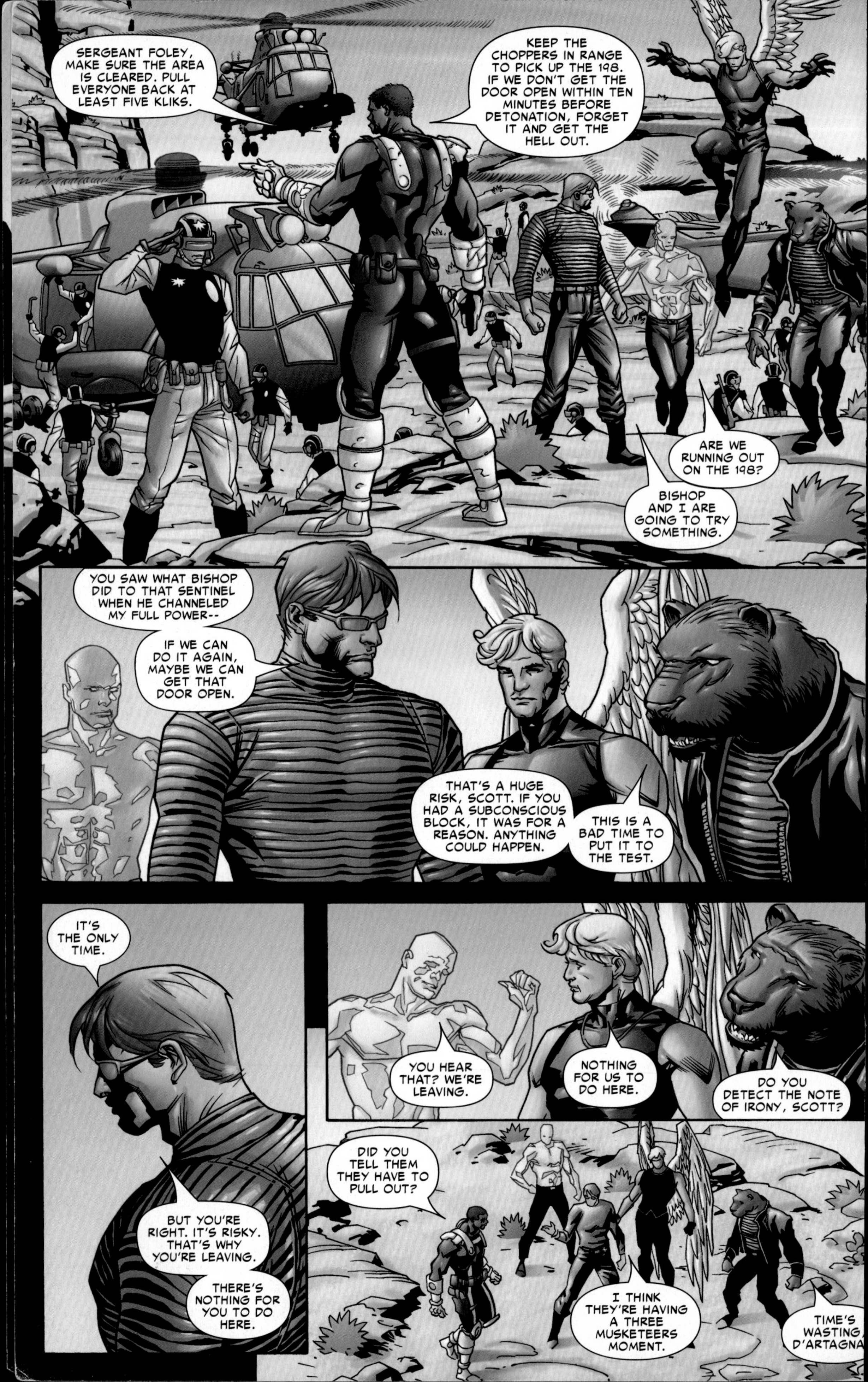
SERGEANT FOLEY, MAKE SURE THE AREA IS CLEARED. PULL EVERYONE BACK AT LEAST FIVE KLIKS.
KEEP THE CHOPPERS IN RANGE TO PICK UP THE 198. IF WE DON'T GET THE DOOR OPEN WITHIN TEN MINUTES BEFORE DETONATION, FORGET IT AND GET THE HELL OUT.
ARE WE RUNNING OUT ON THE 198?
BISHOP AND I ARE GOING TO TRY SOMETHING.
YOU SAW WHAT BISHOP DID TO THAT SENTINEL WHEN HE CHANNELED MY FULL POWER--
IF WE CAN DO IT AGAIN, MAYBE WE CAN GET THAT DOOR OPEN.
THAT'S A HUGE RISK, SCOTT. IF YOU HAD A SUBCONSCIOUS BLOCK, IT WAS FOR A REASON. ANYTHING COULD HAPPEN.
THIS IS A BAD TIME TO PUT IT TO THE TEST.
IT'S THE ONLY TIME.
BUT YOU'RE RIGHT. IT'S RISKY. THAT'S WHY YOU'RE LEAVING.
THERE'S NOTHING FOR YOU TO DO HERE.
YOU HEAR THAT? WE'RE LEAVING.
NOTHING FOR US TO DO HERE.
DO YOU DETECT THE NOTE OF IRONY, SCOTT?
DID YOU TELL THEM THEY HAVE TO PULL OUT?
I THINK THEY'RE HAVING A THREE MUSKETEERS MOMENT.
TIME'S WASTING, D'ARTAGNA

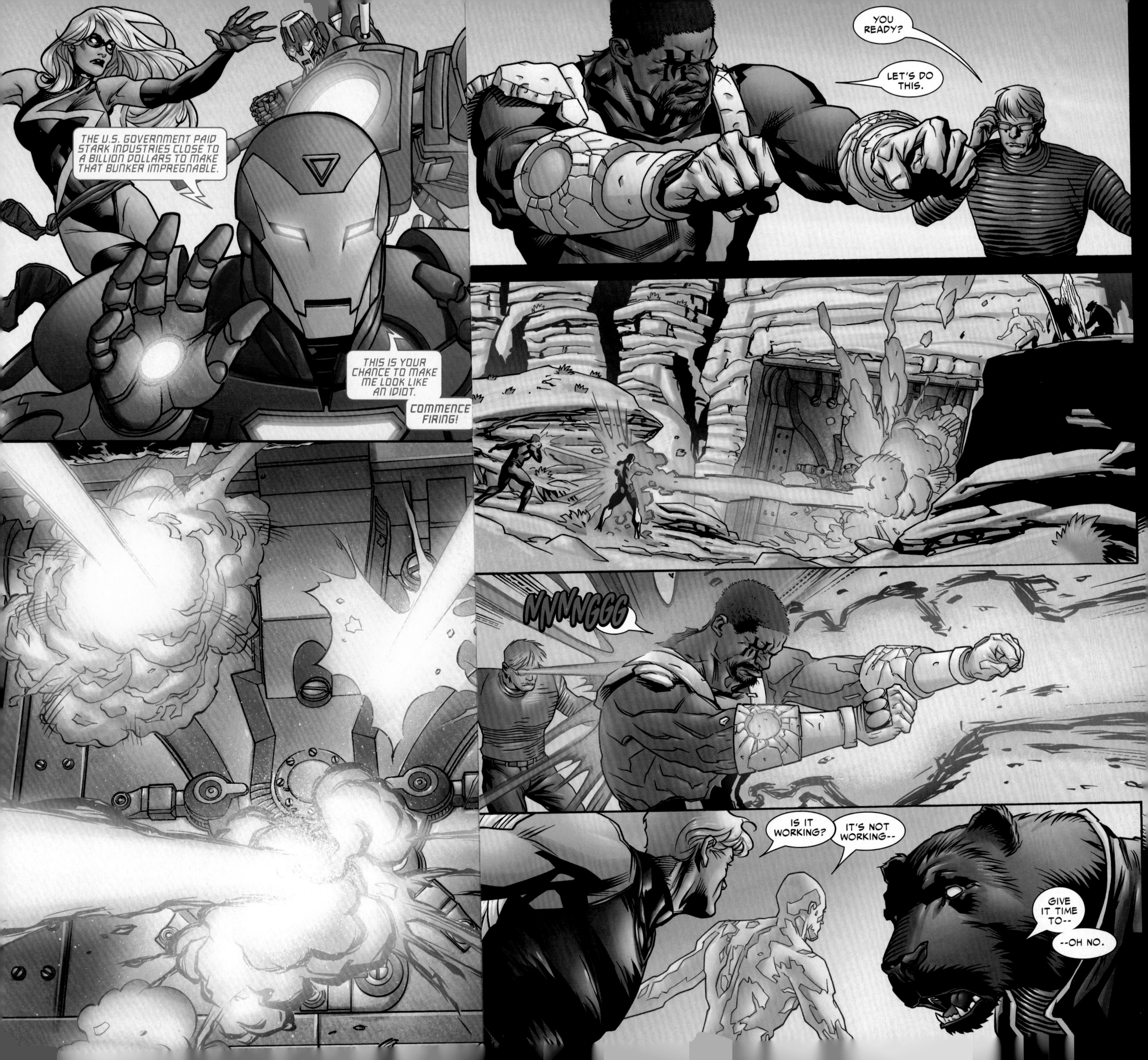
THE U.S. GOVERNMENT PAID STARK INDUSTRIES CLOSE TO A BILLION DOLLARS TO MAKE THAT BUNKER IMPREGNABLE.
THIS IS YOUR CHANCE TO MAKE ME LOOK LIKE AN IDIOT.
COMMENCE FIRING!
YOU READY?
LET'S DO THIS.
MNNNGGG
IS IT WORKING?
IT'S NOT WORKING--
GIVE IT TIME TO--
--OH NO.

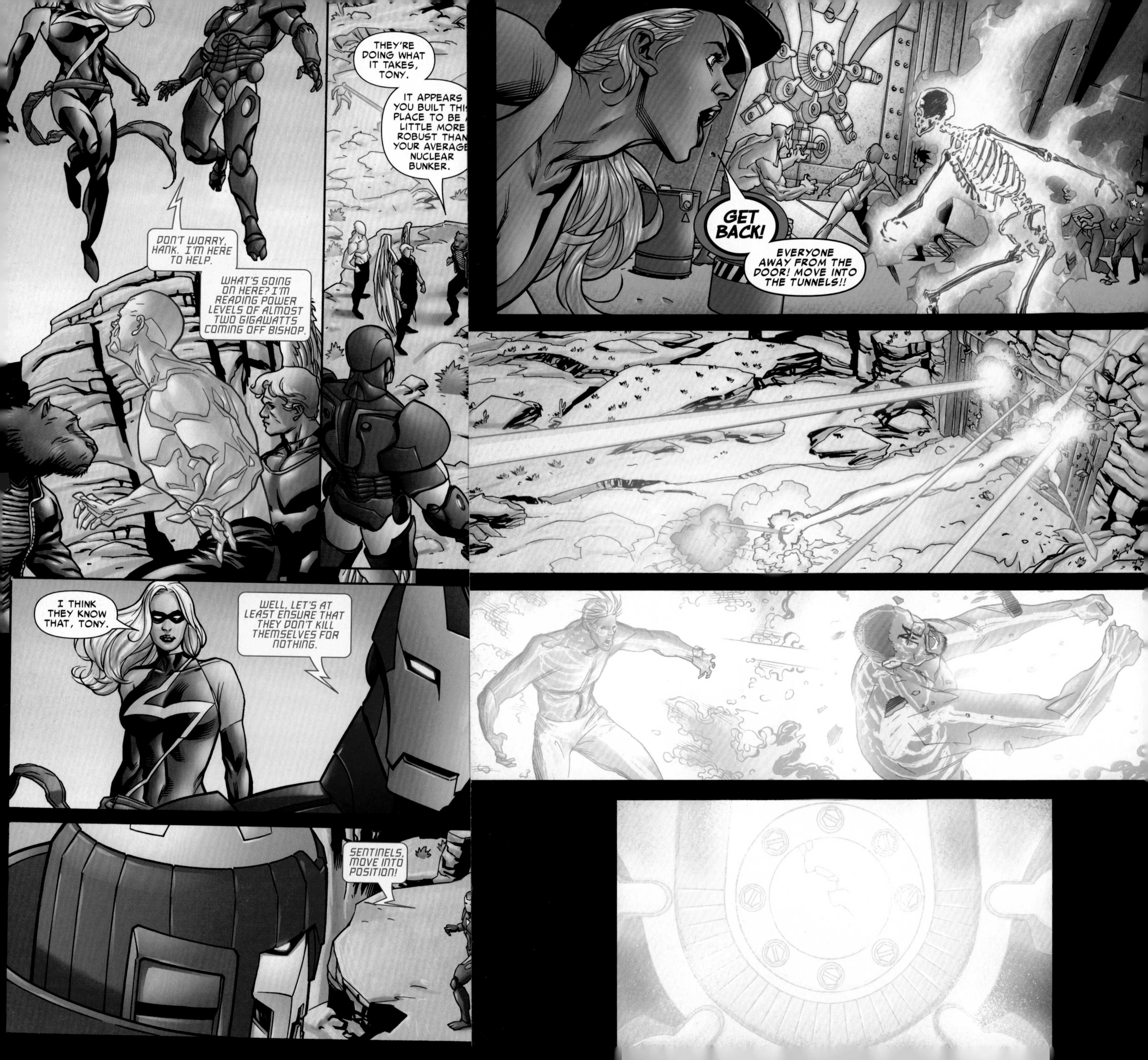

THEY'RE DOING WHAT IT TAKES, TONY.
IT APPEARS YOU BUILT THIS PLACE TO BE A LITTLE MORE ROBUST THAN YOUR AVERAGE NUCLEAR BUNKER.
DON'T WORRY, HANK. I'M HERE TO HELP.
WHAT'S GOING ON HERE? I'M READING POWER LEVELS OF ALMOST TWO GIGAWATTS COMING OFF BISHOP.
I THINK THEY KNOW THAT, TONY.
WELL, LET'S AT LEAST ENSURE THAT THEY DON'T KILL THEMSELVES FOR NOTHING.
SENTINELS, MOVE INTO POSITION!
GET BACK!
EVERYONE AWAY FROM THE DOOR! MOVE INTO THE TUNNELS!!

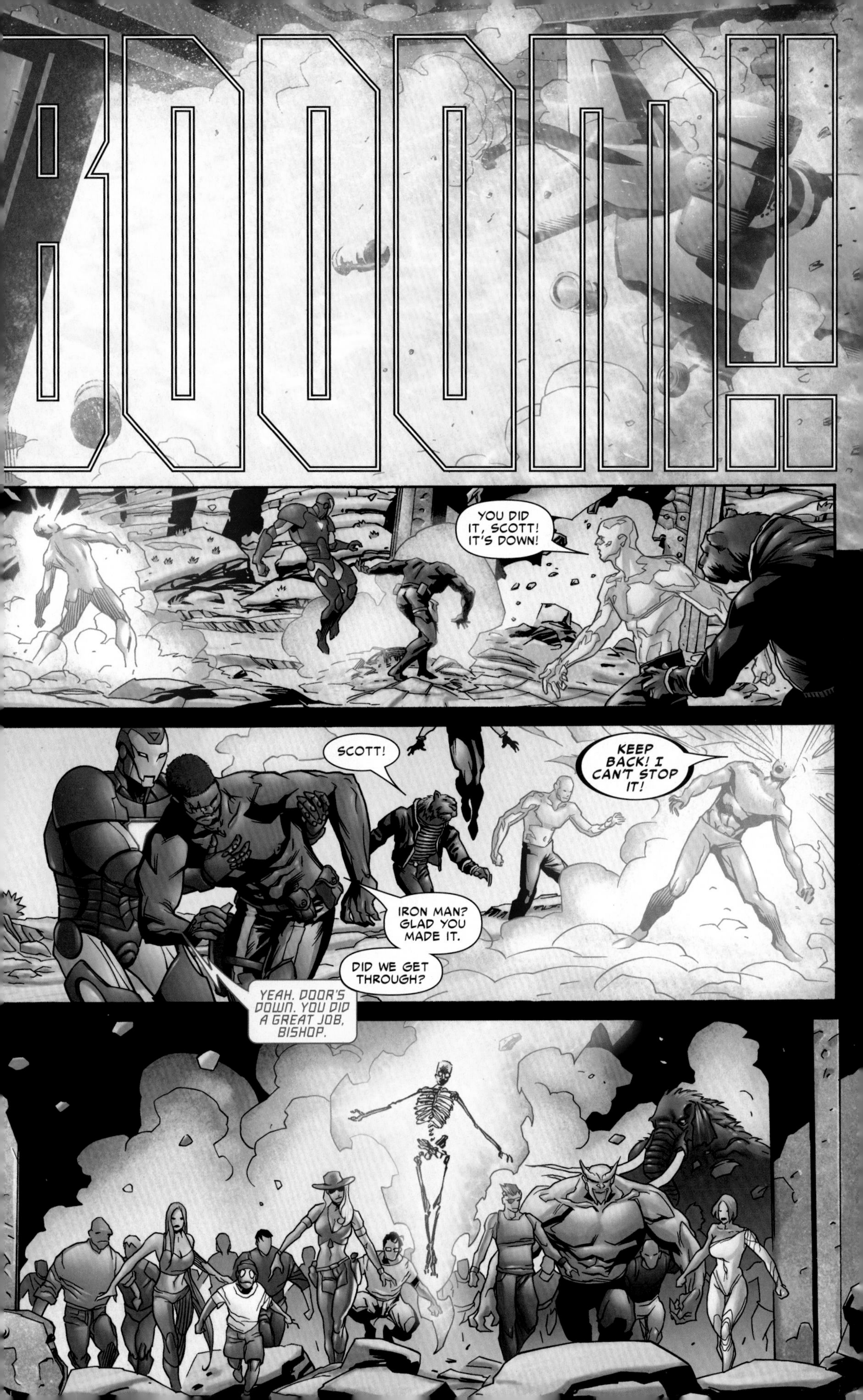
BOOOM!!
YOU DID IT, SCOTT! IT'S DOWN!
SCOTT!
KEEP BACK! I CAN'T STOP IT!
IRON MAN? GLAD YOU MADE IT.
DID WE GET THROUGH?
YEAH. DOOR'S DOWN. YOU DID A GREAT JOB, BISHOP.

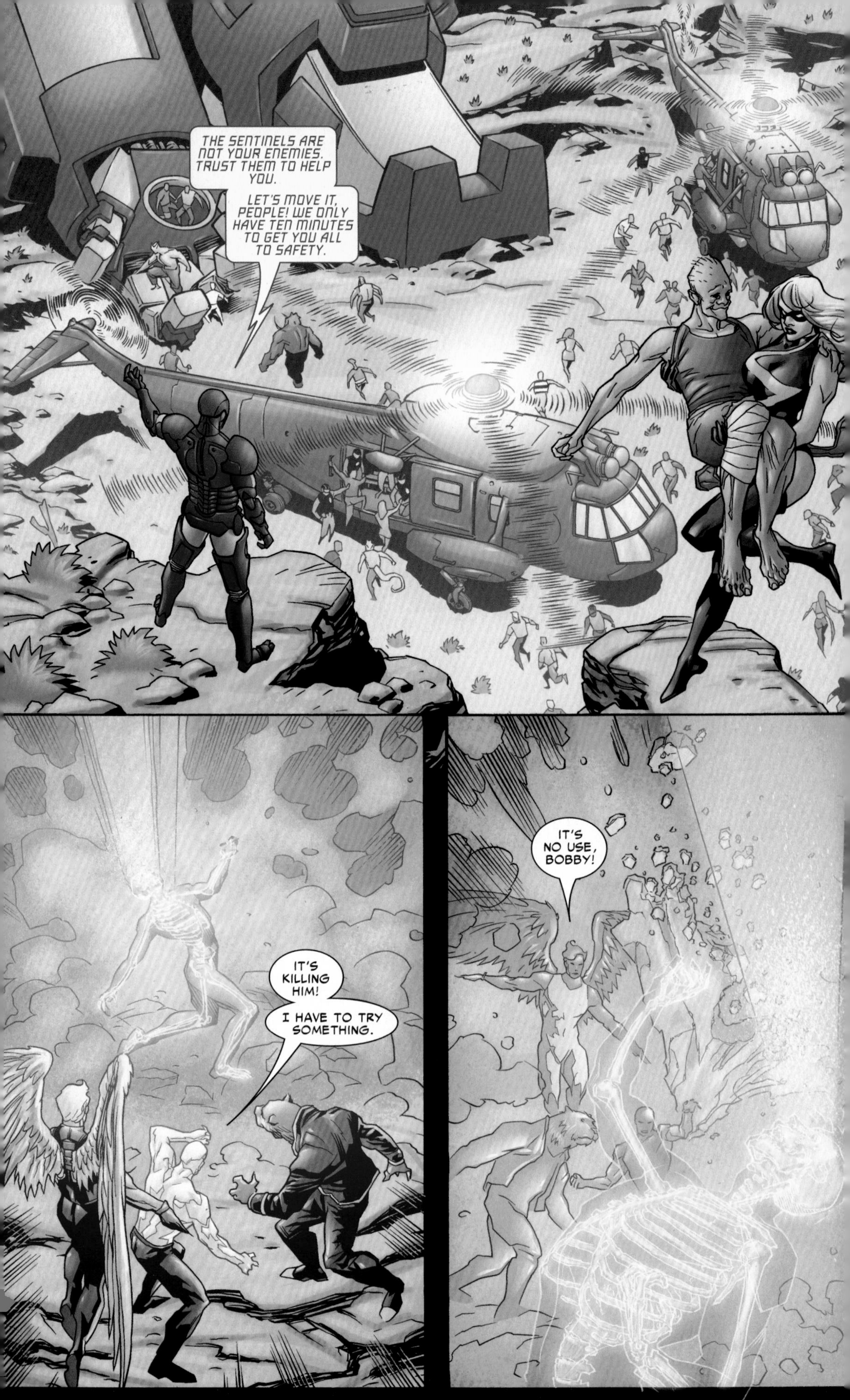
THE SENTINELS ARE NOT YOUR ENEMIES. TRUST THEM TO HELP YOU.
LET'S MOVE IT, PEOPLE! WE ONLY HAVE TEN MINUTES TO GET YOU ALL TO SAFETY.
IT'S KILLING HIM!
I HAVE TO TRY SOMETHING.
IT'S NO USE, BOBBY!

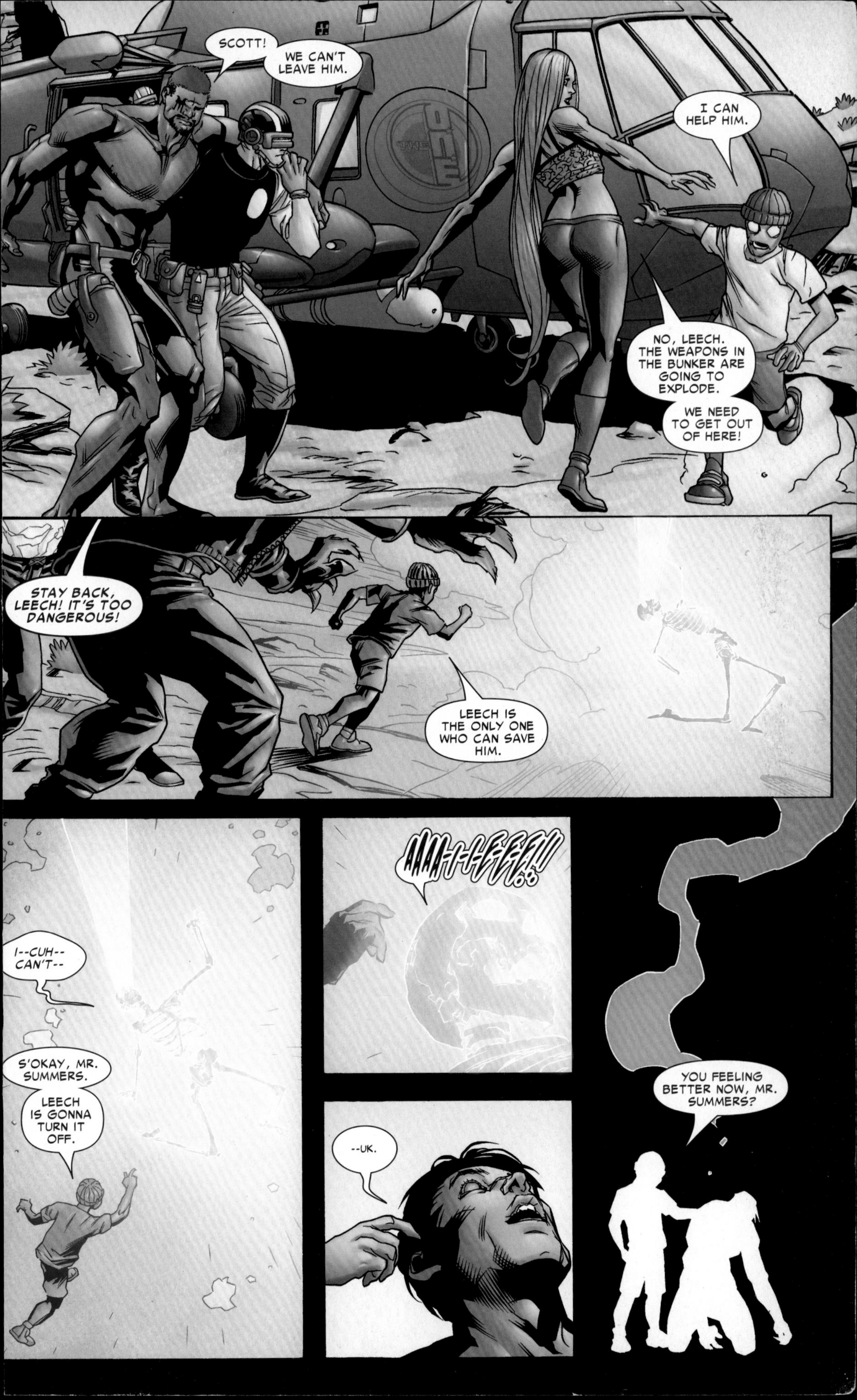
SCOTT!
WE CAN'T LEAVE HIM.
I CAN HELP HIM.
NO, LEECH. THE WEAPONS IN THE BUNKER ARE GOING TO EXPLODE.
WE NEED TO GET OUT OF HERE!
STAY BACK, LEECH! IT'S TOO DANGEROUS!
LEECH IS THE ONLY ONE WHO CAN SAVE HIM.
I--CUH-- CAN'T--
S'OKAY, MR. SUMMERS.
LEECH IS GONNA TURN IT OFF.
AAAA-I-I-EEEE!!
--UK.
YOU FEELING BETTER NOW, MR. SUMMERS?

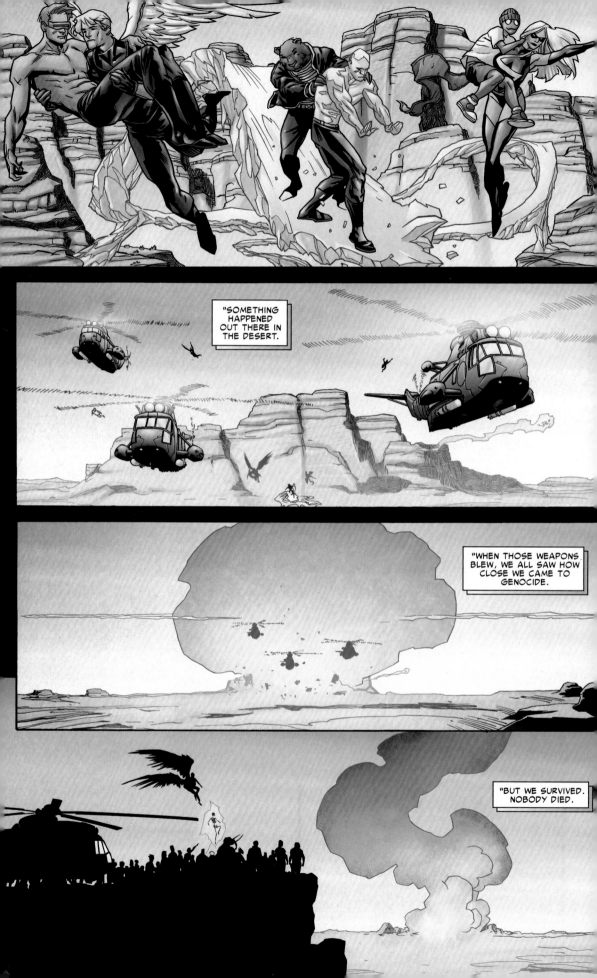

"SOMETHING HAPPENED OUT THERE IN THE DESERT.

"WHEN THOSE WEAPONS BLEW, WE ALL SAW HOW CLOSE WE CAME TO GENOCIDE.

"BUT WE SURVIVED. NOBODY DIED.

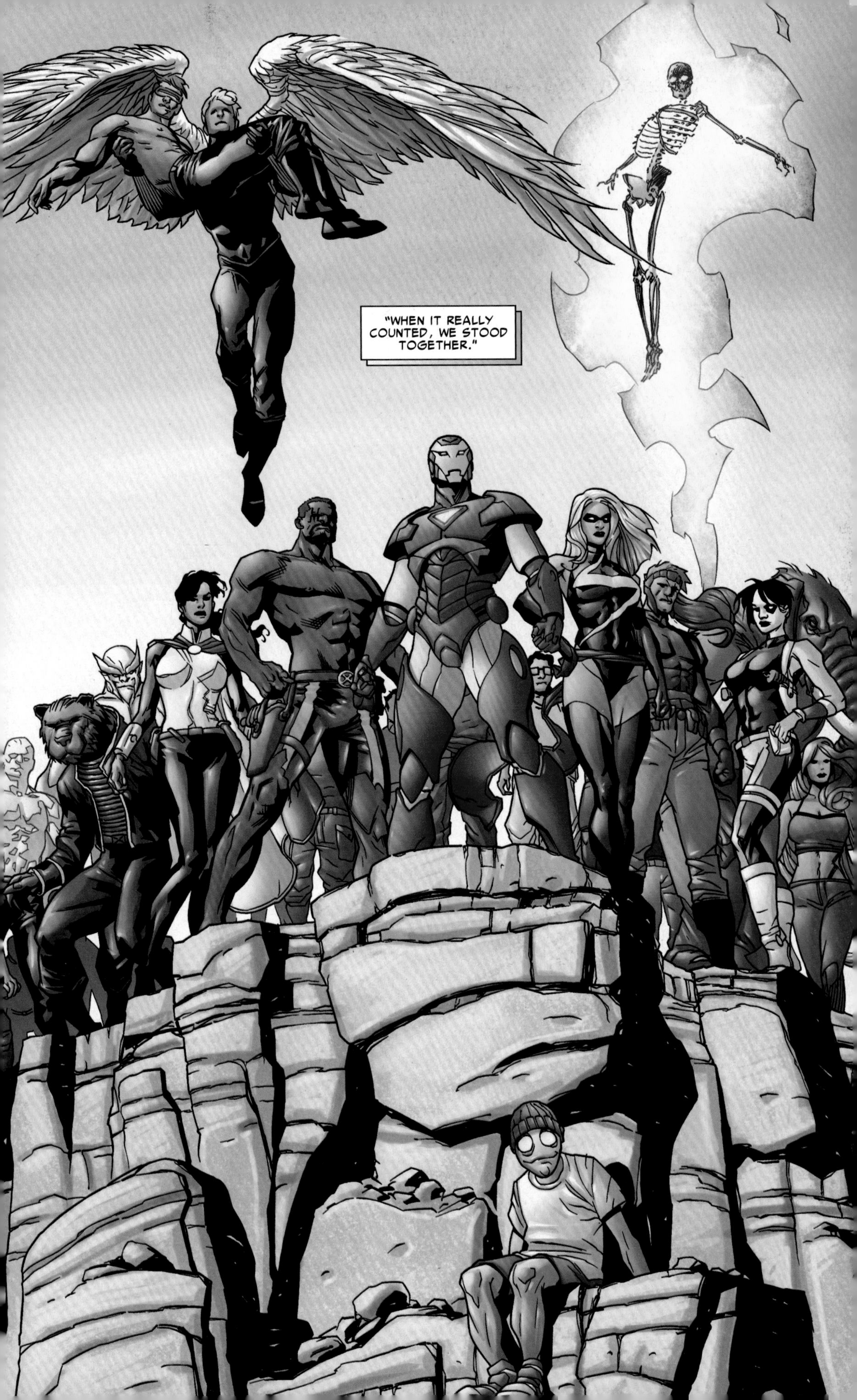
"WHEN IT REALLY COUNTED, WE STOOD TOGETHER."

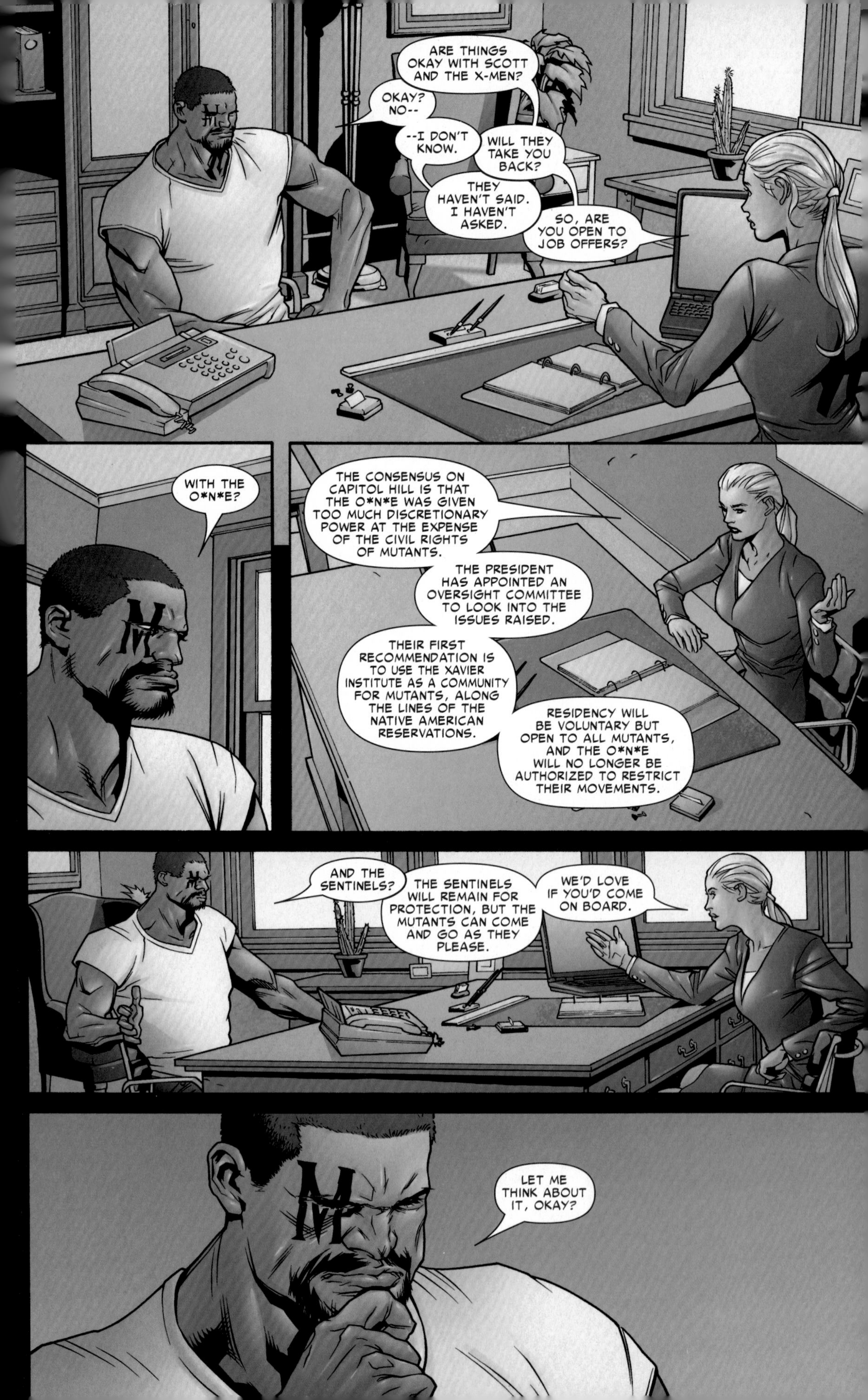
ARE THINGS OKAY WITH SCOTT AND THE X-MEN?
OKAY? NO--
--I DON'T KNOW.
WILL THEY TAKE YOU BACK?
THEY HAVEN'T SAID. I HAVEN'T ASKED.
SO, ARE YOU OPEN TO JOB OFFERS?
WITH THE O*N*E?
THE CONSENSUS ON CAPITOL HILL IS THAT THE O*N*E WAS GIVEN TOO MUCH DISCRETIONARY POWER AT THE EXPENSE OF THE CIVIL RIGHTS OF MUTANTS.
THE PRESIDENT HAS APPOINTED AN OVERSIGHT COMMITTEE TO LOOK INTO THE ISSUES RAISED.
THEIR FIRST RECOMMENDATION IS TO USE THE XAVIER INSTITUTE AS A COMMUNITY FOR MUTANTS, ALONG THE LINES OF THE NATIVE AMERICAN RESERVATIONS.
RESIDENCY WILL BE VOLUNTARY BUT OPEN TO ALL MUTANTS, AND THE O*N*E WILL NO LONGER BE AUTHORIZED TO RESTRICT THEIR MOVEMENTS.
AND THE SENTINELS?
THE SENTINELS WILL REMAIN FOR PROTECTION, BUT THE MUTANTS CAN COME AND GO AS THEY PLEASE.
WE'D LOVE IF YOU'D COME ON BOARD.
LET ME THINK ABOUT IT, OKAY?

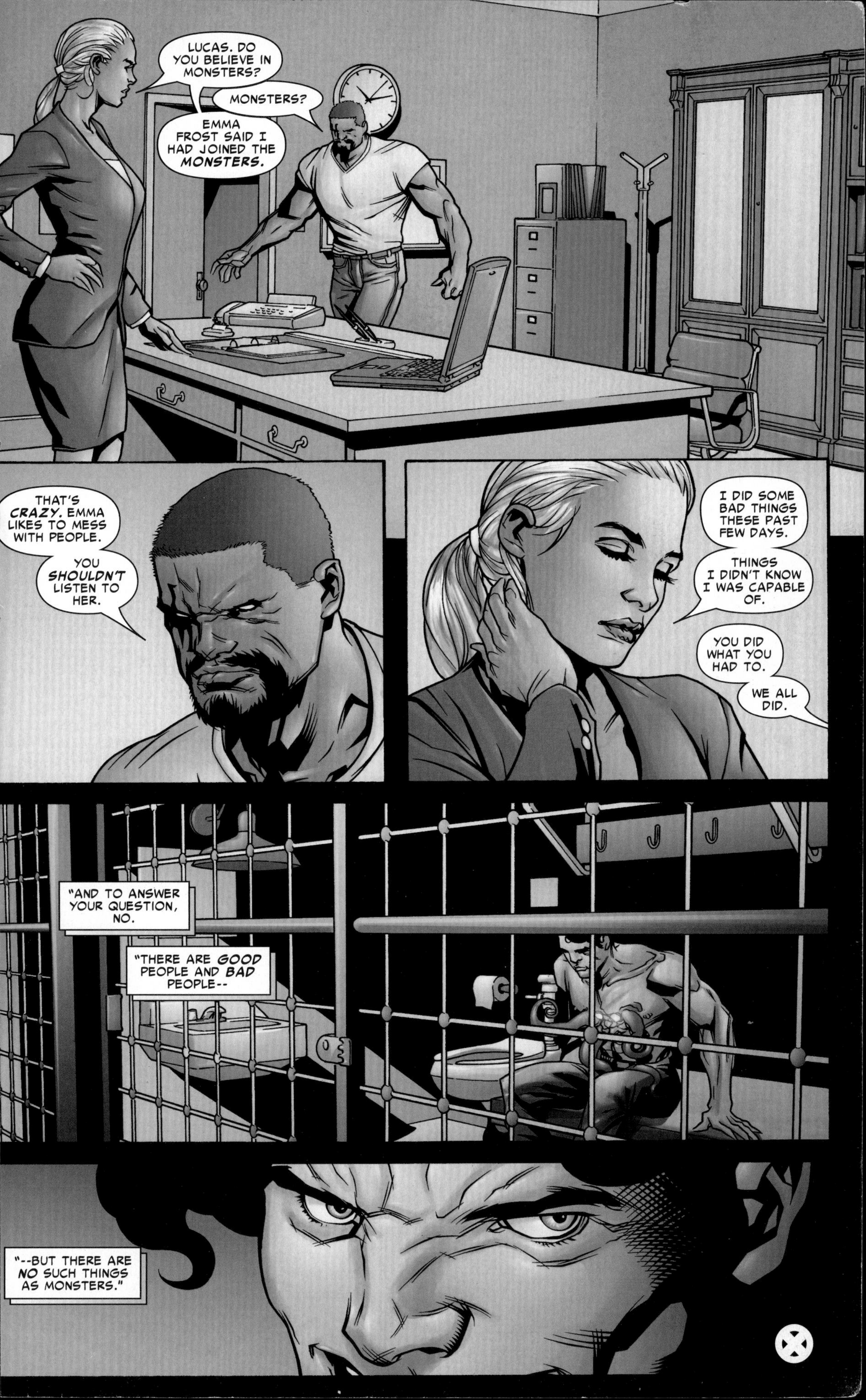
LUCAS. DO YOU BELIEVE IN MONSTERS?
MONSTERS?
EMMA FROST SAID I HAD JOINED THE *MONSTERS.*
THAT'S *CRAZY.* EMMA LIKES TO MESS WITH PEOPLE.
YOU *SHOULDN'T* LISTEN TO HER.
I DID SOME BAD THINGS THESE PAST FEW DAYS.
THINGS I DIDN'T KNOW I WAS CAPABLE OF.
YOU DID WHAT YOU HAD TO.
WE ALL DID.
"AND TO ANSWER YOUR QUESTION, NO.
"THERE ARE *GOOD* PEOPLE AND *BAD* PEOPLE--
"--BUT THERE ARE *NO* SUCH THINGS AS MONSTERS."

CALIBAN

REAL NAME: Unrevealed
ALIASES: Pestilence, Death, Hellhound
IDENTITY: Secret
OCCUPATION: Adventurer; former terrorist, scavenger
CITIZENSHIP: Unrevealed
PLACE OF BIRTH: Unrevealed
KNOWN RELATIVES: None
GROUP AFFILIATION: X-Force; formerly Watchtower, Horsemen of Apocalypse, X-Factor, Morlocks
EDUCATION: Unrevealed
FIRST APPEARANCE: Uncanny X-Men #148 (1981)

HISTORY: The albino mutant known only as Caliban was recruited by Callisto, who used Caliban's mutant-tracking ability to assemble the underground mutant community later known as Morlocks. Caliban was named by Callisto after the grotesque being in William Shakespeare's play "The Tempest." Living in the sewers and abandoned subway tunnels beneath Manhattan's streets with the Morlocks, the naïve Caliban found a renewed sense of family, but still felt lonely among his fellow outcasts. One evening, Caliban sensed the presence of mutants in a New York City nightclub and entered to find the Dazzler (Alison Blaire) performing. Caliban's presence created panic, which X-Men members Storm and Kitty Pryde attempted to quell alongside Spider-Woman (Jessica Drew). During the chaos, Caliban kidnapped Pryde and fled. Intercepted by the heroes, Caliban explained that he only wanted a friend like himself. Invited to join the X-Men, Caliban chose instead to return to the Morlocks.

When Callisto abducted the X-Man Angel (Warren Worthington III) and brought the Morlocks into conflict with the X-Men, Pryde was infected by the Morlock named Plague and found by Caliban. Caring for her, Caliban realized he could not cure her and panicked over what to do. Pryde promised to remain with him forever if he helped her and the X-Men. Unsure of what to do, Caliban sought help from Callisto; however, Callisto refused to allow the X-Men to leave, and only after she was defeated by Storm in ritual combat were the X-Men free to go. Storm offered the Morlocks a home and sanctuary with the X-Men, but Caliban, speaking for the group, declined the offer. When Pryde failed to make good on her promise, Callisto ordered her capture and attempted to force her to marry Caliban; however, Caliban realized Pryde did not truly love him, and released her from her promise. When the sorcerer Kulan Gath warped reality in Manhattan, transforming it to resemble his native era (circa 10, 000 B.C.), Caliban was merged with the X-Men's founder Charles Xavier, and forced to serve as Kulan Gath's familiar.

Soon after, the Morlocks were attacked by the Marauders, who began slaughtering the community. Injured in the massacre, Caliban was saved by his fellow Morlock Leech, and the pair were rescued from the Marauders by Power Pack and X-Factor (Angel, Beast, Cyclops, Iceman & Marvel Girl). Caliban subsequently resided at X-Factor's headquarters, briefly leaving to accompany the surviving Morlocks back underground before returning to join X-Factor in opposing anti-mutant organization the Right. Desperate to avenge the slaughter of his people, Caliban became colder and harder during his brief stint with X-Factor. After a battle against the Horsemen of Apocalypse, Caliban became increasingly frustrated with his passive power's inability to grant him the revenge he sought. When X-Factor subsequently encountered Apocalypse, Caliban swore to serve him as his Hellhound in exchange for power enough to exact revenge. Apocalypse genetically altered Caliban to increase his size and strength. After Caliban proved his worth against the likes of Archangel, Sabretooth and Cable's New Mutants, Apocalypse granted Caliban a place in his Horsemen as Death. With the Horsemen, Caliban fought the X-Men but was defeated, unaware that the Apocalypse he and his fellow Horsemen were serving at the time proved to be Mister Sinister in disguise.

Separated from Apocalypse's influence, Caliban's intelligence began diminishing. He kidnapped the young X-Man Jubilee, holding her hostage in exchange for Sabretooth, an ex-Marauder whom Xavier was trying to rehabilitate. Pryde, now Shadowcat, accompanied Sabretooth into the Morlock tunnels. There, she was left to die by the villain after they encountered a giant subterranean squid. After rescuing Pryde, Caliban faced Sabretooth in a brief yet ferocious fight, which resulted in his face being scarred, and he fled. Later, Caliban was hunted by the Dark Riders, Apocalypse's replacements for the Horsemen. Saved by Cable, Domino and Storm, Caliban helped them to track the Riders back to their base in Egypt and confront their new leader, Genesis. As his intelligence

Art by Tom Raney

MORLOCK LAW
CEREMONY OF MARRIAGE

Art by John Romita Jr.

continued to degrade and he began reverting to his original, non-violent personality, Caliban was recruited by Cable into X-Force. With that team, Caliban faced opponents such as the Mimic, Barrachus the Kalinator, Sabretooth, Holocaust, the Externals, S.H.I.E.L.D., Mr. Sinister, an other-worldly foursome, the alien android Pulse, Mojo, and even Asgardian rock trolls and goblins. For a brief time, Caliban and X-Force fell under the control of Sebastian Shaw, Black King of the Hellfire Club, and were mentally coerced into attacking Cable himself.

Caliban eventually began to suffer crippling seizures with no apparent cause. After aiding Cable against an assault on the Xavier Institute by Bastion's Operation: Zero Tolerance forces, Caliban was taken by Ozymandias, the immortal indentured servant of Apocalypse, who revealed that the seizures were a result of Caliban's past alteration. Returned to Apocalypse, Caliban was reshaped into the Horseman Pestilence. At Apocalypse's behest, Caliban successfully captured both Cable and his alternate reality (Earth-295) counterpart Nate Grey. Caliban and the Horsemen were defeated during battle with the X-Men when they were teleported away by Mikhail Rasputin. Subsequently, Caliban tracked down Cyclops, who had merged with Apocalypse. During a period when Apocalypse's psyche became dominant, he released Caliban from his service. By that time, Caliban had once more begun reverting to his original naïve self, and his intelligence faded until he possessed only a simple, animal-like mind.

Caliban was subsequently captured by the anti-mutant research facility the Watchtower, which sought to train him as a means to ferret out the mutant-devouring Skornn. Caliban was liberated by the combined efforts of Cable, X-Force, Wolverine, Deadpool and the Mutant Liberation Front, and subsequently rejoined X-Force to help fight the Skornn.

Art by Bart Sears

Art by Mary Wilshire

HEIGHT: (Currently) 6'8"; (originally) 5'8"
WEIGHT: (Currently) 275 lbs.; (originally) 150 lbs.
EYES: Black
HAIR: None

ABILITIES/ACCESSORIES: Caliban can psionically sense the presence of other mutants within a 25 mile radius of himself. Originally, as Caliban's adrenaline levels rose, his strength would increase to slightly superhuman levels and he could absorb fear-generated psionic energy from others and redirect that energy against them, overwhelming them. Apocalypse's genetic manipulation enhanced Caliban's strength, speed, stamina, durability, agility and reflexes to superhuman levels, and allowed him to use his fear-casting powers at any time. Apocalypse subsequently altered Caliban's powers to allow him to generate a psychoactive virus that attacks from within on the highest planes of the psyche. After many years underground, Caliban's eyes were once sensitive to even the smallest amount of light, but that no longer seems to be the case.

POWER GRID	1	2	3	4	5	6	7
INTELLIGENCE	■						
STRENGTH	■	■	■	■			
SPEED	■	■					
DURABILITY	■	■	■				
ENERGY PROJECTION	■	■	■				
FIGHTING SKILLS	■	■	■				

MICROMAX

REAL NAME: Scott Wright
ALIASES: Mr. Right
IDENTITY: Known to U.K. authorities
OCCUPATION: Former Brand Corporation Security Chief, Radio 1 Disc Jockey, F.I.6 government agent
CITIZENSHIP: U.K.
PLACE OF BIRTH: Southend-on-Sea, Essex, England
KNOWN RELATIVES: None
GROUP AFFILIATION: Formerly Excalibur, R.C.X. (Resources Control Executive), F.I.6, Bishop's unidentified squad
EDUCATION: Unrevealed
FIRST APPEARANCE: Excalibur #44 (1991)

HISTORY: Shortly after discovering his mutant powers, Radio 1 D.J. Scott Wright was recruited by U.K. national security agency F.I.6, who codenamed him Micromax. After the agency's Esper Division sensed a

sinister presence behind druidic artifact thefts, Micromax was assigned stakeout duty within the premises where robberies were predicted. When Excalibur's Phoenix (Rachel Summers) stumbled into one of the stakeouts, Micromax assumed she was the robber, missing the real thief, an invisible minion of the mage Necrom, whom Phoenix was battling. His interference allowed the real culprit to escape.

During a subsequent stake-out, Micromax clashed with Phoenix's teammate Nightcrawler and his Technet allies, who were assisting Dai Thomas' Inter-Regional Police Taskforce. Four days later, on a Birmingham stake-out, Micromax was knocked out by the robber, whom Nightcrawler's team finally apprehended. When F.I.6's Espers pinpointed the artifact thief's controller, Micromax was disheartened to learn he was being held in reserve while others made the arrest; however, the target, Necrom, easily slaughtered the agents present. Micromax tried to save his superior, Brigadier Blott, but Necrom held him with a force field while the mage absorbed Blott's lifeforce. When Necrom attempted to drain Wright too, Micromax rapidly shrank, passing out from the strain. Mistakenly believing Micromax dead, Necrom departed. Awakening, Micromax learned Necrom was moving to attack Excalibur, then aided the team and their allies in defeating the villain.

Later representing the U.K. at the first Pan-European Conference on Super Human Affairs, Micromax was hypnotized by the Nazi Brain Drain to slay the British Prime Minister, but was stopped by Alpha Flight's Aurora before he could do so. Meanwhile, F.I.6 was dissolved, its surviving members absorbed into rival agency R.C.X.; Micromax turned them down, preferring to concentrate on his show business career. Not accepting his refusal, R.C.X. kidnapped Micromax, placing him in stasis alongside similarly kidnapped Excalibur members. Freed by Nightcrawler, he assisted Excalibur in forcing a change of R.C.X.'s leaders. Soon after, Micromax joined Excalibur, accompanying them into Shi'ar space to rescue their teammate Cerise. His membership was brief; offered a Security Chief post by the Brand Corporation, Micromax moved to New Jersey. After Brand fired him, he attended the Otherworld wedding of Brian Braddock (Captain Britain) and Meggan. Micromax aided the Avengers and le Peregrine when Kang's forces invaded France, and was recently recruited into Bishop's squad hunting renegade mutants.

HEIGHT: Variable; (actual) 5'7"; (usually) 6'1"
WEIGHT: Variable; (actual) 140 lbs; (usually) 175 lbs.
EYES: Blue
HAIR: Brown

ABILITIES/ACCESSORIES: Micromax can control his physical dimensions, increasing or reducing his size and density. He has varied in height between less than an inch and 20 feet tall, but his exact limits are unknown. His durability increases proportionate to his density, and he gains superhuman strength when he grows. His power also permits a degree of shape-shifting; he customarily appears slightly taller and more muscular than he really is, and modifies his facial structure to enhance his looks. It is unclear whether he might be potentially able to shift more dramatically, like Mystique, or stretch like Mr. Fantastic. He tends to rely on size and strength in combat, and is not a skilled fighter.

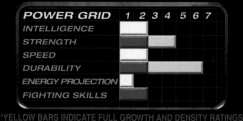

POWER GRID	1	2	3	4	5	6	7
INTELLIGENCE							
STRENGTH							
SPEED							
DURABILITY							
ENERGY PROJECTION							
FIGHTING SKILLS							

*YELLOW BARS INDICATE FULL GROWTH AND DENSITY RATINGS

HISTORY: Arrogant and brusque even as a child, Ruth was recruited into the Israeli Super Soldier program after her mutant powers manifested. She trained in the use of those powers, in myriad forms of combat, and in intelligence gathering. Highly self-motivated, she graduated to the Israeli Super Agents team, where she was given a flight cloak and experimental bracelets which fired paralysis-inducing plasma darts. She took the code name Sabra, which described both a native born Israeli and a sweet prickly pear which grows in Israel.

When Ruth gave birth to a son, Jacob, she requested an in-country position and became a Tel Aviv policewoman, a position she held for years. She worked covertly with the Super Agents, once saving a near-dead addict by giving the addict wind-control powers; as Windstorm, the ex-addict joined the Super Agents. Ruth's son died at age six when terrorists bombed his school bus, but she continued working as a policewoman until the Hulk entered Tel Aviv and she resumed her Sabra identity to oppose him. Sabra was subsequently sent to Washington D.C. to represent Israel when the Hulk was pardoned, and later unwittingly fought for Death in the Grandmaster's "Contest of Champions," where she was unhappily allied with the Arabian Knight (Abdul Qamar). When Windstorm betrayed the Super Agents, leading the "Israelis for Anarchy" in kidnapping an American ambassador's deaf son, Sabra reclaimed the powers she had given her, leaving Windstorm near death. She imbued the ambassador's son with low-level powers to save his life.

Through a misunderstanding, Sabra battled the Hulk again when he entered Israel to protect young mutant Max Meer from Achilles, and Max was left comatose. She was later assigned to protect the Israeli Prime Minister at a secret peace conference in New York, working alongside Syria's super agent Batal and the American New Warriors. Mind-controlled by an undisclosed foe, Sabra attacked the peace mission before the New Warriors' Justice brought her to her senses; Sabra developed a romantic fondness for her rescuer.

With her government's approval, she began working within Charles Xavier's "Mutant Underground," and when Bastion's anti-mutant Operation: Zero Tolerance infiltrated Israeli intelligence, Sabra smuggled data to the X-Men, exposing the infiltration. She became an unofficial liaison between Israel and the mutant community, exposing Magneto's false Erik Lehnsherr identity, aiding the Magneto duplicate Joseph, and

REAL NAME: Ruth Bat-Seraph
ALIASES: SA-1980, Ruth Ben-Sara (mistranscription)
IDENTITY: Known to Israeli authorities
OCCUPATION: Intelligence agent; former policewoman
CITIZENSHIP: Israel
PLACE OF BIRTH: Near Jerusalem, Israel
KNOWN RELATIVES: Jacob (son, deceased)
GROUP AFFILIATION: Mossad, Israeli Super Agents; formerly X-Corporation, Xavier's mutant underground
EDUCATION: Graduate of Israeli Super Soldiers program
FIRST APPEARANCE: (Cameo) Incredible Hulk #250 (1980); (full) Incredible Hulk #256 (1981)

working with Excalibur. Her liaison position was made official, and she joined X-Corporation at their Mumbai, India branch. She retained close contact with the X-Men after that facility's destruction, and when Bishop asked Sabra to join his pro-government super-criminal hunters, her government readily assented after briefly assigning her to aid Union Jack (Joey Chapman), USAgent and a new Arabian Knight (David Hasim) against terrorists in London.

HEIGHT: 5'11"	EYES: Brown
WEIGHT: 150 lbs.	HAIR: Brown

ABILITIES/ACCESSORIES: Sabra possesses superhuman strength sufficient to lift 50 tons, and has superhuman speed, reflexes, and endurance. She is resistant to impacts up to high caliber rifle fire, and recovers from injuries at three times normal human rates. Sabra also can trigger low-level powers in others (she describes this as giving someone else half of her own powers); these powers are permanent, but she can later withdraw them by touch. She uses this power exceedingly rarely. Sabra's bracelets shoot paralytic plasma-charged energy quills. Her cloak enables her to fly at better than 300 mph; she initially wore a large spined cloak to hide its flight technology but later miniaturization has allowed her to use a much sleeker cloak. Her costuming varies with her missions.

POWER GRID	1	2	3	4	5	6	7
INTELLIGENCE							
STRENGTH							
SPEED							
DURABILITY							
ENERGY PROJECTION							
FIGHTING SKILLS							

SENTINELS

CURRENT MODELS: Crazy Train, Megaton, Ogre, Shrapnel, War Machine, possibly others
FORMER MODELS: Mark I: 0, 1, 2, 3-D, 3-R, 4, 5, 6, 7, 8-R, A, B, C, T, others; **Mark II:** Number Two, Number Two-B, Number Three, Number Five, Number Six, Number 10, 23, 66, 86, 99, A3, A4, B7, C6, D3, G9, G12, R7, Z2, Big Bot, others; **Mark III:** 26, 27, 28, 29, A1, A3, A7, D3, D7, G7, K9, L-1, R-71, T-20, others; **Mark IV:** A-3, A-4, Psi-Ber, others; **Mark V:** Lambda-Three, Lambda-Four, Lambda-Seven, Lambda-One-Nine; **Mark VI:** 47139-B, BB-14, HG-12, Metallak (728-67), Seyfert's Sentinel, Source, others; **Fitzroy's Sentinels:** 3.14159, 2007, 2016, 2024; **Prime Sentinels:** Delilah Fremont, Ekatarina Gryaznova, Lance C. Gwynn, Samuel Mbende, Lao Mei-Ling, Mustang, Number Five, Angie Quail, Karima Shapandar, Jürgen Tiebold, Unit Three (Sanjit Shaara), Unit #1031 (Ginny Mahoney), others; **Wild Sentinels:** 1701AgL9914, others; **Others:** Bot, Cynthia Chalmers, Conscience, Machine Man (X-51), Nano-Sentinels, Protectorate, Russian Sentinels, Sentinel Squad O*N*E, Tri-Sentinel, X-Sentinels
BASES OF OPERATION: Office of National Emergency Sentinel Squad Central Command, New Mexico; formerly Sentinel base, Chicago; Master Mold facility, Ecuador; Operation: Zero Tolerance facility, New Mexico; Cape Hayden military base, Kentucky; Ophrah Industries complex, Adirondack Mountain Preserve, New York; Life Foundation facility, New Jersey, New York; Interdefense, Okanagan Valley, Washington; Master Mold's asteroid base; Shaw Industries, New York City, New York; Project Armageddon base, orbital S.H.I.E.L.D. platform; Ant Hill, Great Australian Desert; Lawrence Trask's mountain base, New York; Bolivar Trask's secret base, New York
FIRST APPEARANCE: X-Men #14 (1965)

HISTORY: When noted anthropologist Bolivar Trask discovered that his children, Lawrence and Tanya, were mutants, he studied the rapidly increasing emergence of mutants in the world. Convinced that mutants would eventually dominate mankind, Trask used his considerable fortune to create a prototype 30' tall robot he dubbed the Master Mold, designed to automate production of the first wave of Mark I Sentinels — 10' tall humanoid robots equipped with a variety of weapons that were designed to protect mankind from mutants. As a safeguard, Trask programmed them to preserve the DNA of the Trask line, thus permitting his descendants control over them. He also had his son wear a medallion that prevented the Sentinels detecting his mutant nature. Trask first revealed the Sentinels' existence during a live televised debate on the alleged "mutant menace" with geneticist Professor Charles Xavier, secretly the mutant founder of the X-Men. The Sentinels' logic deemed that the best way to guard mankind was to rule it, and they rebelled, kidnapping their creator. Opposed by the X-Men, the Sentinels were defeated after Trask, realizing his mistake, sacrificed his life to destroy the Sentinel's ionic power source, causing an explosion that wrecked the Master Mold.

Wrongfully blaming the X-Men for his father's death, Lawrence spearheaded the construction of a new fleet of Sentinels adapted from his father's designs. The Mark II's were 20' tall and more powerful, with computers to counter virtually any threat, self-repair programs, great strength, and specialized weapons. Lawrence sent them against the X-Men, and they successfully captured Havok, Lorna Dane, Iceman, and several other mutants. Seeking to halt Lawrence's desire to destroy mutants, his ally Judge Chalmers removed the medallion, causing the Sentinels to turn on Lawrence. After the remaining X-Men arrived to rescue their teammates, Cyclops convinced the Sentinels' leader Number Two to find and neutralize the cause of human mutation. The Sentinels determined this to be the Sun, and they left to investigate. Subsequently, several damaged Mark II's merged into a single unit which was found by young mutant Ashley Martin, who named it "Big Bot." When Xavier and the Beast came to investigate Ashley's mutant nature, the Sentinel attacked them until Ashley used her psychokinetic bonding power to stop it. Ultimately, the Sentinel's original programming resurfaced, forcing Ashley to cause it to destroy itself.

Reed Richards of the Fantastic Four later sought to borrow a pair of Mark I Sentinels that the X-Men had captured and deactivated to employ them as sentries. Richards was unaware that his nemesis Doctor Doom had taken control of the X-Men's training robot Colosso and used it to reprogram the Sentinels to self-destruct in the heart of New York City, a disaster that was halted by numerous heroes. Meanwhile, Number Two and its Sentinels concluded that they lacked the means to destroy the Sun. Returning to Earth, they established a base called the Ant Hill in the Australian outback and captured the Avengers' Scarlet Witch with the intent of using her probability-affecting power to control solar flares with which to sterilize all of humanity, thus preventing any more mutant births. The Sentinels were opposed by the Avengers, and, with the aid of a repentant Lawrence Trask, Number Two was revealed to have been itself mutated by solar radiation. The other Sentinels turned on their leader and destroyed it, then deactivated themselves. Lawrence was killed by a falling Sentinel, after which the Avengers sealed the base.

The Sentinels subsequently came under the control of the U.S. Government's Project Armageddon, a federal study of mutants headed by Steven Lang, a fanatical mutant hater. He illegally appropriated billions from the government in his quest to exterminate mutants, and, after obtaining Lawrence's notes on Sentinel construction, gained additional funding from the Hellfire Club. With this backing, he constructed a new series of Mark III Sentinels purposefully designed to be less intelligent than their predecessors to ensure they would not rebel; a new Master Mold that could project its artificial consciousness into the smallest mechanical parts as well as create duplicates of itself and maintain its consciousness in each; and an orbital base from which he sent the Sentinels to capture members of the X-Men. When their teammates arrived to rescue them, they were faced with Lang's X-Sentinels, robotic duplicates of the original X-Men. Wolverine's senses ultimately uncovered their true nature, after which the X-Sentinels were destroyed. Injured in an explosion, Lang believed himself to be dying and copied his brain engrams into his Master Mold which then left to construct a new base on an orbiting asteroid. Soon after, another captive, the mutant Vanisher, awoke to find the base abandoned. Upon discovering some incomplete Sentinels, he finished their construction and modified their programming to obey his commands in an effort to destroy the X-Men; however, the Sentinels were easily destroyed by the former X-Men Angel and Iceman and their teammates in the Champions of Los Angeles. Meanwhile, the Master Mold had come to believe that it truly was Lang, and sought revenge on the X-Men. Capturing Iceman and Angel, the robot ran afoul of the Hulk, who ultimately crippled it, forcing it to self-destruct its base. The Master Mold tumbled in a decaying orbit until finally falling to Earth where it crash-landed, inactive, into the Bering Strait near Alaska.

Following an assassination attempt on Senator Robert Kelly by Mystique's Brotherhood of Evil Mutants, the U.S. President inaugurated Project: Wideawake, a covert operation tasked with creating a new series of Sentinels. The contract was granted to Shaw Industries, whose owner, Sebastian Shaw, was secretly a mutant and leader of the Hellfire Club's Inner Circle. As a test of his new remote-controlled Mark IV Sentinels, Shaw sent them against the X-Men, but the heroes prevailed. Shaw improved on the design, and sent new Mark V Sentinels against the neophyte New Mutants, but they also triumphed. Soon after, the Falcon (Sam Wilson) encountered a lone Mark III Sentinel that had repaired itself after its initial battle with the X-Men. The Falcon ultimately deactivated it with the aid of his pet falcon, Redwing. Later, a prototype Nimrod Sentinel from the future of Earth-811 arrived on Earth-616 tracking the mutant Rachel Summers. The ultimate mutant-hunting machine, Nimrod possessed complete control of its component elements down to the molecular level, allowing for nigh-instantaneous repairs. It also possessed hunter/slayer systems that allowed it to track mutants, predict and counter virtually any threat, super-strength, teleportation systems and advanced weaponry. Locating the X-Men in battle against the Juggernaut, Nimrod attacked but was defeated. The omnipotent Beyonder then summoned a pair of Omega Sentinels from Nimrod's time to oppose Rachel and the X-Men. Despite being composed of non-ferrous materials and possessing advanced warsystems that could modify the Sentinel's internal systems to counter threats, the Omega Sentinels were destroyed. Later, Nimrod attacked the X-Men once more during a clash with Shaw's Inner Circle, but was again defeated. Around this time, the Russian government began building their own Sentinels as a safeguard against the perceived mutant threat, but Xavier convinced the Russians to dismantle most of these Sentinels.

Subsequently, the Interdefense group had several Mark III's upgraded by Dr. Carmody Whyte to include stealth capabilities. Field testing them by sending them to recapture the mutant hypnotist Mesmero, who had fled to Canada, the Sentinels clashed with the Canadian super-team Alpha Flight, who destroyed them. Meanwhile, the Lang Master Mold reactivated, and upon detecting the presence of Cyclops it renewed its mission to destroy the X-Men. Rebuilding itself, the Master Mold was seemingly destroyed after Cyclops tricked it into causing an explosion. Its core unit survived, and after it was inadvertently reactivated it rebuilt itself once more. It sought to eliminate the powerful young mutant Franklin Richards, but was opposed by Power Pack and was again seemingly destroyed in an explosion. Some time later, Chalmers' daughter Cynthia sought to claim the Sentinels as her own and reopened their Australian base, reawakening the surviving Mark II's therein. They reassembled Number Two and resumed their intent to sterilize mankind, this time by using gamma radiation from solar flares. The Sentinels targeted gamma-influenced humans such as the Abomination and Doc Samson to act as catalytic agents; however, the X-Men freed the captives and destroyed the Sentinels. Cynthia then struck a deal with the Abomination to rebuild a Sentinel in order to destroy the X-Men before she died of cancer. Secretly, Cynthia intended to transfer her consciousness into the Sentinel so as to cheat death. Upon beginning the transfer, the Sentinel's programming reactivated and regained control. It sought to complete its mission to sterilize humanity, but was opposed by the X-Men. When Cynthia's body died, her remaining consciousness transferred to the Sentinel, and to prevent its programming regaining control she flew her new body into the sun to destroy it.

After the Lang Master Mold rebuilt itself once more, it realized that Lang's consciousness was a weakness and so constructed a robotic assistant named Conscience into which it downloaded the creative and emotional sides of Lang's mind. The Master Mold then mentally enslaved geneticist Moira MacTaggert and compelled her to weaponize a virus to kill all mutants, but it was later discovered this "Retribution Virus" would also kill 92.4% of all humans. Conscience was disturbed by the thought of killing normal humans and joined with Cyclops, Banshee and MacTaggert's bodyguard Callisto in opposing the Master Mold. MacTaggert implemented a cure for the virus, while the Master Mold was demolished by Banshee's newly-regained sonic powers. Conscience then sacrificed itself to destroy the Master Mold's ship. Later, when Nimrod discovered the Master Mold's core unit, its programming usurped control of Nimrod's body and rebuilt itself. Seeking once more to destroy mutants by exterminating all mankind, the Master Mold fought the X-Men, who ultimately sought to lure the Master Mold into the pan-dimensional Siege Perilous portal. As the Master Mold resisted, Nimrod's resurfaced intelligence contended that the Master Mold was now itself a mutant and urged it to fulfill its prime directive, which it did by allowing itself to be pulled into the portal. However, passage through the unpredictable Siege Perilous saw the merged Master Mold/Nimrod reborn as Bastion, who founded the government-sponsored Operation: Zero Tolerance anti-mutant organization.

Shaw Industries then created three prototype Sentinels to use as the cornerstone of the U.S. Government's new Project: Nimrod anti-mutant operation. Unbeknownst to Shaw, the Norse trickster god Loki sought revenge on mankind for his most recent defeat at the hands of the Avengers. He magically merged the prototypes into a single "Tri-Sentinel" and reprogrammed its prime directive to destroy the Amity Point Nuclear Plant. To prevent a meltdown, the cosmic Uni-Power possessed Spider-Man, transforming him into Captain Universe and granting him enough power to destroy the Tri-Sentinel. Subsequently, the Life Foundation gathered the Tri-Sentinel's remains and rebuilt it as a prototype for a proposed new security force. They added a failsafe in the form of a small piece of Antarctic Vibranium ("anti-metal") encased in a shielded box which would melt the Sentinel's control center when triggered. Upon activation, the Tri-Sentinel rejected the Life Foundation's programming, deactivated the failsafe, and restored Loki's prime directive. Spider-Man and Nova joined forces to oppose the robot and activated the failsafe, causing an overload that destroyed it. Later, the time-displaced criminal

SENTINEL CREATORS/CONTROLLERS

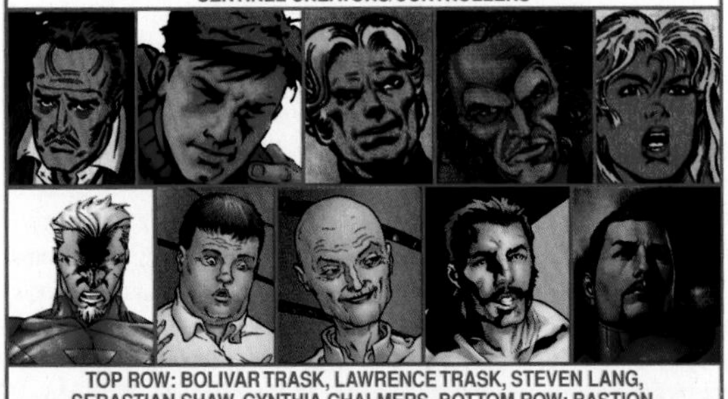

TOP ROW: BOLIVAR TRASK, LAWRENCE TRASK, STEVEN LANG, SEBASTIAN SHAW, CYNTHIA CHALMERS BOTTOM ROW: BASTION, DONALD TRASK III, CASSANDRA NOVA, MADISON JEFFRIES, TONY STARK

Trevor Fitzroy utilized Sentinels from his native Earth-1191's future to attack the criminal cyborg Reavers. When the Reavers' leader, Donald Pierce, fled to the New York Hellfire Club, the Sentinels followed and attacked the resident White Queen (Emma Frost) and her Hellions as well as the visiting X-Men, seemingly killing Frost and the X-Man Jean Grey. Soon after, the British super-team Excalibur traveled to the future of Earth-811 and encountered Gamma, Delta and Omega Class Sentinels as well as the ruling Sentinel Hierarchy which they were able to reprogram to preserve all life.

Subsequently investigating the Reavers' Australian base, Wolverine and Jubilee inadvertently reactivated a Sentinel which had been bathed in the electrolytes that Pierce had used to create the Reavers, resulting in it becoming self aware. Naming itself 3.14159, it decided to erase humanity and create an ordered, disciplined Sentinel society. To that end, it reopened the Ant Hill and took up Number Two's quest to sterilize mankind; however, when one of its subordinates displayed empathy for a fellow Sentinel during a clash with Wolverine and Jubilee, 3.14159 sought to better understand human emotions and re-dedicated the Ant Hill's computer systems to create binary algorithms for them. Determining this would take 2137.23 years to complete, the Sentinels entered processor sleep until that time. Later, a Mark IV Sentinel was appropriated by mutant businessman Gideon's Ophrah Industries and endowed with psychic energy. To empower this "Psi-Ber" Sentinel, Gideon coerced the mutant Karma to aid the mercenary Deadpool and the Juggernaut in capturing the X-Men's psychic members. Seeking to rescue their teammates, the other X-Men clashed with the Psi-Ber Sentinel until Karma freed the captives, thus disconnecting the Psi-Ber Sentinel from its power source. The Psi-Ber Sentinel was subsequently destroyed in an explosion.

Meanwhile, the U.S. Government continued with Project: Wideawake, creating prototype Mark VI Sentinels that combined the finest features of their predecessors with the evolving and far superior Nimrod models, as well as the ability to absorb psionic energy. Cable and X-Force sought to abort the Nimrod project, but were too late to prevent a prototype becoming active by means of a self-awareness program previously hidden in the military cybernet by the future Nimrod. Using his telepathy to link with Nimrod's artificial intelligence, Cable made it realize that a Nimrod unit existing sixty years before it was originally intended would result in incalculable loss of human life from the inevitable war that would follow if it fulfilled its directive to eliminate mutants, which caused it to shut down. After the psionic being Onslaught learned of the Mark VI's psionic absorption ability, it abducted scientists from Cape Hayden to create an army of Sentinels. It unleashed them on Manhattan to foment panic in order to exacerbate the level of ambient psionic energy, but they were destroyed by numerous heroes. S.H.I.E.L.D. buried the remains in a New Jersey landfill which was later uncovered by the Avengers' former technician Fabian Stankowicz, who rebuilt and redesigned the Sentinels as the Protectorate, robotic versions of the then-missing Avengers; however, the Protectorate enslaved Stankowicz and set out to "protect" New York, bringing them into conflict with the true Avengers. Their butler Jarvis destroyed Stankowicz's cybernetic interface, freeing him and immobilizing the Protectorate.

In the aftermath of Onslaught's assault, Bastion's Operation: Zero Tolerance (OZT) launched an attack on mutants utilizing Prime Sentinels — ordinary humans who had been clandestinely bio-engineered by a new Master Mold to be outfitted with cybernetic nanotech implants which activated into armor and weapons systems upon receipt of a signal transmitted from OZT. Following OZT's shut down, Bastion was remanded into S.H.I.E.L.D. custody, where he was studied by a team of technologists who inadvertently reawakened his true identity. Escaping, Bastion returned to the OZT facility and absorbed the Master Mold's power, transforming himself into a Nimrod Sentinel. Intending to reprogram the robotic hero X-51 into the Sentinel Supreme, vanguard

of a new Prime Sentinel army, Bastion was opposed by Cable, who restored X-51's original identity. Subsequently, X-51 caused the facility to self-destruct, seemingly destroying Bastion. However, X-51 was unaware that he now possessed Sentinel programming, and subsequently began attacking mutants, such as Mystique's Brotherhood, the Avengers' Firestar and Justice, and Shaw. Concerned that X-51 would expose his mutant nature, Shaw oversaw construction of a new series of remote-controlled Mark VII Sentinels which he sent to destroy X-51. This drew the attention of the X-Men, and during the clash X-51 had a crisis of conscience and self-destructed to end the Sentinel threat.

Later, the cyborg Lady Deathstrike sought the X-Men's help in preventing the future despot Stryfe accessing the Prime Sentinel's catalyst codes within her mind. After Stryfe was defeated, Deathstrike gave the codes to the X-Men to allow them to revert all remaining Prime Sentinels. Later, during an attempted invasion of Earth by the chronal villain Kang, the U.S. Government sent enhanced Sentinels to oppose him; however, Kang easily overrode their programming and turned them against Washington, D.C. where they were destroyed by the Avengers. During this time, Xavier's sister Cassandra Nova uncovered a years-old shadow U.S. Government program that had assigned Bolivar Trask to create a Master Mold in the Ecuadorian jungle that was precision-engineered to adapt to its environment and programmed to build "Wild" Sentinels using any and all technology within its test radius. Locating Trask's last living relative, Albuquerque dentist Donald Trask III, Cassandra took him to the Master Mold facility where she absorbed his DNA and, now recognized as a Trask, ordered two Wild Mega-Sentinels to decimate the 16 million mutants on the island nation of Genosha. Injecting herself with Nano-Sentinels, Cassandra subsequently confronted the X-Men and, after switching minds with her brother, had him shoot her physical body, exposing the X-Men to the Nano-Sentinels in her blood. The Nano-Sentinels began dismantling the X-Men's immune structures until they were destroyed by the mutant healer Xorn.

The U.S. Government then expanded its Sentinel program, establishing Sentinel bases in other major cities. In Chicago, a band of subterranean-dwelling mutant Morlocks found themselves hunted by Sentinels. One of the Morlocks, Litterbug, was a former U.S. Army mechanic who had worked on Sentinel construction, and his knowledge enabled the Morlocks to infiltrate and destroy the local Sentinel base. Meanwhile, a group of Wild Sentinels began killing mutants in Chicago, but were opposed by the former X-Man Shadowcat and her allies Karma and Shola Inkosi. Soon after, Xavier learned that two Russian Sentinels had been sold on the black market to Cuba and coerced Mystique into finding them. She became involved with an extremist pro-mutant group whose leader was seeking to rescue his sister Evangelina, a machine-controlling mutant who had been captured by the Cuban military. After discovering that Evangelina was being used to control the Sentinels, her brother was forced to kill her to end their threat. With their remote control ended, the Sentinels' programming forced them to eliminate all evidence of the project, including themselves. Following a change of leadership in the Weapon X Project, ousted Director Malcolm Colcord tasked the technomorph Madison Jeffries with creating an army of Sentinels to use in a renewed war against mutants. Soon after, the last remaining Prime Sentinel, the Omega Class Karima Shapandar, was ferried to Genosha by the Magistrates in an effort to regain control of the island. Karima was intercepted by Xavier and Magneto, who used their powers to reboot the nanites in her system, thus restoring her original personality. Karima subsequently joined the effort to rebuild the shattered nation. Soon after, the X-Men's Danger Room gained sentience and created the humanoid form Danger. It then uploaded its programming into one of the Wild Mega-Sentinels that had decimated Genosha, granting it a conscience. As it battled the X-Men, Shadowcat phased inside the robot and reactivated its memories of the Genoshan destruction that Danger had repressed. Horrified at what it had done, the Sentinel overrode Danger's consciousness and left.

When young student Juston Seyfert repaired a damaged Mark VI Sentinel and reprogrammed it to obey him, he was unaware that it had previously been used as a disposable murder weapon by U.S. Army Colonel Archie Hunt and Senator Jeff Knudsen. Upon learning of the Sentinel's reactivation, Hunt and Knudsen sought to again cover their tracks by deploying a new prototype Mark VII-A Sentinel which was quieter, faster, and had stealth capabilities, flight, self-repair systems, and numerous weapons systems; however, it could only utilize one tactical component at a time. Hunt operated the Mark VII-A via remote control in an effort to destroy Juston and his Sentinel, but when the ensuing clash endangered innocents, Knudsen sought to stop Hunt, allowing Juston and his Sentinel to defeat the prototype.

The U.S. Government next sought to overcome the Sentinels' difficulty in weighing contradictory input, the Office of National Emergency (O*N*E) commissioned Stark Industries to create a new model Sentinel operated by human pilots via a command suit that translated the pilot's movements and reflexes to the Sentinel. These new Sentinels came in a variety of units such as brawler, recon, stealth, and ballistics. One team of Sentinel Squad recruits had a trial by fire against the android Growing Man before being sent to the Savage Land to rescue survivors of a decimated Squad. They prevailed against telekinetic dinosaurs controlled by the Savage Land Mutates and rescued the captives, after which they were sent to eradicate a Wild Sentinel colony in Ecuador. Following the depowering of many of Earth's mutants, the Sentinel Squad was sent to the Xavier Institute to oversee its burgeoning mutant refugee camp. After a misunderstanding with the resident X-Men, the Sentinel Squad helped them repel an attack by the Leper Queen's anti-mutant Sapien League. Around this time, the anti-mutant Reverend Stryker put into action a plan years in the making after he discovered a deactivated future Nimrod Sentinel and accessed its memory of future events, using them to strike at the students of the Xavier Institute.

The Sentinel Squad subsequently aided the X-Men against the Shi'ar Death Commandos, sought to prevent Mister M from liberating the mutant refugees the 198, opposed an attack on the Institute by Stryker and his Purifiers during which Stryker usurped control of the Sentinels by using Nimrod technology, and clashed with Apocalypse and his new Horsemen. After the Sentinel Squad was disabled by Apocalypse, the O*N*E sent two new model Sentinels — Crazy Train and War Machine — to oppose him. The Sentinel Squad were subsequently decimated during a breakout by the 198, and were replaced by other new O*N*E Sentinels including Ogre, Shrapnel and Megaton. Recently, the X-Men liberated Karima Shapandar from experimentation by the mysterious Pan and took her back to the Institute to recover. The Sentinels then sought to aid the X-Men against an attack by the Children of the Vault and their agents Northstar and Aurora, but were unable to enter the mansion due to their size.

FIRST ROW: MASTER MOLD, MARK I, MARK II, NUMBER TWO
SECOND ROW: MARK III, LANG'S MASTER MOLD, MARK IV, MARK V
THIRD ROW: NIMROD, CHALMERS' SENTINEL, CONSCIENCE, TRI-SENTINEL
FOURTH ROW: FITZROY'S SENTINEL, PSI-BER SENTINEL,
MARK VI, PRIME SENTINEL
FIFTH ROW: PROTECTORATE, MARK VII, SHADOW MASTER MOLD
SIXTH ROW: WILD SENTINEL, NANO-SENTINELS, RUSSIAN SENTINEL,
KARIMA SHAPANDAR
SEVENTH ROW: JEFFRIES' SENTINEL, MARK VII-A, SENTINEL SQUAD O*N*E,
WAR MACHINE, CRAZY TRAIN

SHATTERSTAR

REAL NAME: Gaveedra-Seven
ALIASES: Benjamin Russell, "Shatty-buns"
IDENTITY: Unknown to general public
OCCUPATION: Adventurer; former ultimate fighter
CITIZENSHIP: Mojoverse
PLACE OF BIRTH: Mojoverse
KNOWN RELATIVES: Windsong (wife)
GROUP AFFILIATION: X-Force; formerly Cadre Alliance
EDUCATION: Trained in combat and technology in Mojoverse
FIRST APPEARANCE: New Mutants #99 (1991)

HISTORY: Though he is rumored to be an offspring or a genetic duplicate of the lucky X-Man Longshot, Shatterstar's true origins remain unknown. Shatterstar was born Gaveedra-Seven one hundred years in the future of the Mojoverse, an extradimensional world where the Spineless Ones, ruled by Mojo V, used humanoids as slaves and television stars because ratings in the Mojoverse meant power. Genetically engineered to be an ultimate fighter and trained in the finest skills of swordsmanship and war, Gaveedra-Seven was destined to slay Mojo V. Shatterstar was also given the ability to channel a powerful blast through his swords; though this act left him weak, his regenerative abilities and enhanced strength, senses and stamina made up for it. Shatterstar fought for years in the arena, and was assigned a wife, Windsong, whom Shatterstar had never met. Eventually, Shatterstar escaped the arena and lived in the shadows for two years, joining the humanoid rebels who opposed Mojo V. The rebels frequently fought Mojo V's Imperial Protectorate, regenerative biochemical constructs. Shatterstar's rebel force, the Cadre Alliance, decided to send Shatterstar to Earth to seek the aid of the X-Men, as the famous Longshot had once done against the original Mojo a century before. Sent into the past, Shatterstar landed in the X-Men's Danger Room, where he and the New Mutants slew several pursuing members of the Imperial Protectorate. His technology to return to the future destroyed, Shatterstar made a deal with the New Mutants' leader, Cable: he would aid Cable's cause if Cable would someday help Shatterstar return home and win his rebels' war.

The New Mutants soon rechristened themselves X-Force. Shatterstar continually trained and challenged himself, constantly longing for battle and distancing himself from his team. He fought many foes with X-Force, including the New Warriors, who soon became allies when the teams teamed up to take down the reality-warping Piecemeal. The team fought the Mutant Liberation Front, whose member the scythe-wielding Reaper had his hand sliced off by Shatterstar twice, and against whom Shatterstar refused to back down against even when teammate Siryn was held hostage; Black Tom and Juggernaut, whose face Shatterstar slashed; Toad's Brotherhood of Evil Mutants, whose member Blob had his face savagely sliced by Shatterstar; and the underground-dwelling Morlocks, whose leader the flesh-warping Masque was seemingly slain by Shatterstar. Shatterstar also fought alongside Wolverine against the young gang Vid-Kids. The team went through several changes when Cable seemingly abandoned them (though he later returned), leaving X-Force to face Weapon: PRIME (PRototype Induced Mutation Echelon), an international group seeking revenge on Cable for various reasons, on their own. X-Force later fought the long-lived X-Ternals, who held some of their members captive. X-Force clashed with the X-Men and their allies when X-Force was implicated in an assassination attempt on Charles Xavier; Wolverine took down Shatterstar by stabbing him through his abdomen, but the wound quickly healed. X-Force also fought the anti-mutant Friends of Humanity and the self-proclaimed heir of Magneto, Exodus. Shatterstar continued acclimating to his new culture, even learning other languages by watching television, but focused mostly on improving his battle skills. He resisted the romantic advances of teammates Feral, who lusted after him, and Siryn, who hit on him while she was drunk.

Shatterstar formed a lasting friendship with his seismic-powered teammate, Rictor, who understood what it was to be an outcast. Major Domo from Shatterstar's future hired the gamesman Arcade to test Shatterstar's skills, and Shatterstar had to fight the Imperial Protectorate to save human lives. Making Shatterstar think that Windsong was being held captive, Arcade forced him to fight the blood-electrifying mutant X-Treme to save her. After X-Treme and Shatterstar teamed up to defeat Arcade, Shatterstar realized that Windsong's presence had been a ruse. X-Force soon teamed up with the New Warriors to oppose the Upstarts and their leader Gamesmaster, a telepathic mutant. Shatterstar and Domino helped expose the government's plan to rebuild Nimrod, the advanced mutant-hunting Sentinel, then fought the techno-organic Phalanx. When the computer-intelligence Prosh used much of X-Force's technology to incorporate a body for himself to launch into space, Shatterstar impressed his teammates with his technological know-how. X-Force changed headquarters to Arcade's former Murderworld base and, after battles with Feral and Reignfire, Arcade destroyed their base and X-Force moved into the X-Mansion. When Cable made changes to the team that Rictor disagreed with, Rictor quit the group, causing Shatterstar much anguish. Shatterstar next fought Genoshan Magistrates alongside Cable and Domino. His ribs were broken in this battle, and his injuries did not heal quickly as they had in times past. Shatterstar was side-lined from X-Force's next few missions while the Beast (Dr. Hank McCoy) studied him, discovering several fascinating facts, such as his DNA matching Longshot's.

While Siryn was imprisoned in the Weisman Institute for the Criminally Insane, she saw a file on a patient named Benjamin Russell, who greatly resembled Shatterstar. Meanwhile, Sebastian Shaw and Tessa of the Hellfire Club mind-controlled X-Force into battling Cable and Domino. Shatterstar began struggling when his warrior instinct seemed to be progressively lessening. When the police confronted Shatterstar with records of Benjamin Russell's criminal career, he began to doubt himself even more. After X-Force infiltrated the S.H.I.E.L.D. Helicarrier to rescue Cyclops, Shatterstar accompanied Siryn to the Weisman Institute to rescue Deadpool, but was mentally manipulated by Gamesmaster and began having memories of being Benjamin Russell. After X-Force narrowly survived a psychic assault by Mr. Sinister, Rictor returned to the team to aid Shatterstar in his identity crisis and X-Force stormed the Weisman Institute. Sending his monstrous soldiers Gog and Magog to subdue X-Force, Mojo kidnapped and tortured Shatterstar and Cable. In a broadcast mimicking the future moment when Shatterstar was destined to slay Mojo, Mojo mortally wounded Shatterstar instead, then turned his attentions to invading Earth. Mojo's assistant, the six-armed sorceress Spiral, took the nearly dead Shatterstar back to the Weisman Institute and combined his essence with that of Benjamin Russell, a Chicago-born mutant who had been comatose since his powers manifested. Spiral claimed close ties to both Russell and Shatterstar, though those ties have not been revealed. Mojo's invasion plans were stopped and he was defeated. Now with clear memories of Russell's life, Shatterstar felt whole again, and his warrior instinct returned; he even began using Russell's name at times. Shatterstar participated in more X-Force missions: fighting Shinobi Shaw's soldiers Clearcut and Mindmeld; retrieving Dr. Doom's equipment alongside Nathaniel Richards; battling Nazi Baron Strucker during World War II; and fighting the anti-mutant government Sentinels of Operation: Zero Tolerance. Shatterstar chose to leave the team with

Rictor and went to Rictor's family home in Mexico, where he helped his friend clean up his family's criminal dealings. Mojo hired Arcade to test Shatterstar's prowess, and Arcade kidnapped Rictor to force Shatterstar into battling Domino, a fight Shatterstar lost. Shatterstar and Rictor also aided the mutant Hanrasha against Martin Henry Strong.

Separating from Rictor, an aimless Shatterstar ended up in Madripoor, engaging in arena-style fights for sport until he became involved in a battle of wits between Spiral and Dominicus Pierce; Spiral and Pierce both sought the Five Fingers of Annihilation, an ancient blade capable of slaying the Skornn, an entity that could feed on the mutant gene. When Spiral obtained the blade, she took Shatterstar to the alternate reality Earth-2055, where she ruled the planet and was known as Apocalypse, though Shatterstar, with alternate versions of his X-Force teammates, defeated her. After returning to Earth-616, Shatterstar sought solace at a monastery in Tibet charged with protecting the Five Fingers. He briefly trained with the monk Zed, who was killed by a group called the Helix seeking the blade. Shatterstar joined with Cable and X-Force in defeating the Skornn, though Cable was believed killed. Most recently, Shatterstar teamed with Domino and Caliban to free the 198, a group of mutants who had retained their powers after "M-Day" and were living in a tent city on the grounds of the X-Mansion under supervision by government Sentinels.

Art by Scott S. Miller

| HEIGHT: 6'3" | WEIGHT: 195 lbs. (formerly 95 lbs.) |
| EYES: Blue (sometimes clear) | HAIR: Red-Blond |

ABILITIES/ACCESSORIES: Shatterstar is genetically bred to be the perfect fighting machine. His DNA initially matched Longshot's, but there were physical differences, such as Shatterstar having five digits per hand; since his spirit merged with Russell he no longer has hollow bones or lacks white blood cells. Shatterstar has an enhanced biorestorative metabolism and heals from injuries at a superhuman rate. He has enhanced speed, strength, stamina and senses. He can resonate a vibratory shockwave through the metallurgic properties of his swords, even from a distance, though this power physically weakens him. Shatterstar's vast technological knowledge enables him to repair even alien technology. Shatterstar has been trained in several combat techniques and in military strategy, though his weapons of choice are the swords he brought with him from his homeworld. Forged from science and magic, his swords can slice through highly durable materials such as the moorings on Juggernaut's helmet, and they are equipped with a bio-electric current to make them difficult for others to wield. Shatterstar's costumes are actually bulletproof battle armor. Whatever powers Benjamin Russell possessed prior to his coma and whether they are accessible to Shatterstar are unknown.

POWER GRID	1	2	3	4	5	6	7
INTELLIGENCE							
STRENGTH							
SPEED							
DURABILITY							
ENERGY PROJECTION							
FIGHTING SKILLS							

Art by Rob Liefeld

TOAD

REAL NAME: Mortimer Toynbee
KNOWN ALIASES: Terrible Toad-King; impersonated the Stranger
IDENTITY: Known to government officials
OCCUPATION: Freelance mercenary; former amusement park manager, fast food worker, subversive
CITIZENSHIP: U.K.
PLACE OF BIRTH: York, England, United Kingdom
KNOWN RELATIVES: Unidentified parents
GROUP AFFILIATION: 198; formerly Brotherhood of Mutants, Kings of Pain, Misfits, Defenders impersonators, Brotherhood of Evil Mutants
EDUCATION: Unrevealed
FIRST APPEARANCE: X-Men #4 (1964)

HISTORY: Born a mutant to parents he never knew, the infant Mortimer Toynbee was given to the Alamogordo research center, where the leading physician, Black Womb (Amanda Mueller), noted his unstable genetic matrix. Soon placed in an orphanage, Toynbee was ridiculed by his peers throughout his adolescent years. Due to learning disabilities and a chemical imbalance in his mutant physiology, his mental and physical states fluctuated widely over the following years, shifting between depressed, manic, psychotic and narcissistic states. He began to crouch almost constantly, and developed a fawning and subservient personality toward anyone who paid him positive attention. Fleeing a crowd of persecutors who sought to harm him in Manchester, Toynbee was rescued by the powerful mutant terrorist Magneto (Magnus), who was then organizing his Brotherhood of Evil Mutants. Slavishly loyal to his new master Magneto, Toynbee joined the Brotherhood as the jester-costumed Toad, a demeaning alias Magneto chose for him based on Toynbee's powers, personality and appearance. Unconsciously regarding Magneto as a father figure of sorts, Toad saw himself as Magneto's valued right hand, but the often-abusive Magneto saw Toynbee as little more than an expendable pawn.

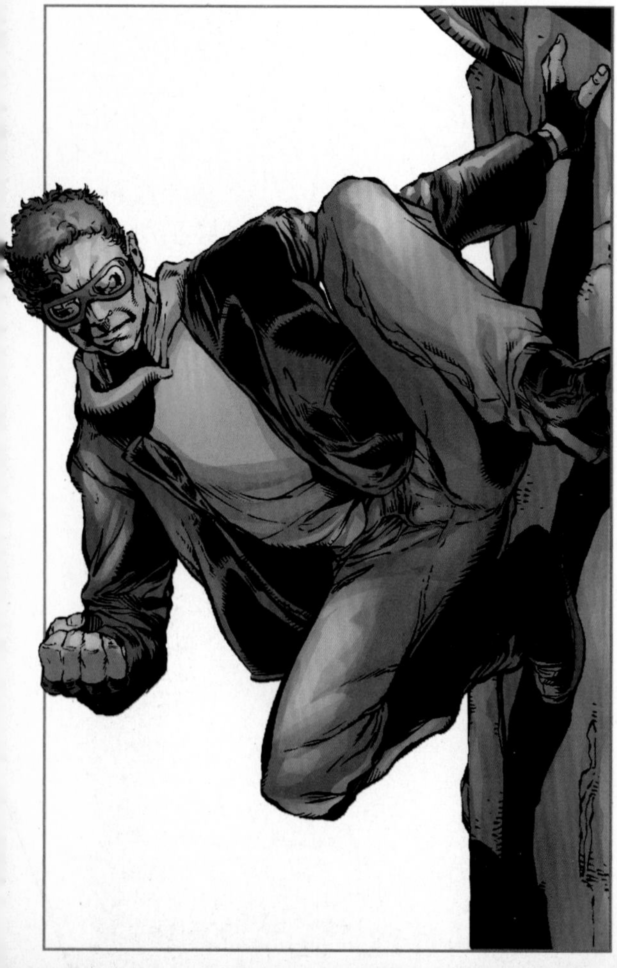

Toad constantly worked to earn Magneto's affections and had occasional conflicts with his Brotherhood teammates, mutant twins the speedster Quicksilver and the probability-altering Scarlet Witch, and the illusion-casting Mastermind (a.k.a. Jason Wyngarde). Toad began to think of the Scarlet Witch as the ideal woman and developed an unrequited crush on her. The Brotherhood frequently clashed with the X-Men, led by Magneto's arch-rival, Charles Xavier. The Brotherhood made their public debut by conquering the small nation of Santo Marco, though the X-Men drove them out. At some point, the Brotherhood set up headquarters in an orbiting asteroid, called Asteroid M. The Brotherhood encountered the X-Men at least five more times during revenge schemes and attempts to gain new recruits. When the giant alien Stranger appeared on Earth, the Brotherhood attempted to enlist him, but the Stranger was far too powerful. He took Magneto and the Toad as captives to his own planet in order to observe them, where they spent months trapped and learning his technologies. When Magneto finally escaped, he left Toad behind, leaving Toynbee wondering why Magneto treated him so poorly; Magneto was soon recaptured by the Stranger.

Toad and Magneto were brought back to Earth after they made contact with scientist Dane Whitman (later the new heroic Black Knight). They battled the Avengers to bring Quicksilver and Scarlet Witch back to their ranks, which they did successfully. The Toad fell into his old patterns of seeking Magneto's attentions by sniveling and tattling on his teammates, but Magneto became more verbally and physically abusive towards the Toad in response, even forcing Toad to wear a magnetic belt so that Magneto could "chastise" him more effectively. When the X-Men and the Avengers attacked, defeat seemed imminent and Magneto set his island base to self-destruct. Though Magneto sought to retreat, Toad, finally fed up with his treatment at Magneto's hands, betrayed Magneto and left his former master behind to perish with the island as Toad escaped in a ship with Quicksilver and the Scarlet Witch.

Toad traveled Europe with them for a time, though the trio was briefly captured by the mutant-hunting Sentinels. Toad unrelentingly helped his allies search books for a way to restore the Scarlet Witch's waning powers; when a certain spell was recited, Arkon, the ruler of the other-dimensional Polemachus, appeared and took Toad captive in his home dimension. Though briefly kept as a prisoner, Toad had opportunities to study Polemachus' technology and built himself a ship, with which he traveled back to the Stranger's homeworld. Toad spent the following months pilfering and studying enough technology to make himself powerful enough to impress the Scarlet Witch so that he could finally win her affections and get revenge on those who had rejected him. Toad took his ship and technology back to Earth where he learned that the Scarlet Witch had married the Vision, her synthozoid teammate. Furious, Toad attacked the Avengers at Yankee Stadium, using deadly mines, mental waves and imaging technology to impersonate the Stranger; Toad seriously injured the diminutive Wasp before being exposed and imprisoned. After escaping, he joined the balance-seeking android Libra in a short-lived team of villainous Defenders.

Financially backed by the hitman Arcade, Toad set up elaborate traps in a stateside castle of Doctor Doom, determined to get revenge on his enemies. Toad captured Angel (Warren Worthington III), and accidentally got the Fantastic Four's Thing as well, and subjected them to traps until he was exposed. Rather than turning Toynbee in, the Angel agreed to finance Toad in turning the castle into an amusement park. Toad considered this one of his life's happiest times until Dr. Doom reclaimed the land and ejected Toad. Aimless and suicidal, Toad attempted to jump to his death, but Spider-Man (Peter Parker) saved him. Toad tried to become Spider-Man's sidekick, but Spider-Man wasn't interested. When Toad met two other awkward Spider-Man allies, Frog-Man (Eugene Patilio) and Spider-Kid, the trio formed a short-lived team, the Misfits.

Toad later returned his attentions to winning Scarlet Witch's affections; with the Stranger's technology, Toad designed robots to resemble the Brotherhood and attacked her home, but was repelled and imprisoned by Vision, Quicksilver and Magneto. After escaping, Toad used a powerful force field to fight the Vision, but he was defeated again, sent drifting in space. Donning a powerful suit of toad-like armor, Toynbee defeated Vision and Spider-Man, whom Toad was embarrassed to see. Finally reaching Scarlet Witch, Toad was disgusted by her large, pregnant abdomen, and she quickly defeated him. In between major battles, Toad worked at various fast food restaurants and contemplated his very existence. Focusing on developing power and respect for himself in the mutant community, Toad enhanced his powers to include secreting a sticky resin from his hands, and made contacts with other powerful mutants to make deals for power. Toad allied with the billionaire External Gideon, the two calling themselves the Kings of Pain, in an ill-fated plot to resurrect the reality-altering Proteus. Toad then recruited other mutants to form a new Brotherhood of Evil Mutants. Toad led the team, with the Morlocks, in battle with X-Force, but his forces failed. While trying to recruit others, the Brotherhood lost battles against the government-sponsored X-Factor and unlikely allies Spider-Man, Darkhawk and Sleepwalker. The Toad's Brotherhood soon fell apart.

In his most psychotic state yet, Toad teamed with the mutant Surgeon who altered frogs and toads to be able to communicate with Toad. Toad and Surgeon had been denied a promised place in the Hellfire Club by the White Queen (Emma Frost), who had gone on to run a school for the team Generation X. Seeking revenge, Toad led his flock of frogs and toads in an attack on Generation X, but was quickly defeated and taken in for psychiatric help. His psychiatrist prescribed Ritalin for Toad and the drug finally stabilized his chemical imbalances and mental fluctuations. When Professor X's mutant-tracking machine, Cerebro, came to life and worked to catalogue the world's mutants, Toad joined Professor X and others to form a new Brotherhood of Mutants. The Brotherhood was catalogued by Cerebro before being rescued by the X-Men. The shape-shifting Mystique then took over the Brotherhood and led them into battle against Machine Man, who easily defeated them. While planning a heist with the Blob, Toad and his allies briefly lost their powers due to the influence of the High Evolutionary.

The space-faring mechanical man Prosh recruited Toad as one of five who would influence the future of the world. Alongside Mystique, the unstoppable Juggernaut and X-Men members Phoenix (Jean Grey) and Iceman, Toad was sent back in time to various points in his past, giving him the opportunity to reflect on his life and granting Toad insight into his origins. In time, Toad's knowledge was crucial for the five to defeat the attacking Stranger. During the battle, Toad was injured and Prosh healed him, taking the time to repair Toad's genome so that Toad could experience the full benefit of his mutation. Now much taller and leaner, Toad discovered greater strength, self-confidence and a long prehensile tongue he could use in combat.

With a new lease on life, Toad rejoined Mystique's Brotherhood and participated in an attack on Muir Island, fighting the X-Men. Toad soon took part in an ultimate fighting competition in Madripoor; he defeated the Eel before being taken down by Wolverine. After the mutant-hunting Sentinels wiped out the mutant population of Genosha, Toad migrated there and joined other mutants in acknowledging the seemingly deceased Magneto as their leader; Toad — alongside his protégé, Toad-in-waiting — even helped construct a monument to Magneto. When the powerful Xorn posed as Magneto and called all of Magneto's followers to New York, Toad helped form a new Brotherhood, assaulting the humans of New York before turning against the false Magneto; Toad briefly returned to Genosha. After the events of M-Day, Toad retained his powers. He moved to the mutant protection camp on the grounds of Xavier's estate, where he saw fellow mutants persecuted. Toad was among the mutants who escaped the grounds after Domino (Neena Thurman) and Shatterstar (Gaveedra-7) broke them out.

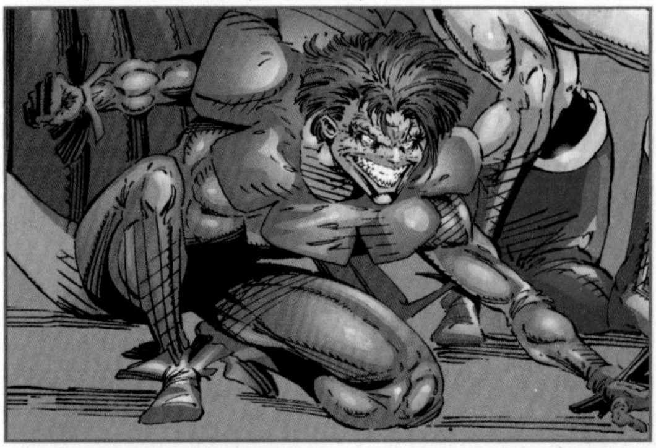

Art by Rob Liefeld

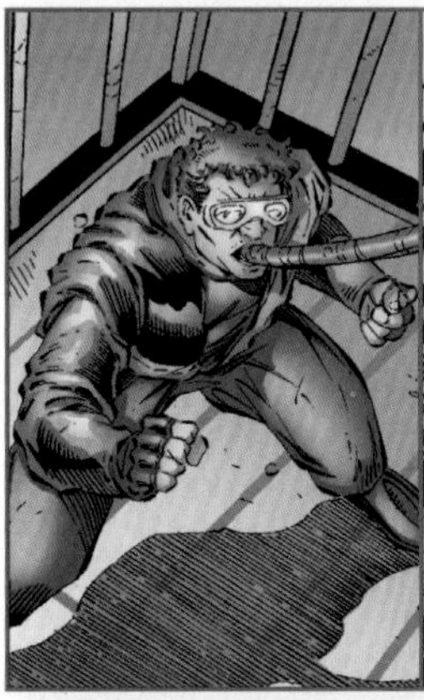

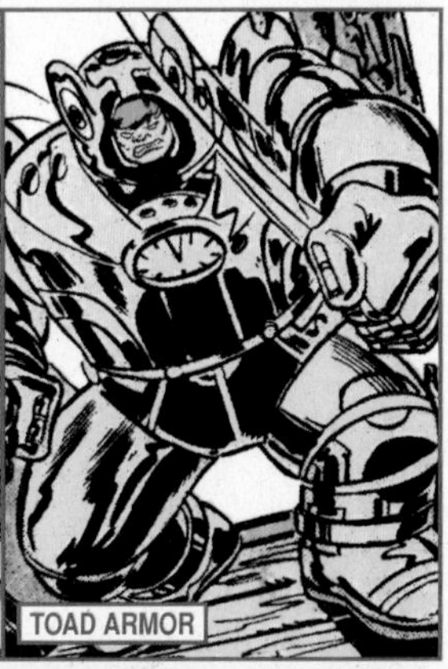
TOAD ARMOR

Art by Dan Fraga & Richard Howell

HEIGHT: 5'8" **WEIGHT:** 169 lbs.
EYES: Yellow; originally brown **HAIR:** Brown

SUPERHUMAN POWERS: Toad's initially imperfectly developed powers included low level superhuman strength and a superhuman leaping ability, allowing him to reach heights of 24 feet and cover distances of 36 feet. More recently, Toad has developed the additional abilities to exude a sticky resin from his hands, to secrete new pheromonous venoms with which he can control minds, to stick to walls; he now has a prehensile tongue which can reach up to 25 feet, support his weight and deliver blows. Toad was briefly able to talk to specially prepared amphibians. He has manipulated a wide array of advanced technology, including machines capable of delivering mindwaves, illusion-casting and constructing robots and spaceships; Toad briefly wore a powered suit of toad-armor. These technologies have been pilfered from various sources, such as the Stranger, Magneto, Arcade and Arkon.

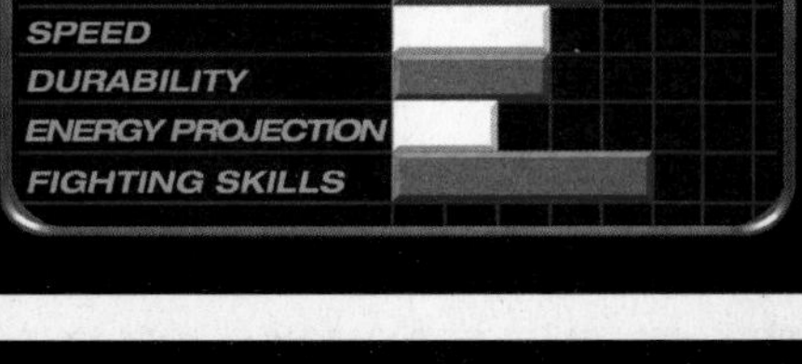
POWER GRID
1 2 3 4 5 6 7
INTELLIGENCE
STRENGTH
SPEED
DURABILITY
ENERGY PROJECTION
FIGHTING SKILLS